MONEY IN CONGRESSIONAL ELECTIONS

Gary C. Jacobson ☆ MONEY IN
CONGRESSIONAL
ELECTIONS

New Haven and London
Yale University Press
1980

Designed by Sally Harris
and set in VIP Times Roman type.
Printed in the United States of America by
Vail-Ballou Press, Binghamton, N.Y.

Published in Great Britain, Europe, Africa, and
Asia (except Japan) by Yale University Press,
Ltd., London. Distributed in Australia and
New Zealand by Book & Film Services, Artarmon,
N.S.W., Australia; and in Japan by Harper & Row,
Publishers, Tokyo Office.

Library of Congress Cataloging in Publication Data

Jacobson, Gary C
    Money in congressional elections.

    Includes index.
    1. Elections—United States—Campaign funds.
    2. United States. Congress—Elections. I. Title.
JK1991.J32   329'.025'0973   79-20669
ISBN 0-300-02442-8

For my Mother and Father

CONTENTS

TABLES AND FIGURES

ACKNOWLEDGMENTS

My debts for varying combinations of assistance, criticism, advice, and encouragement—all equally essential—I happily acknowledge. John Ferejohn and Roger Noll provided the strongest stimulus by combining a thorough skepticism about my early findings with invaluable suggestions about how to retest them. I suspect they will remain unconvinced. Christopher Achen, Steven Rosenstone, and William P. Welch offered many helpful comments, criticisms, and ideas. Herbert E. Alexander kindly shared the Citizens' Research Foundation library—and his own unexcelled knowledge of campaign finance—with me; he was also instrumental in arranging forums in which many of the ideas and findings that make up this book were first presented. Roland D. McDevitt allowed me access to his own research findings while providing useful suggestions about mine. I am especially obliged to David Mayhew for steady encouragement, good advice, and an unmatched standard of scholarship.

I am grateful also to Trinity College for funding computer time, manuscript preparation, and the sabbatical leave during which several drafts of this book were written.

The data used in chapters 1 and 5 were made available in part by the Inter-University Consortium for Political Research; I am solely responsible for all analyses and interpretations. Some of the material presented in this book originally appeared in "The Effects of Campaign Spending in Congressional Elections," *American Political Science Review* 72 (June 1978), in "Public Funds for Congressional Campaigns: Who Would Benefit?" in *Political Finance*, ed. Herbert E. Alexander, Sage Electoral Studies Yearbook 5 (Beverly Hills, Calif.: Sage Publications, 1979), and in "Campaign Finance Regulation: Politics and Policy in the 1970s," *Paths to Political Reform*, ed. William Crotty (Lexington, Mass.: D.C. Heath–Lexington Books, forthcoming).

INTRODUCTION

The principal thesis of this book is that money has an important effect on what happens in congressional elections. Campaign spending matters, and it matters most to candidates who are not incumbents. Indeed, for reasons examined at length, what incumbents spend makes relatively little difference. Whether or not campaigns are seriously contested depends on the resources mobilized by nonincumbents.

The thesis bears a variety of implications. One is that people and groups supplying campaign funds largely determine which races are to be competitive and which are not, which go by default to an incumbent and which threaten him with immediate retirement. Another is that changes in the laws regulating campaign finance can alter the competitive environment decisively. Others are easily imagined; many are explored in due course. A general theory of how money works in congressional elections necessarily intersects a wide range of scholarly and policy issues.

Congressional campaign spending has these effects because of the particular conditions of congressional electoral politics. The same conditions underscore the critical importance of carefully assessing the consequences of campaign finance regulation for electoral competition. In the first chapter, I undertake a broad examination of the context of congressional elections, beginning with a brief review of the familiar and well-documented decline of competition. An account of that decline requires consideration of voting behavior, which is central to this chapter, as it is to any clear delineation of campaign spending effects. I argue that what we know about voting in congressional elections provides ample ground for supposing that campaign spending makes a difference, most especially to nonincumbents.

However plausible, the central thesis is only persuasive if it can be shown that how much (at least nonincumbent) candidates spend on the campaign has a strong and direct effect on how well they do at the polls. In chapter 2, I exploit the data on campaign expenditures by House and Senate candidates in 1972, 1974, and 1976 (data generated by campaign finance reforms enacted at the beginning of this decade) to test a preliminary model of the effects of campaign expenditures on election results. Multiple regression estimates confirm that, with other variables controlled, campaign spending by nonincumbents has a substantial impact on their share of the vote; incumbent campaign expenditures have little effect. And spending by Republicans, candidates of the much weaker party, evidently has a greater electoral impact, *ceteris paribus*, than spending by Democrats.

The findings are preliminary at this point because they do not confront the possibility fhat the connection between spending and votes may be reciprocal: candidates may attract campaign funds because they are expected (correctly) to do well. A more convincing defense of the thesis thus requires an examination of the sources of campaign funds and the motives and strategies of those who provide them. Who contributes? For what reasons? To which candidates? Such questions merit attention in their own right, and chapter 3 includes, among other things, a detailed analysis of the funds contributed by individual and institutional donors to candidates in diverse electoral circumstances. It establishes that contributors of all kinds vary their contributions radically depending on the incumbency status of the candidate and the expected level of electoral competition—related, although distinguishable, phenomena.

As a result, challengers, incumbents, and candidates for open seats face fundamentally different fund-raising tasks. The problem of raising money observed from the candidates' perspectives is the principal subject of chapter 4. A nonincumbent's capacity to raise funds depends primarily on the chances of winning—which are largely controlled by the actions of the incumbent. "Strong" challengers attract money, and the availability of money attracts strong challengers, but the effectiveness with which an incumbent exploits available resources has a critical impact on his ability to avoid facing both. Incumbents who appear vulnerable inspire effective, well-financed challenges; most do not, however, and the great majority of challengers remain severely underfinanced.

Incumbents, on the other hand, are able to raise and spend as much money as they think necessary. Evidence from their campaign spending patterns over several elections indicates that they adjust their campaign finances to the gravity of the challenge they face. It is also clear, however, that upward adjustments do not offset the gains made by challengers that inspire them. Simply stated, the more incumbents spend, the worse they do. Greater spending does not, to be sure, cost them votes, but indicates a serious challenge that does cost them votes.

This interpretation is supported by a revised and expanded version of the regression model estimated in chapter 2. The variables found in chapters 3 and 4 to influence the pattern of contributions to congressional campaigns are used in chapter 5 to develop and test a simultaneous equation system which acknowledges potential reciprocal causation between money and votes. Even with adjustments for simultaneity, campaign spending affects electoral outcomes as predicted: the challenger's spending is what matters. This result is reinforced by an analysis of the connection between campaign spending and voters' recall of candidates, with possible reciprocal causation again taken into account. The marginal gains in voter recall for a given increase in campaign spending are greater for nonincumbent than for incumbent congressional candidates.

The balance of evidence indicates that the relationship between campaign spending and election results is, in fact, basically recursive. Although potentially formidable nonincumbent candidates usually do attract more campaign money, their potential is not fulfilled if the funds are not forthcoming. It is not popular appeal, but rather anticipated capacity for winning popular support, that fills campaign coffers. Support among voters depends on the funds actually being contributed and spent. An extension of this idea leads to an explanation of some puzzling survey findings about the effects of Watergate on voting in 1974. It also suggests how aggregate political conditions and events may be translated into aggregate electoral results without necessarily having any direct impact on individual voters.

The understanding of money in congressional elections developed in the first five chapters forms a basis for interpreting the politics of campaign finance reform and for projecting the electoral effects of enacted and proposed changes in campaign finance regulations. Chapter 6 traces the politics of campaign finance legislation through the past decade. Its main conclusion is that, regardless of what other benefits they may have produced, changes in campaign finance policy have consistently tended to dampen electoral competition, thus favoring the very people who do the legislating. Because of the divergent utility of campaign money to challengers and incumbents, members enhance their own security each time they restrict the flow of funds into or out of campaigns.

The potential consequences of further changes in campaign finance policy—in particular, of extending public funding to congressional campaigns—are similarly predictable. Campaign subsidies will help challengers; restrictions on spending will help incumbents. Chapter 7 offers evidence that the combination of public funds and spending limits proposed in major bills before both Houses during the 95th Congress would hinder challengers (and, other things equal, Republicans) except in years when exceptionally strong short-term forces were at work. I conclude with some speculation on the future of campaign finance regulation in light of continuing problems with current campaign finance practices and of equally disconcerting consequences that are likely to flow from presently contemplated changes in campaign finance laws.

Neither the electoral cycle nor congressional politics waits for the scholar to catch up. Since the manuscript for this book was completed, another election has passed and Congress has once again considered—and rejected—extending public subsidies to congressional campaigns. Because data on campaign finances in 1978 and congressional action on public funding came too late to be discussed in the main body of the text, they are treated in a separate epilogue that follows chapter 7.

This brief summary ignores a host of related issues that are at least touched upon, but this book does not, by any means, exhaust the topic of money in congressional elections or congressional politics. I do not, for example, attempt to discover how campaign finance practices affect what candidates do once they have been elected. Neither do I consider what difference it makes how the money is spent. Both are clearly important questions that deserve full treatment on their own. So do many others. Happily, the opportunities for detailed empirical research on money in politics have expanded enormously since effective reporting requirements were implemented. And they can only grow with the increasingly rich supply of campaign finance data. My purpose is to begin the sifting of data and ideas, to establish some propositions that lay the groundwork for understanding how an important element of our politics works.

1 ☆ THE CONTEXT OF
CONGRESSIONAL ELECTIONS

This is a book about money in congressional elections—where it comes from, who gets and spends it and to what effect, how it is treated as a policy issue. But neither the role of money in congressional elections nor campaign finance as a political issue can be understood apart from the broader context of congressional politics, electoral and otherwise. In this chapter I delineate some salient elements of that context; my purpose is to establish a foundation for the theoretical propositions and empirical investigations that follow in subsequent chapters.

Specific changes in the congressional context over the past twenty years explain the recent prominence of campaign finance issues. The most striking manifestation of change has been the decrease in competition for congressional seats; consideration of its causes leads directly to crucial questions about voting behavior in congressional elections.

COMPETITION FOR CONGRESSIONAL SEATS: LONG-TERM TRENDS

By any measure, elections to the House of Representatives are not very competitive. In elections from 1956 through 1976, 91.1 percent of the incumbents sought reelection; 92.2 percent of them were successful. A mere 1.7 percent lost primary contests; only 6.2 percent met defeat in general elections. The smallest percentage of incumbent general election victories in any of these election years was 86.9 percent; the largest was 96.8 percent.[1] Election odds

1. William J. Keefe, *Parties, Politics, and Public Policy in America*, 2d ed.

1

overwhelmingly favor incumbents.

The persistent and successful pursuit of reelection by incumbents is not a new development. The long-term trend toward stability in House membership is more than a century old. Since about 1850, the percentage of first-term members (or, to use a slightly different measure, the percentage of replacements) has declined steadily, from over 50 percent before the Civil War to under 20 percent in the two most recent decades.[2] The average number of terms served by members has increased, as has the proportion of members who have served ten or more terms.[3] The number of seats switching from one party to the other has correspondingly diminished.[4] A decline in competition has been, from the beginning, a major component of this trend.[5]

House incumbents have experienced an additional quantum jump in security since the mid-1960s. They do not win any more *frequently*—their reelection rate left little room for improvement—but they do win more *easily*. By any definition (the standard thresholds are 55 and 60 percent of the two-party vote), the number of close elections—and hence marginal seats—has dropped sharply. Typically, about 75 percent of the incumbent House candidates now win with more than 60 percent of the major party vote; this is up from two-thirds prior to 1966.[6] Mayhew's

(Hinsdale, Ill.: The Dryden Press, Inc., 1976), p. 39; *Congressional Quarterly Weekly Report* 34 (November 6, 1976): 3119–22.

2.   Nelson W. Polsby, "The Institutionalization of the U.S. House of Representatives," *American Political Science Review* 62 (1968): 146; Morris P. Fiorina, David W. Rohde, and Peter Wissel, "Historical Change in House Turnover," in *Congress in Change: Evolution and Reform*, ed. Norman J. Ornstein (New York: Praeger Publishers, Inc., 1975), pp. 29–32.

3.   Polsby, "Institutionalization of the House," p. 147; Charles S. Bullock III, "House Careerists: Changing Patterns of Longevity and Attrition," *American Political Science Review* 66 (1972): 1296.

4.   Charles O. Jones, "Inter-party Competition for Congressional Seats," *Western Political Quarterly* 17 (1964): 465–66.

5.   Samuel Kernell, "Toward Understanding 19th Century Congressional Careers: Ambition, Competition, and Rotation," *American Journal of Political Science*, 21 (1977): 679–82.

6.   Albert D. Cover and David R. Mayhew, "Congressional Dynamics and the Decline of Competitive Congressional Elections," in *Congress Reconsidered*, ed. Lawrence C. Dodd and Bruce I. Oppenheimer (New York: Praeger Publishers, Inc., 1977), pp. 55–56.

graphic evidence depicts the remarkable transition to a strongly bimodal distribution of vote percentages in elections involving House incumbents—with the developing trough centered on the marginal range.[7] In contrast, the distribution for elections to open seats remains strongly unimodal; these contests are, by the same measures, thoroughly competitive.

Further indication of the increased electoral value of incumbency is found in data on elections involving first-term incumbents and on contests in districts where incumbents have voluntarily retired. The average "sophomore surge"—the gain in percentage of the major party vote between a member's first and second election, adjusted for national trends—was +2.7 percent from 1962 through 1966, +6.6 percent from 1968 through 1974. Similarly, the "retirement slump"—the falloff in the vote for the candidate of a retiring incumbent's party—averaged −2.2 percent in the earlier period, −7.7 percent more recently.[8] Using related though somewhat different calculations, Erikson determined that about 1966 the value of running as an incumbent increased from 2 to 5 percent of the vote.[9]

Two recent elections confirm the particularly striking ability of first-term incumbents to hold on to their seats. Burnham made the surprising discovery that, in 1974, "the first-generation or 'new incumbent' Republicans as a group actually improved their position very slightly in the face of an exceptionally large national shift toward the Democrats."[10] In 1976, no fewer than forty-eight of the forty-nine Democrats elected to formerly Republican seats in 1974 (in the wake of the Watergate debacle) won a second term; seventy-two of the seventy-four freshman Democrats who sought reelection won.[11]

7. David R. Mayhew, "Congressional Elections: The Case of the Vanishing Marginals," *Polity* 6 (1974): 298–301.

8. Cover and Mayhew, "Congressional Dynamics," p. 60.

9. Robert S. Erikson, "Malapportionment, Gerrymandering, and Party Fortunes in Congressional Elections," *American Political Science Review* 66 (1972): 1240.

10. Walter Dean Burnham, "Insulation and Responsiveness in Congressional Elections," *Political Science Quarterly* 90 (1975): 419.

11. Charles M. Tidmarch, "The Second Time Around: Freshman Democratic House Members' 1976 Reelection Experiences" (Prepared for delivery at the 1977

Incumbent senators have been notably more vulnerable. Indeed, this important difference between the two Houses visibly shades the approach each takes to questions of campaign finance reform. Aggregated by decade, the data reveal that from the 1920s through the 1950s, between 75.0 and 76.6 percent of Senate incumbents seeking reelection were successful. In the 1960s this figure jumped to 92.2 percent, but for the first four elections of the 1970s it has fallen back to 78.5 percent.[12]

Senate elections are typically much closer than House elections. Most are won with less than 60 percent of the major party vote. No overall decline in Senate marginality has occurred, but when southern and nonsouthern states are viewed separately, a greater number of competitive seats now appear in the former, significantly fewer in the latter.[13] However, in 1976 (a year not yet included in studies of electoral competition), no fewer than nine of twenty-five incumbents were defeated, eight of them in nonsouthern states.

Why Has Competition Declined?

The decline in competition for congressional seats—at least in those in the House—bears important implications for many aspects of American politics, and it is no surprise that its causes have been the subject of extensive research and controversy. The competing explanations suggest different perspectives for assessing the role of money in congressional elections, so a brief account of them is essential. The two most promising approaches—which are by no means mutually exclusive—are grounded in data that are crucial to campaign finance questions in any case.

One major hypothesis can be disposed of quickly. Tufte proposed that the increase in incumbent security—and the consequent

Annual Meeting of the American Political Science Association, Washington, D.C., September 1–4 1977), p. 8.

12. From data in *Congressional Quarterly's Guide to U.S. Elections* (Washington, D.C.: Congressional Quarterly, Inc., 1975), pp. 457–509, and *Congressional Quarterly's Guide to the 1976 Elections: A Supplement to CQ's Guide to U.S. Elections* (Washington, D.C.: Congressional Quarterly, Inc., 1977), pp. 36–44.

13. Cover and Mayhew, "Congressional Dynamics," p. 56.

dampening of partisan swings in the House corresponding to given changes in the partisan distribution of the vote—was a function of redistricting.[14] Incumbents took advantage of the Supreme Court's decision in *Baker* v. *Carr* to design (with a little help from their friends in the state legislatures) safer districts for themselves. The trouble with this hypothesis is that competition has decreased evenly across districts that were and were not redrawn.[15] And the "sophomore surge" and "retirement slump" figures do not vary with redistricting.[16]

The remaining explanations focus on (1) changes in the behavior of incumbents, (2) changes in the behavior of voters, or (3) some combination of the two. In this last case, the question is: Which brought about the other?

The broader purposes of this book require that special attention be given the behavior of incumbents. They make campaign finance policy, and it will become clear that incumbency status has a decisive effect both on a candidate's ability to raise money and on the consequences of his spending it. Mayhew argues persusasively that much of what congressmen do is best explained by the simple premise that they are "single-minded seekers of reelection."[17] The Congress is itself organized to maximize reelection of its members. Its rules and procedures support what amounts to a permanent campaign. Members enjoy ample opportunities for what Mayhew terms *advertising* (keeping their names and faces before the home folks, maintaining a favorable personal image), *credit claiming* (convincing constituents that the member is responsible for desirable government decisions—casework is the greatest part of this), and *position taking* (roll-call votes and pronouncements from which members reap benefits by taking the correct stand quite apart from any effective policy impact). The legislative consequences of these

14. Edward R. Tufte, "The Relationship between Seats and Votes in Two-Party Systems," *American Political Science Review* 67 (1973): 531–46.
15. John A. Ferejohn, "On the Decline of Competition in Congressional Elections," *American Political Science Review* 71 (1977): 168.
16. Cover and Mayhew, "Congressional Dynamics," p. 63.
17. David R. Mayhew, *Congress: The Electoral Connection* (New Haven, Conn.: Yale University Press, 1974), p. 5.

activities are almost entirely incidental to the more immediate goal of shoring up constituency support.[18] Party discipline within Congress is minimal. On the premise that the basic duty is to get reelected, members are encouraged to "vote the district first"; the advice is rarely ignored. Party conflict has increasingly given way to activity that enhances the ability of incumbents of both parties to retain office. Mayhew argues that "in a good many ways the interesting division in congressional politics is not between Democrats and Republicans, but between politicians in and out of office. Looked at from one angle . . . it has the appearance of a cross party conspiracy among incumbents to keep their jobs."[19]

Individual members have adopted a complementary approach to dealing with constitutents back in the district. They typically cultivate personal images surprisingly empty of partisan or programmatic content. They present themselves as trustworthy, hardworking, concerned individuals who merit support on the basis of personal character rather than political beliefs or goals.[20] And what is known about voting behavior in congressional elections suggests that they are not misguided; more on this shortly.

This pattern of behavior clearly antedates the recent jump in incumbent security and so cannot explain it, although it certainly helps account for the long-term electoral success enjoyed by incumbents. What has changed is the volume of resources available to members pursuing reelection. The quantity and dollar value of offical perquisites have grown rapidly since 1960, and an end to growth is not yet in sight. Recent estimates place the value of salary, staff, travel, communications, and office allowances at about $400,000 per year for a representative;[21] even more is provided

18. Ibid., pp. 115–38.
19. Ibid., p. 105.
20. Richard F. Fenno, Jr., "U.S. House Members in Their Constituencies: An Exploration," *American Political Science Review* 71 (1977): 898–908.
21. Albert D. Cover, "One Good Term Deserves Another: The Advantage of Incumbency in Congressional Elections," *American Journal of Political Science* 21 (1977): 537.

senators, the amount being scaled to the size of the state (staff allowances alone may come to more than $900,000).[22] Travel allowances, to pick one example, went from twelve to twenty-six free trips to the district per year while Wayne Hays was chairman of the House Administration Committee, which handles these matters. Hays was notorious for adding to congressional perqs, but his departure has not made any noticeable difference. In the first session of the 95th Congress, the allowance was increased to thirty-two.[23] Senators now enjoy from forty to forty-four free trips home per year.[24]

The most important official perq is no doubt the frank. Mail flow increased by more than 600 percent between 1954 and 1970, with a particularly large spurt between 1965 and 1966. It peaks—or it did before a recent tightening of regulations[25]—in Octobers of even-numbered years.[26] In 1973, it was estimated that the volume of mail had doubled—and the cost tripled—over the previous five years; the prediction was that 476 million pieces of mail would be sent out in 1974—900,000 for each member—at a cost of $38.1 million.[27] The most recent figures on the cost of congressional mail for a twelve-month period appear in table 1.1. The total works out to more than $117,000 per member.

Other avenues of communication with voters have not been ignored. A survey taken in the 1960s found that more than half the sample of congressmen reported giving regular radio and television reports to constituents; those doing so averaged eight radio and four television appearances per month during the session.[28] The facilities for preparing radio and television tapes and films are available

22. *CQ Weekly Report* 34 (July 3, 1976): 1700.
23. Lewis Perdue, "The Million Dollar Advantage of Incumbency," *Washington Monthly* 9 (March 1977): 51.
24. *CQ Weekly Report* 34 (July 3, 1976): 1700.
25. Members are now prohibited from sending out mass mailings at public expense during the sixty days prior to a primary or general election.
26. Mayhew, "Congressional Elections," p. 311.
27. Norman C. Miller, "Yes, You Are Getting More Political Mail, and It Will Get Worse," *Wall Street Journal*, March 6, 1973, p. 1.
28. John S. Saloma III, *Congress and the New Politics* (Boston: Little, Brown and Company, 1969), p. 174.

Table 1.1   Cost of Congressional Mail (12 Months, 1976–77)

Postage	$52,973,703
Handling	
House	1,400,000
Senate	443,249
Government Printing Office	150,000
Computer addressing	
House	1,027,170
Senate	671,000
Printing	
House	2,001,401
Senate	560,643
Agricultural publications	1,585,000
Child care publications	228,696
Consumer information	194,000
Franked envelopes	1,002,000
Wall calendars	164,500
Historical society calendars	345,076
Total	$62,746,438

Note: Total does not include salaries of staff preparing letters, cost of paper for printing Senate newsletters, or office overhead expenses.

Source: *Hartford Courant*, March 28, 1977, p. 6.

to members free of charge. And recently, members voted themselves an unlimited WATS line for long-distance calls.[29]

There is no question that members use this increasingly formidable array of official resources to pursue reelection, if only because the campaign never really ends. An obvious hypothesis is that incumbents are now simply reaping the electoral rewards of a more extensive and more effective interelection campaign. The prevalent understanding of voting behavior in congressional elections adds plausibility to this explanation, but studies of the congressional electorate also provide evidence that voting behavior itself has changed in a way that benefits incumbents independently of more extensive self-promotion.

29.   Perdue, "Advantage of Incumbency," p. 51.

VOTING BEHAVIOR IN CONGRESSIONAL ELECTIONS

Congressional voters have recieved much less attention than presidential voters. Perhaps for this reason, the findings about voting behavior in congressional elections are unusually consistent and lend themselves to a relatively clear, straightforward interpretation. The basic determinant of congressional voting is, by all accounts, the party identification of the voter. Although the concept of party identification is not without ambiguities and has undergone extensive criticism in recent years,[30] its utility for explaining the behavior of congressional electorates has not been questioned. A manifest tribute to its importance is the frequency with which partisan defection is taken to be the phenomenon requiring explanation. It is of no small significance, then, that partyline voting has decreased, and defection increased, in congressional elections since the mid-1960s, as the data in table 1.2 attest.

The weakening of partisanship as an electoral force has been observed at a variety of electoral levels, although the true extent of the change is the subject of some controversy.[31] It has two additive components: (1) a greater proportion of voters disavowing attachment to any party, and (2) less consistent party-line voting among the remaining self-designated partisans. The figures in table 1.2 indicate that the second component has been more important at the congressional level. Ferejohn's analysis supports the same conclusion.[32]

Partisan defection is on the upswing in congressional elections;

30. See, for example, H. Douglas Price, "Party Identification in History and the History of Party Identification" (Prepared for delivery at the 1977 Annual Meeting of the American Political Science Association, Washington, D.C., September 1–4, 1977).
31. For example, Norman H. Nie, Sidney Verba, and John R. Petrocik argue that the decline has been dramatic. See *The Changing American Voter* (Cambridge, Mass.: Harvard University Press, 1976), chap. 4. Contrary evidence is presented by Bruce E. Keith et al., "The Myth of the Independent Voter" (Prepared for delivery at the 1977 Annual Meeting of the American Political Science Association, Washington, D.C., September 1–4, 1977).
32. Ferejohn, "Competition in Congressional Elections," pp. 173–74.

Table 1.2. Party-Line Voting in House Elections, 1956–76 (percent)

Year	Party-Line Voters	Defectors	Independents	Total
1956	82	9	9	100
1958	84	11	5	100
1960	80	12	8	100
1962	83	12	5	100
1964	79	15	5	99
1966	76	16	8	100
1968	74	19	7	100
1970	76	16	8	100
1972	73	17	10	100
1974	74	18	8	100
1976	72	19	9	100

Note: Party-line voters are those who voted for the party with which they identified. (Independents leaning toward a party are treated as partisans, not as independents.) Defectors are those who voted for the party other than that with which they identified. Data may not sum to 100 because of rounding.

Source: Thomas E. Mann, *Unsafe at Any Margin: Interpreting Congressional Elections* (Washington, D.C.: American Enterprise Institute for Public Policy Research, 1978), p. 14. Data are originally from SRC/CPS National Election Studies.

so is voting for incumbents, regardless of party. It follows that a substantially greater proportion of defections must now favor incumbents, as, indeed, the data in table 1.3 confirm. Defection rates of voters identifying with the incumbent's party have fluctuated; no trend is evident. In striking contrast, voters sharing the challenger's partisan orientation defect more than twice as frequently as they did ten years ago. Cover, who compiled these data, emphasizes the point: *"Since 1972 about half of those identifying with the challenger's party have deserted their party's congressional candidate in contested elections involving an incumbent."*[33]

The weakening of partisan ties has clearly redounded to the benefit of incumbent candidates. As Cover points out, no logical necessity demands that this be so; defections might go equally to incumbents and challengers or might even favor the latter.[34] An ex-

33. Cover, "Advantage of Incumbency," p. 535.
34. Ibid., p. 532.

Table 1.3.   Defection Rates for Incumbents and Challengers, 1958–74
(percent)

Year	Incumbent Partisans		Challenger Partisans	
1958	8.9	(406)[a]	16.2	(291)
1960	7.7	(534)	19.3	(394)
1962		b		b
1964	10.9	(430)	25.1	(311)
1966	9.1	(296)	32.5	(200)
1968	13.5	(355)	32.5	(286)
1970	4.7	(253)	32.1	(190)
1972	5.9	(323)	56.0	(168)
1974	12.9	(255)	48.6	(181)

[a]Number of cases from which percentages were computed.
[b]Data not available.

Source: Albert D. Cover, "One Good Term Deserves Another: The Advantages of Incumbency in Congressional Elections," American Journal of Political Science 21 (August 1977): 535. Data are originally from SRC/CPS National Election Studies.

planation of why incumbents have been favored derives from the second crucial element affecting voting behavior in congressional elections: information.

A critical difference between presidential and congressional elections (and an important difference between House and Senate elections) arises from the pronounced differences in the amount of information voters have about the candidates. A variety of data argue this point. Table 1.4 presents one set of items. It lists the percentage of respondents who could name the candidates they reported voting for in elections for president, governor, senator, and representative in SRC/CPS surveys between 1952 and 1972. Almost everyone remembers the name of his presidential choice (or at least can accurately name one of the candidates, which is what the question really requires). And a large percentage, particularly in the two most recent elections listed, remember who they voted for for governor.

Congressional choices are not so readily recalled. Respondents make a respectable showing of remembering their Senate choice, especially in recent years, but at rates still about 20 percent below president, 10 percent below governor. Not many more than half the

Table 1.4.   Percentages of Voters Able to Name Candidate They Voted For,
1952–72

		Office		
Year	President	Governor	U.S. Senator	U.S. Representative
1952	99.9	73.3	60.3	44.8
	(1239)[a]	(706)	(922)	(1201)
1954	b	b	b	b
1956	99.8	b	50.1	32.8
	(1273)		(938)	(1249)
1958		81.0	53.0	49.1
		(781)	(761)	(1038)
1960	100.0	b	55.1	47.7
	(1428)		(744)	(1253)
1962		b	b	54.0
				(709)
1964	100.0	77.8	63.4	47.0
	(1113)	(491)	(840)	(1082)
1966		84.6	78.4	64.5
		(540)	(394)	(705)
1968	98.8	82.2	71.8	59.5
	(1027)	(321)	(710)	(898)
1970		91.1	78.5	55.3
		(628)	(665)	(765)
1972	98.8	93.6	79.4	55.4
	(1625)	(455)	(826)	(608)

[a]Number of cases from which percentages were computed.
[b]Data not available.

Source: SRC/CPS Codebooks for each survey.

respondents recall the name of the House candidate they voted for. Respondents' memories do seem to have improved over the years surveyed.

Voters also have relatively little information about congressional candidates apart from their names. In 1958, for example, 59 percent of the SRC sample had neither read nor heard anything about either House candidate; fewer than one in five knew something about both candidates. Forty-six percent cast their ballots

Table 1.5. Percentages of "Don't Know" Responses to Requests to Place Self,
Parties, and Candidates on Issue and Ideological Dimensions
(Wisconsin Survey)

	Self	Party		Presidential Candidates		House Candidates	
		Dem.	Rep.	Dem.	Rep.	Dem.	Rep.
Vietnam	3.4	12.4	11.2	10.1	8.7	59.3	60.2
Welfare	2.5	15.5	13.9	13.2	11.1	59.8	59.3
Liberalism– Conservatism	7.2	17.3	16.3	18.3	16.7	57.8	56.2

Note: Table includes those who could not place the person or party at any point on
a seven-point scale.

Source: Barbara Hinckley, "Issues, Information Costs, and Congressional Elections," *American Politics Quarterly* 4 (1976): 139. The data are from a sample survey of 841 Wisconsin residents taken in the winter following the 1972 election.

without having received any information about either candidate.[35]
It is no surprise, then, that respondents find it difficult to specify
congressional candidates' stands on issues. The figures in tables
1.5 and 1.6 show how far this is the case. The data for table 1.5 are
from a survey of Wisconsin residents taken during the winter following the 1972 election. Respondents were able to place parties
and presidential candidates on the seven-point issue and ideology
scales at least 80 percent of the time. House candidates could be so
placed less than 45 percent of the time. Similarly, table 1.6 indicates that respondents in the 1972 and 1974 SRC/CPS surveys had
much more difficulty placing Senate candidates on seven-point issue and ideology dimensions than they did presidential candidates,
parties, themselves, or a sitting president. The samples are of
course quite different, but it seems safe to conclude from these data
that more is known about Senate candidates than about House candidates, hardly a counterintuitive discovery. It should be noted that
respondents in these surveys are not required to make accurate or

35. Donald E. Stokes and Warren E. Miller, "Party Government and the Saliency of Congress," in *Elections and the Political Order* (New York: John Wiley &
Sons, Inc., 1966), p. 204.

Table 1.6. Percentages of "Don't Know" Responses to Requests to Place Self, Parties, and Candidates on Issue and Ideological Dimensions (National Election Surveys)

	Self	Nixon[a]	McGovern[a]	Ford	Party Dem.	Party Rep.	Senate Candidates Dem.	Senate Candidates Rep.
Government job guarantee	17.8 (2504)[b]	9.9 (955)	16.9 (954)	26.9 (2049)	23.7 (2040)	24.0 (2041)	45.1 (1499)	48.9 (1429)
Urban unrest	17.9 (2480)	9.8 (947)	18.3 (944)	26.2 (2013)	26.4 (2009)	25.6 (2009)	45.6 (1484)	53.2 (1429)
Rights of accused	17.5 (2482)	14.8 (1935)	23.1 (1930)	31.4 (2030)	31.3 (2030)	31.8 (2030)	48.9 (1499)	53.7 (1453)
Liberalism–conservatism	26.8 (2478)	5.2 (1543)	9.8 (1543)	18.0 (1799)	17.9 (1795)	17.7 (1799)	38.2 (1341)	45.0 (1304)

[a]From the 1972 CPS Survey.

[b]Number of cases from which percentages were computed. The 1974 sample is weighted.

Source: 1972 and 1974 CPS American National Election Study Codebooks.

even plausible assessments of where the candidates and parties belong; any placement at all is sufficient for them to be considered knowledgeable.

The relative paucity of information voters have about congressional candidates is crucial because of the connection between information about candidates and voting decisions in congressional elections. This has customarily been demonstrated in the literature by assessing the effects of one item of information—the name of the candidate—on partisan defection. Stokes and Miller's groundbreaking study of voting in the 1958 congressional elections showed that partisan defection was directly related to differential awareness of the candidates, and their results have been confirmed without exception in subsequent national surveys. Table 1.7 displays the relevant data. The name recall question was asked of Senate candidates for the first time in 1974; notice that partisan voters respond to differential recall of Senate candidates in essentially the same way as to differential recall of House candidates. Any recall of the other party's candidate increases the likelihood that a partisan voter will defect; those few who remember only the other party's candidate are more likely to defect than not in elections from 1966 onward.

The evident importance of candidate familiarity provides some insight into why incumbents usually do so well in congressional elections: they are much more likely than their opponents to be known by voters. The data in table 1.8 show this clearly. In every election for which data are at hand, incumbents are recalled significantly more frequently than nonincumbents. And these data underestimate the incumbent's advantage, since they include candidates for open seats in the "nonincumbent" category. In 1972, for example, 40.9 percent of the voters recalled the names of nonincumbents seeking open seats; only 26.5 percent recalled those challenging incumbents. The comparable figures for 1974 are 35.3 percent and 31.0 percent; for the 1974 Senate elections, they are 53.9 percent and 44.2 percent. This gap can be traced to differences in campaign resources available to the two types of nonincumbents; the pertinent evidence is presented later.

Table 1.7.   Effects of Candidate Recall on Partisan Defection in House
and Senate Elections

Percentage Who Defected	Voter Recalled			
	Both Candidates	Own Candidate	Other Candidate	Neither Candidate
House elections				
1958	17	2	40	8
	(196)[a]	(166)	(68)	(368)
1966	19	4	66	14
	(198)	(98)	(41)	(231)
1968	23	5	51	19
	(303)	(97)	(57)	(267)
1970	24	1	57	13
	(152)	(148)	(37)	(256)
1972	23	7	62	21
	(151)	(100)	(26)	(242)
1974	29	1	58	15
	(281)	(154)	(79)	(374)
Senate elections				
1974	25	2	62	10
	(317)	(138)	(87)	(205)

[a]Number of cases from which percentages were computed. The 1974 sample is weighted.

Source: 1958–70, Robert B. Arseneau and Raymond Wolfinger, ''Voting Behavior in Congressional Elections'' (Presented to the 1973 Annual Meeting of the American Political Science Association, New Orleans, September 4–8, 1973), p. 14; 1972 and 1974, CPS American National Election Studies.

By the measure of name recall, then, the incumbent's advantage in voter familiarity is unmistakable. Its effect is even more telling—in light of the data in table 1.7—when we observe that when the contest is between an incumbent and a challenger and only one of the candidates is remembered (the two middle columns), that candidate is almost invariably the incumbent. This is true in more than 96 percent of the cases in the 1972 and 1974 surveys, for example.

What's in a Name?

Since remembering a candidate's name has been given no weighty theoretical significance, it requires some more substantive

Table 1.8.   Percentages of Voters Recalling Names of Candidates in
Contested Congressional Elections

	Incumbents		Nonincumbents	
House elections				
1958	57.6	(738)[a]	38.0	(947)
1964	63.0	(856)	39.8	(920)
1966	55.9	(583)	37.6	(703)
1968	63.7	(703)	46.5	(861)
1970	54.7	(548)	31.3	(630)
1972	50.0	(498)	30.9	(718)
1974	57.2	(856)	32.2	(1230)
Senate elections				
1974	72.7	(595)	48.3	(1023)

[a]Number of cases from which percentages were computed.

Source: 1958–70, John A. Ferejohn, "On the Decline of Competition in Congressional Elections," American Political Science Review 71 (1977): 170; 1972 and 1974, CPS Surveys.

interpretation. Stokes and Miller concluded from their study of the 1958 election that, in general, "recognition carries a positive valence; to be perceived at all is to be perceived favorably."[36] More recent evidence casts doubt on that conclusion.[37] One plausible suggestion is that name recall is at least a threshold indicator; that is, it should not be assumed that respondents who answer positively and correctly know nothing but the name of the candidate (although for some this may be true), but rather, the ability to remember a candidate's name is best understood as a sign that the respondent has crossed a minimal threshold essential to the acquisition of further information and to the elaboration of opinions about the candidate.

But the issue turns out to be more complicated. Abramowitz found that many of his respondents were quite ready to offer and amplify opinions on how one incumbent had performed his job without being able to recall his name.[38] If it is not necessary to re-

36.   Ibid., p. 205.
37.   See Alan J. Abramowitz, "Name Familiarity, Reputation, and the Incumbency Effect in a Congressional Election," Western Political Quarerly 28 (1975): 673–83.
38.   Ibid., pp. 673–77.

Table 1.9.   Voter Recall and Evaluation of 1974 Senate Candidates

Percent Evaluating	Evaluation				
	Positive	Negative	Positive and Negative	None	
Own party's candidate					
Recalled	56.4	12.5	15.4	15.7	(479)[a]
Not recalled	38.1	4.6	1.5	55.8	(260)
Difference	18.3	7.9	13.9	−40.1	
Other party's candidate					
Recalled	21.9	40.0	15.7	22.4	(402)
Not recalled	5.6	26.9	1.0	66.6	(305)
Difference	16.3	13.1	14.7	−44.2	
Independent voters, candidate is:					
Recalled	36.4	27.3	18.2	18.2	(77)
Not recalled	10.0	8.3	1.7	80.0	(66)
Difference	26.4	19.0	16.5	−61.8	

[a]Number of cases from which percentages were computed. The sample is weighted.

Source: 1974 CPS Survey.

member the candidate to have an opinion about him, what difference *does* name recall make? The 1974 CPS survey included some items that allow the question to be probed further. Regarding Senate races, respondents were asked, in addition to the name recall questions, a series of questions that can be summarized as: "Was there anything in particular about the Democratic (Republican) candidate that made you want to vote for (against) him (her)? What was that?"[39] Responses to these questions were first coded simply as positive (if there was anything that made the respondent want to vote for the candidate), negative (if there was anything that made the respondent want to vote against the candidate), or no response (the respondent mentioned nothing for or against the candidate) and were cross-tabulated with responses to the recognition question. The results, broken down by partisanship, appear in table 1.9.

39.   See variables 2177 to 2192 in Warren E. Miller, Arthur H. Miller, and F. Gerald Kline, *The CPS 1974 American National Election Study*, ICPR ed. (Ann Arbor, Mich.: The Center for Political Studies, The University of Michigan, 1975).

Respondents (and only those who reported voting are included in this sample) who know the name of the candidate are also much more likely to have something else to say about him. Nearly two-thirds of the voters who could not recall the candidate's name had nothing to say about him either. Less than one-fifth of those accurately naming a candidate had no further comment. Although the effects of partisanship are quite apparent, aware voters more frequently find something both good and bad about both their own and the other party's candidate. Familiarity does not, by any means, invariably produce a favorable evaluation. The relative gain in positive evaluations associated with recognition occurs primarily among a candidate's fellow partisans and, to a lesser extent, independent voters; among the other party's supporters the greater proportion of positive responses arising from awareness is more nearly matched by the increased in proportion of negative responses.

From another perspective, table 1.9 makes it clear that ignorance of a candidate's name does not preclude expressing an opinion about him; one-third of the voters in this category were willing to do so. Do respondents who do not remember the candidate's name use different evaluative criteria than those used by respondents who know the candidate? A more detailed recoding of the survey answers provides a way of finding out. All positive and negative responses (up to three of each were recorded by the interviewers) were classified as *personal* (those referring specifically to characteristics of the candidates themselves), *party* (references to one of the parties or to the candidate exclusively as a partisan), or *mixed*.[40] These were cross-tabulated with responses to the recognition question; the results are in table 1.10. Not surprisingly, voters who do not remember a candidate's name resort more readily to partisan criteria to evaluate him; personal comments are much more frequent among voters knowing the candidate. Still, nearly one-third of the unaware group employ purely personal criteria without recalling who the person is. Notice, incidently, that aware voters are

40. Responses coded 00, 01, and 05 in the hundred series for these questions were considered party references; those coded 02, 03, and 04 were classified as personal references; and those coded 06 through 12 were considered mixed. See ibid., pp. 400–15.

Table 1.10. Voter Recall and Criteria for Evaluation of 1974 Senate Candidates

		Evaluative Criteria:			
Percentage of Evaluations	*Personal*	*Party*	*Mixed*	*Number of Comments*	*Number of Respondents*
Positive					
Recalling candidate	60.7	8.9	30.4	957	538
Not recalling candidate	37.1	31.1	31.7	167	134
Negative					
Recalling candidate	44.4	14.5	41.1	601	393
Not recalling candidate	24.6	43.0	32.5	114	108

Source: 1974 CPS Survey. The sample is weighted.

more likely to offer multiple comments about candidates; they average 1.7 responses, the unaware group, 1.2.

In general, assessments of the candidates' personal qualities predominate; 51 percent of all evaluative comments refer to these exclusively; only 15 percent refer to purely partisan characteristics; the other 34 percent combine these and other criteria. Candidates themselves believe that their personal standing among voters is the most important determinant of how well they do—or at least the winners do.[41] They seem to have judged the situation correctly, unless we wish to argue that voters respond to the personal characteristics of candidates because this is what the candidates emphasize.

Although the ability to remember a candidate's name is not a precise thereshold—voters are often able to evaluate candidates without this item of information—differences in both the frequency and character of evaluative comments between voters who do and do not recall the candidate are substantial. It is plainly to a candidate's advantage to impress voters enough to be remembered, par-

41. John W. Kingdon, *Candidates for Office: Beliefs and Strategies* (New York: Random House, Inc., 1968), p. 24; Stokes and Miller, "Party Government," p. 206.

ticularly if the voters are of the candidate's party. But the evaluations that accompany greater familiarity are not invariably positive, and they have an important influence on the vote. Table 1.11 displays the connection between the simplified candidate evaluation index and the reported vote for senator in 1974. Evaluations of both candidates have a very noticeable impact on voting. The effects are as we would anticipate: controlling for partisanship, posi-

Table 1.11. Evaluation of Senate Candidates and Voting Behavior in 1974

Percentage of Partisan Voters Defecting

Evaluation of Other Party's Candidate	Evaluation of Own Party's Candidate			
	Positive	Positive and Negative	Negative	Marginal Totals
Positive	28.6	77.1	77.1	65.9
	(21)	(35)	(35)	(91)
Positive and negative	4.5	31.1	56.0	16.3
	(139)	(45)	(25)	(209)
Negative	4.2	3.4	40.0	4.8
	(167)	(59)	(5)	(231)
Marginal totals	5.8	30.9	66.2	19.8
	(327)	(139)	(65)	(531)

No evaluation: 16.5 (115)

Independent Voters: Percentage Voting for Democrat

Evaluation of Republican	Evaluation of Democrat			
	Positive	Postive and Negative	Negative	Marginal Totals
Positive		0.0	20.0	6.3
		(11)	(5)	(16)
Positive and negative	88.9	66.7	0.0	58.8
	(9)	(3)	(5)	(17)
Negative	100.0	83.3	100.0	88.9
	(2)	(6)	(1)	(9)
Marginal totals	90.0	35.0	18.2	45.2
	(11)	(20)	(11)	(42)

No evaluation: 40.0 (15)

[a]Number of cases from which percentages were computed. The sample is weighted.

Source: 1974 CPS Survey.

tive evaluations increase the probability of voting for a candidate, negative evaluations decrease that probability, and the effect in either case depends also on the evaluation of the other candidate. Defections are concentrated in the upper right-hand corner of the partisan table, party loyalty is predominant in the lower left-hand corner. A corresponding pattern emerges among independent voters.

Comparable data on House candiates and elections tend toward the same conclusion: personal evaluations predominate, and evaluations affect the vote. Stokes and Miller noted that "a long series of open-ended questions asked of those who said they had any information about the Representative produced mainly a collection of diffuse evaluative judgments: he is a good man, he is experienced, he knows the problems, he has done a good job, and the like."[42] They also found that evaluations, positive and negative, affected the vote in the expected direction.[43] Abramowitz concluded from his study of a small sample ($N = 208$) of voters in one Oregon district in 1974 that the evaluations of the incumbent (assessments of the challenger were not investigated) were a more important determinant of the vote than either party identification or name recall, particularly among voters who could give reasons for their judgments. Personal evaluations were most common (48 percent), followed by those related to issues (25 percent; most had to do with Nixon's impeachment), and constituency services (10 percent); the remaining 14 percent were undifferentiated.[44]

Mann reaches the same conclusion from his analysis of telephone surveys taken for the Democratic Study Group in selected congressional districts in 1974 and 1976: most reasons offered for judgments about candidates are personal. He also notes that "the number of references to issues was very small . . . but they were disproportionately negative. That is, when issues are sufficiently salient to become part of the public's image of the incumbent, they will probably do the incumbent more harm than good."[45]

42. Stokes and Miller, "Party Government," p. 207.
43. Ibid., p. 205.
44. Abramowitz, "Incumbency Effect," p. 678.
45. Thomas Edward Mann, "Candidate Saliency and Congressional Elections" (Ph.D. diss., University of Michigan, 1977), p. 36.

Mann's surveys are unique in asking a name recognition as well as a name recall question. Respondents (all were registered voters) were asked if they knew the candidates' names, and if they did not, they were given the names and asked if they recognized them. The second question is clearly the more pertinent, since voters are given a list of candidates in the voting booth. The difference in responses is striking and shows once again that name recall is not necessarily a critical threshold. The mean frequency of name recall in the 1976 surveys was 50 percent for incumbents, 25 percent for challengers, and 22 percent for candidates for open seats.[46] The mean recognition frequency was 92 percent for incumbents, 68 percent for challengers, and 76 percent for other nonincumbents.[47]

Recognition, rather than recall, appears to be the more crucial variable. "Visibility does not insure popularity, but it is an essential prerequisite. Voters who fail to recognize a challenger, as opposed to those who fail to recall the name of the challenger, invariably move disproportionately into the incumbent's camp. . . . Among those who did not recognize them, challengers lost on the average 38 percent of their own partisans."[48] Once candidates are recognized, however, the critical variable becomes the voter's assessment of the candidates. Mann's findings match those reported above for the 1974 Senate elections: "the association between candidate reputation and vote choice is strong for both incumbents and challengers. The ability of both candidates to hold their own partisans and attract opposition partisans is dependent upon their reputation with voters; a positive reputation is also critically important for minimizing their opponent's support among independents."[49]

A reasonable conclusion from these findings is that variations in the amount of information projected (and, by assumption, absorbed) about congressional candidates produces variations in voter support—although the voters' intervening evaluations of candidates based on that information are by no means irrelevant. This implies

46. Ibid., p. 36.
47. Ibid., p. 41.
48. Ibid., p. 82.
49. Ibid., p. 87.

that congressional campaigns actually matter; the quantity of resources expended—as well as the quality of the candidates—will affect the outcome. Money, as the basic and most flexible resource for acquiring means to reach voters, can make a difference in congressional contests. It also follows that campaign expenditures should be more helpful to nonincumbent candidates, who must do without the official resources for communicating with constituents enjoyed by incumbents.

The same findings also suggest an explanation of why incumbent security has risen. Incumbents are using their augmented perquisites to reach more voters more frequently and are simply reaping the electoral rewards greater familiarity brings. The most serious objection to this hypothesis is found in the data in table 1.8. These reveal neither an increase in the frequency with which incumbents' names are recalled nor an increase in the size of the advantage incumbents have over nonincumbents on this dimension. The greater support incumbents now attract has nothing to do with their advantage in name recall. Partisan voters are more likely to defect to incumbents than to nonincumbents, even when they cannot remember their names.[50]

This objection loses much of its force in light of the difference between name recall and name recognition. Indeed, if voters consistently prefer incumbents to challengers without recognizing *or* recalling either one, the phenomenon defies rational explanation. On this ground, and recognizing the importance of candidate evaluations in voting decisions, the hypothesis that incumbents are doing better because they advertise themselves more effectively cannot be dismissed out of hand. The question remains open.

An Alternative Explanation: The Bureaucracy Did It

Partisan voting has declined, partisan defection to incumbent candidates had increased, yet there is no clear evidence that incumbent self-advertising is the primary cause. One interpretation of these changes is that voters with weakened party ties have simply

---

50. Ferejohn, "Competition in Congressional Elections," p. 171.

substituted one simple cue—incumbency—for another—party.[51]
Such a view reflects the dominant conception of voters as poorly
informed, uninvolved, and unsophisticated in their approach to
voting decisions. Fiorina has advanced an alternative interpretation
from the premise that voters can and do make rational voting
choices. He argues that a change in the behavior of congressmen
has altered the decision criteria employed by voters in a way that
benefits incumbents of both parties.

The growth of the federal bureaucracy, fostered by congressional
policies, has encouraged congressmen to emphasize their role as
ombudsman for their constituents. The greater demand for such
services provides more opportunities for credit claiming, and "the
nice thing about case work is that it is mostly profit; one makes
many more friends than enemies."[52] It is also nonpartisan. The
party of the member delivering, or the constituent receiving the
service is irrelevant. What counts is a member's ability to deliver
services, which increases with his tenure in Washington and his
consequent mastery of the administrative apparatus. The rational
voter thus supports him on the basis of his incumbency rather than
his party or policy positions. As long as potentially marginal
districts—as determined by their political and social compo-
sition—"are represented by Congressmen who function primarily
as national policy makers . . . reasonably close Congressional elections will naturally result. But given Congressional incumbents who
place heavy emphasis on nonpartisan constituency service, the district will shift out of the marginal category."[53]

Based as it is on close analysis of only two congressional districts, Fiorina's thesis is admittedly speculative; a great deal more
supporting evidence will have to be uncovered for it to remain a serious rival of hypotheses that assume a much less sophisticated
electorate. But it does have the attraction of explaining the change

51. Ibid., p. 174.
52. Morris P. Fiorina, "The Case of the Vanishing Marginals: The Bureaucracy
Did It," *The American Political Science Review* 71 (1977): 180.
53. Ibid., p. 179.

in behavior of voters as a rational response to an equally rational change in strategy by incumbent congressmen.

Incumbency in Senate Elections

If party ties have weakened and if, for any reason, incumbency has replaced party as a positive cue for voters, Senate incumbents should also benefit. That incumbency is also a valuable asset in Senate elections is clear from the data in tables 1.7 and 1.8. Like House voters, Senate voters are more likely to vote for a candidate they can recall and are much more likely to recall incumbents than challengers. Additional survey evidence lends support. Hinckley, Hofstetter, and Kessel's analysis of data from the Comparative State Election Project uncovered "many more positive references for incumbents" than for nonincumbents in response to open-ended questions about them. "The pattern is consistent for both Republican and Democratic senatorial . . . candidates. Negative references do not seem similarly affected. What seems to be happening is that in a generally low information context, incumbency provides one item of positive information."[54]

Cowart's investigation of various SRC surveys taken between 1956 and 1970 showed that incumbency provided Senate candidates with a residual advantage when party and issue attitudes were controlled.[55] He had no data on candidate familiarity, however, so this factor could not be controlled. Little study has been made of changes over time in individual voting behavior at the Senate level, although there is some evidence that defections have increased rather steadily since the 1950s.[56] Aggregate data do, however, support the conclusion that incumbency is an increasingly important factor in Senate as well as House elections. Kostroski's study of postwar Senate elections found strong indication that the "importance of party has undergone a sharp, secular decline, while the im-

54.   Barbara Hinckley, Richard Hofstetter, and John Kessel, "Information and the Vote: A Comparative Election Study," *American Politics Quarterly* 2 (1974): 137.

55.   Andrew T. Cowart, "Electoral Choice in the American States," *American Political Science Review* 67 (1973): 840.

56.   Nie, Verba, and Petrocik, *Changing American Voter*, p. 51.

portance of incumbency has experienced an almost commensurate increase."[57] His regressions suggest that incumbency was worth less than 5 percent of the vote prior to 1952, whereas by the period 1966–70 its value had increased to more than 10 percent of the vote.[58] A replication of Kostroski's analysis for the years 1972–76 shows the value of Senate incumbency to have remained at this level.[59]

Still, incumbent senators have never been as consistently successful as their counterparts in the House. The reasons have not been very carefully studied yet, but several explanations come easily to mind. Senators are not nearly so well situated to follow a constituency service strategy for building and maintaining bipartisan support. States are, with six exceptions, larger and more populous than House districts, in some cases very much so. The opportunities for personal contact with constituents and attention to individual problems are, proportionately, diminished. The rewards for adopting a national, or even international orientation are more likely to tempt senators; the payoffs from attending to casework may be less appealing than the opportunity to make history. The six-year term reduces the pressure to keep electoral coalitions in good repair, and a careless senator may discover that he must begin almost from scratch when it is time to run once more. Action in the Senate is more visible; senators are fewer, they are given more attention by the news media, and they more easily become identified with policy stands and issues. And states tend to be much more socially and politically diverse than congressional districts. Whatever the reasons, incumbent senators remain twice as vulnerable as representatives at election time. The evident loosening of partisan ties has not redounded so directly to their benefit. The 1974 survey found a defection rate of 12.2 percent among incumbent partisans, 32.9 percent among challenger partisans in the Senate election. The

57. Warren Lee Kostroski, "Party and Incumbency in Postwar Senate Elections: Trends, Patterns, and Models," *American Political Science Review* 67 (1973): 1229.
58. Ibid., p. 1228.
59. Susan Rodnon, "Follow-Up to Warren Lee Kostroski's 'Party and Incumbency in Postwar Senate Elections: Trends, Patterns and Models' " (Unpublished paper, Trinity College, May 1978), p. 8.

comparative defection rates for House voters were 12.9 percent and 48.6 percent, respectively (see table 1.3).

ISSUES IN CONGRESSIONAL ELECTIONS

Partisanship, incumbency, and candidate saliency (and affect) dominate voting in congressional elections, but they are not the only influential variables. Political issues also enter into the equation, although in a peculiar way. Positions taken by candidates on the issues of the day have little discernible impact on congressional voters.[60] This is hardly surprising in light of the data in tables 1.5 and 1.6; voters often simply do not know where the candidates stand. Neither does the congressional vote appear to be a referendum on the performance of the party controlling Congress, as a "responsible parties" model would require.[61] There is, however, reason to believe that the congressional vote is, at least in off-year elections, a referendum on the performance of the president and his handling of the economy, and that his party is rewarded (or, more frequently, punished) according to how voters feel about him and current economic conditions. Coattail effects are also discernible in presidential election years, suggesting that presidential candidate evaluations may play a similar role for some voters in these elections.[62]

The strongest evidence that assessments of the president's performance and economic conditions affect off-year congressional voting emerges from studies of aggregate election results. The most striking findings are Tufte's, although work by Kramer, Bloom and Price, and Kernell provide additional evidence on these points.[63] Tufte found that he could explain fully 91 percent of the

60. Stokes and Miller, "Party Government," pp. 199 and 207.
61. Ibid., p. 209.
62. Gary C. Jacobson, "Presidential Coattails in 1972," *Public Opinion Quarterly* 40 (1976): 194–200.
63. Edward R. Tufte, "Determinants of the Outcomes of Midterm Congressional Elections," *American Political Science Review* 69 (1975): 812–26; Gerald H. Kramer, "Short-Term Fluctuations in U.S. Voting Behavior, 1896–1964," *American Political Science Review* 65 (1971): 131–43; Howard S. Bloom and H. Douglas Price, "Voter Response to Short-Run Economic Conditions: The Asymmetric Effect

variance in the standardized midterm loss in the share of the national two-party vote for U.S. Representatives of the president's party with just two variables: presidential popularity (measured by the Gallup Poll in the September before the election) and the change in real disposable income per capita over the year preceding the election. His equation indicates that a change of 10 percent in presidential popularity is associated with a change of 1.3 percent in the aggregate midterm House vote; a difference of $100 in per capita income is associated with a difference of 3.5 percent of the vote.[64] In aggregate, the off-year congressional electorate looks like a rational god of vengeance and reward: "the vote cast in the midterm elections is a referendum on the performance of the President and the administration's management of the economy."[65]

Tufte makes no claim that individual voters necessarily make a rational assessment of the president and the economy and cast their ballots accordingly. But his findings have given this question a prominent place on the research agenda. So far, the results have been inconclusive. Kernell found evidence that evaluation of the president's performance did directly affect individual voting behavior in off-year elections; assessments of the president's performance affect both turnout and the direction of the vote. Disapproval of the president inspires greater turnout and more partisan defection than does approval, leading Kernell to conclude that negative voting is the fundamental source of the off-year shift away from the president's party.[66]

Miller and Glass, on the other hand, used a normal vote analysis to argue that, at least in 1974, voters' reactions to the economy, particularly to inflation, were decisive. They found presidential approval to be strongly related to respondents' evaluations of the government's handling of economic problems, so that with party

of Prosperity and Recession," *American Political Science Review* 69 (1975); 1240–54; Samuel Kernell, "Presidential Popularity and Negative Voting: An Alternative Explanation of the Midterm Congressional Decline of the President's Party," *American Political Science Review* 71 (1977): 44–66.

64. Tufte, "Midterm Elections," p. 817.
65. Ibid., p. 824.
66. Kernell, "Presidential Popularity," pp. 60–61.

identification and economic evaluations controlled, presidential popularity had no additional effect on the vote. Economic evaluations did have an independent impact when the other two variables were taken into account. Their most startling conclusion, however, is that "contrary to popular opinion, *Watergate and the distrust in government it fostered was not the most important factor in the Democratic landslide of 1974.*"[67]

Conway and Wyckoff's investigation of the same data using path regression models reaches a similar conclusion: "The effects of Watergate on the congressional vote in 1974 were found to be indirect and complex" and, it should be added, very weak.[68] Their models support the familiar thesis that party identification, candidate familiarity, and incumbency are the most important determinants of the House vote; the addition of presidential and economic evaluations, attitudes toward Nixon, and other issue dimensions adds almost nothing to the explanatory power of their equations.[69]

The findings about Watergate are strongly counterintuitive and require further analysis. For now they must remain a puzzle, but the interpretation of the role of money in congressional elections developed in the next four chapters will produce an attractive and plausible solution. It will also suggest a more general link between aggregate and individual patterns of congressional voting.

The evidence for issue voting apart from presidential and economic evaluations is not entirely negative. If the relationship between party identification and issue attitudes is nonrecursive —certainly a possibility—then issue effects could be buried, statistically, in the ordinary least-squares regression models usually estimated. Achen estimated a simultaneous equation model which takes this possibility into account and found that even in the 1950s

67.   Arthur H. Miller and Richard Glass, "Economic Dissatisfaction and Electoral Choice" (Unpublished paper, Center for Political Studies, University of Michigan, 1977), p. 34.

68.   M. Margaret Conway and Mikel L. Wyckoff, "Vote Choice in the 1974 Congressional Elections: A Test of Competing Explanations" (Prepared for delivery at the 1977 Annual Meeting of the Midwest Political Science Association, Chicago, April 21–23, 1977), p. 24.

69.   Ibid., table 10.

(he uses Stokes and Miller's data), issues had a consistent, if small, effect on voting for House candidates.[70] Wright and Arseneau and Wolfinger also found some indication that issues have a small, but statistically significant effect on congressional voting when party and incumbency are controlled.[71] But there is no question that these latter two variables, plus candidate familiarity and affect, are far more important.

CONCLUDING COMMENTS

The patterns of voting behavior in congressional elections allow ample opportunity for campaign expenditures to influence election results. Although congressional voters have relatively little information about the candidates, both the extent and content of information they do have has a decisive effect on how they vote. Normally, incumbents are much better known than their challengers and so win with relative ease. Challengers have a fighting chance only if they are able to use the campaign period to neutralize the incumbent's informational advantage—which is built up at the public expense over his term of office. Mann points out that "the crucial difference between safe and marginal districts . . . rests with the challenger, not the incumbent. The several safe incumbents in my sample were as distinctly visible as marginal incumbents. Challengers who oppose safe incumbents, on the other hand, often generate so little campaign activity that their candidacies go largely unnoticed by the public. This no doubt accounts in part for the safeness of the incumbent."[72]

The more extensive the campaign, the more information will reach the electorate; the more extensive the campaign, the more ex-

70. Christopher H. Achen, "Issue Voting in the 1950's" (Unpublished paper, September 1976), pp. 15–17.

71. Gerald C. Wright, Jr., "Candidates' Policy Positions and Voting in Congressional Elections" (Prepared for delivery at the 1976 Annual Meeting of the American Political Science Association, Chicago, September 2–5, 1976), p. 20; Robert B. Arseneau and Raymond E. Wolfinger, "Voting Behavior in Congressional Elections" (Prepared for delivery at the 1973 Annual Meeting of the American Political Science Association, New Orleans, September 4–8, 1973), p. 17.

72. Mann, "Candidate Saliency," p. 65.

pensive it is likely to be. A serious challenge, then, is usually costly. It follows that, other things equal, the more a challenger spends, the better he will do at the polls. The same should also hold for nonincumbent candidates for open seats. The next four chapters will use campaign spending data from the 1972, 1974, and 1976 congressional elections to test these and some related propositions about money in congressional elections.

2 ☆ THE EFFECTS OF CAMPAIGN SPENDING: PRELIMINARY FINDINGS

"As it is now," House Speaker Tip O'Neill once said, "there are four parts to any campaign. The candidate, the issues of the candidate, the campaign organization, and the money to run the campaign with. Without money you can forget the other three."[1] Most students of campaign finance agree: money is not *sufficient*, but it is *necessary* for successful campaigns.[2] It is not sufficient because many factors quite apart from campaigns (and, therefore, campaign resources) affect election outcomes: district partisanship, national tides, presidential coattails, issues, candidates' personalities and skills, scandals, incumbency, and many others. Money is necessary because campaigns do have an impact on election results, and campaigns cannot be run without it. "In virtually all campaigns a basic amount of organizational work, communication through the commercial media, and getting-out-the-vote must be accomplished if the candidate expects to compete seriously. These things require money. Unless money to meet these minimum, essential expenses is available—regardless of how small the amount—candidates lacking it will be decisively handicapped."[3]

How much money is essential, and what difference it actually makes, are more difficult and controversial questions. Writing in 1960, Heard reached the unexceptionable, it not very satisfactory

---

1. Quoted in Jimmy Breslin, *How the Good Guys Finally Won: Notes from an Impeachment Summer* (New York: Ballantine Books, Inc., 1975), p. 14.

2. Alexander Heard, *The Costs of Democracy* (Chapel Hill, N. C.: The University of North Carolina Press, 1960), pp. 10–16; Herbert E. Alexander, *Money in Politics* (Washington, D.C.: Public Affairs Press, 1972), p. 10.

3. Heard, *Costs of Democracy*, p. 34.

conclusion that ''under some conditions the use of funds can be decisive. And under others no amount of money spent by the loser could alter the outcome.''[4] More than a decade later, Alexander could not be much more precise: ''The conventional wisdom is that pocketbook advantage spells the difference between success and failure at the polls, but the outcome of elections usually depends upon much more than money. . . . Many frugal campaigns triumph over lavish competition. . . . Not enough is known, however, about the bedrock minimum needed to reach the electorate. Few losers are satisfied they had ample resources.''[5]

Before the campaign finance reforms of the 1970s, scholars were severely handicapped by the lack of trustworthy data on how much was actually spent in specific campaigns. But from 1972 onward reasonably comprehensive data have been gathered and published on campaign contributions and expenditures in federal election campaigns.[6] These data provide the basis for a much more thorough investigation of the role of money in congressional elections. They are used in this and the next three chapters to develop and test several statistical models of campaign finance processes and to support some less formal hypotheses about money in elections. My intention is to develop a broad, empirically based understanding of the political consequences of current campaign finance practices.

This chapter presents the results of a preliminary analysis of the effects of campaign spending on the outcomes of House and Senate elections. Some of the hypotheses to be tested grow naturally out of the discussion in chapter 1; they will be considered shortly. Before that, however, I suggest several reasons why money should be particularly important in congressional elections—and why it is more important now than it was prior to the 1960s. This, in turn, helps

4. Ibid., p. 16.

5. Alexander, *Money in Politics*, p. 37.

6. The law requiring the first detailed reporting of campaign contributions and expenditures, the Federal Elections Campaign Act of 1971 (PL 92-225), did not take effect until April 7, 1972; contributions or expenditures made before that date may or may not have been reported, so the campaign finance data for 1972 are not as accurate as those available for 1974 and 1976.

account for the emergence of campaign finance as an important political issue; the politics of congressional campaign finance reform will be the subject of the concluding two chapters of this book.

CONGRESSIONAL CAMPAIGNS

Congressional elections are conducted by and for individual candidates. Even when party organizations were still relatively robust, congressional candidates were hardly the center of attention; little patronage was at stake, and House district boundaries rarely coincided with the locally more important divisions, the counties or cities. The continuing atrophy of party organizations has merely reinforced this circumstance; candidates must acquire the necessary financial and organizational resources on their own. Incumbents realize this. Even before the 1960s, their consensus was that "if we depended on the party organization to get elected, none of us would be here."[7] Nonincumbents, often to their surprise and dismay, learn the same lesson.[8] It is not simply that parties provide only a small proportion of the necessary campaign funds (pertinent data are presented in chapter 3); they give relatively little assistance of any kind to most congressional candidates.

The weakening of partisanship among voters has made individual campaigning strategically attractive; the personal approach pays off; the demise of parties as organizations has made individual campaigning essential. The decline of parties has been paralleled by the development of professional campaign management. Professional campaign managers set about doing what professionals traditionally do: rationalizing their field as much as possible. They adapted modern techniques of market research, advertising (particularly broadcast advertising), and personnel management for use in election campaigns. They reinforced the customary campaign arsenal

7. Charles L. Clapp, *The Congressman: His Work As He Sees It* (Washington, D. C.: The Brookings Institution, 1963), p. 397.

8. Robert J. Huckshorn and Robert C. Spencer, *The Politics of Defeat* (Amherst, Mass.: University of Massachusetts Press, 1971), p. 133; Jeff Fishel, *Party and Opposition: Congressional Challengers in American Politics* (New York: David McKay Company, Inc., 1973), pp. 99–100.

with professionally conducted polls, computerized data processing, and individualized mailing, and they brought modern managerial approaches to bear on traditional campaign operations.[9] In doing so, they probably hastened the transition to campaigns that were increasingly candidate-centered. They also drove up the cost of campaigning; the new technology is expensive.

Senator Muskie made a revealing observation during the 1971 hearings on broadcast expenditure restrictions. In 1954, he ran with three candidates for the House and one for governor on a combined budget of $18,000; his most recent campaign (1966), he said, cost about ten times that amount.[10] His intended message concerned the dramatic rise in campaign costs. At least as significant, I think, is the distinction between the earlier party campaign and the recent individual effort. Parties could provide economies of scale that are now lost to congressional candidates.

The question of just how great the increase in campaign expenses has actually been is complicated; it will be taken up in detail in chapter 6. Campaign costs have most certainly risen in the last twenty years, of course. For now, the important point is that the present circumstances of congressional campaigning would elevate money to a crucial role apart from any growth in actual costs—and that costs have increased on top of this.

CAMPAIGN SPENDING AND THE INCUMBENCY FACTOR

Money is necessary, but in congressional elections, it is more necessary to some candidates than to others. Or so it would certainly appear in light of the information and discussion in chapter 1. Put simply, money should be more important to challengers and other nonincumbent candidates than to congressional incumbents. The reasoning is obvious. The more information voters have about a candidate, other things equal, the more likely they are to vote for

9. For a full account of these changes, see Robert Agranoff, ed., *The New Style in Election Campaigns* (Boston: Holbrook Press, Inc., 1972).

10. U.S., Congress, Senate, Committee on Commerce, Subcommittee on Communications, *Federal Election Campaign Act of 1971*, 92nd Cong., 1st sess., hearings March 2–5 and 31, and April 1, 1971, p. 358.

him. Not that familiarity invariably breeds approbation; awareness does not always carry a positive valence. But it is generally much better for a candidate to be known than to be unknown by voters.

Incumbents can and do use the resources of office to publicize themselves, their views, and their accomplishments on a continuous basis. The additional campaigning that occurs during the formal campaign period should have relatively little additional impact (consider that recall of incumbents has not increased despite their more extensive self-promotion); the law of diminishing returns applies. Campaign spending should not make a great deal of difference for an incumbent who has been properly attentive to his state or district.

With rare exceptions, nonincumbent candidates enjoy nothing like incumbents' easy access to voters before the actual campaign. It is essential that they make the most of the campaign period. Their fundamental problem is usually to attract the attention of potential voters—to make themselves known—although they must of course also take pains to assure that they are perceived in the best possible light. The data in chapter 1 show their typically limited success in this endeavor. Money is a critical resource in the project. It buys access to the means of reaching voters—radio, television, newspapers, billboards, telephones, mailings, bumper stickers, and so on—and supports the campaign organization as well. How much nonincumbents manage to raise and spend should have an important impact on how well they do at the polls.

Indeed, the argument can be extended to any group of candidates suffering from serious electoral handicaps. Winter argues that "those pursuing established policies will generally have the advantage in nonmonetary campaign resources . . . to the point where the law of diminishing returns applies to their spending. Dollar for dollar, spending will generally yield much greater benefits to those seeking change" as well as to those challenging incumbents.[11] Alexander suggests that "money is capable of at least reducing se-

11. Howard R. Penniman and Ralph K. Winter, Jr., *Campaign Finances: Two Views of the Political and Constitutional Implications* (Washington, D. C.: American Enterprise Institute for Public Policy Research, 1971), p. 53.

vere handicaps for all candidates. Certainly no candidate can make much of an impression without it, especially a maverick who fights the regulars or one who challenges an incumbent."[12] At present, Republicans as a group probably ought to be considered handicapped; they certainly were in 1974. It might be expected, then, that campaign spending is, other things equal, more important to Republican than to Democratic congressional candidates.

The Preliminary Regression Model for House Elections

Straightforward multiple regression analysis of the spending–votes connection provides an initial test of these hypotheses; it will also suggest some additional propositions needing further investigation. However, an ordinary regression model ignores some crucial complications in the relationship between campaign expenditures and election results, so any conclusions derived from it are necessarily preliminary.

The first hypothesis to be tested is that money is more important to challengers than it is to incumbents in congressional elections. In other words, the amount spent by challengers has a greater effect on the outcome of the election than does the amount spent by incumbents. In the language of economics, the marginal returns for a given expenditure are greater for challengers. The model chosen to test this proposition for House elections is

$$CV = a + b_1CE + b_2IE + b_3P + b_4CPS + e \qquad (2.1)$$

where CV = challenger's share of the two-party vote[13]

$\quad\quad CE$ = challenger's campaign expenditures, thousands of dollars[14]

---

12. Alexander, *Money in Politics*, p. 39.

13. The election results for 1972 and 1974 are from Richard M. Scammon, *America Votes 11: A Handbook of Contemporary American Election Statistics* (Washington, D.C.: Congressional Quarterly, Inc., 1975); those for 1976 are from *Congressional Quarterly's Guide to the 1976 Elections: A Supplement to CQ's Guide to U.S. Elections* (Washington, D. C.: Congressional Quarterly, Inc., 1977), pp. 36–44.

14. The data for 1972 are from Common Cause Campaign Finance Monitoring Project, *1972 Congressional Campaign Finances*, 10 vols. (Washington, D.C.: Common Cause, 1974); those for 1974 are from the same organization, *1974 Con-*

IE = incumbent's campaign expenditures, thousands of dollars

P = challenger's party (1 if Democratic, 0 if Republican)

CPS = strength of the challenger's party in his district (approximated here by the percentage of the vote won by the challenger's party's candidate in the last election for this seat)[15]

a = intercept

b = regression coefficient

e = error or disturbance term

The challenger's share of the vote is taken to be a function of what he spends, what his opponent spends, his party, and the strength of that party in the district. Note that the same equation with observations on incumbents (with the incumbent's vote percentage as the dependent variable) would generate estimates which exactly mirror those derived from this model; either one would support the same substantive conclusions.

Our main concern is with the effects of campaign spending, so the variables P and CPS serve principally as controls in this equation. The party variable measures the short-term national trend favoring one party or the other in a particular election year. District party strength is measured by the vote for the candidate representing the challenger's party in the most recent previous election for the seat. Although far from ideal as an approximation of the expected or "normal" vote—which is what ought to be controlled—it has the advantage over the other possible index (percentage of registrants with the challenger's party in the district) of being available for a much larger proportion of the districts. At one stage of the re-

gressional Campaign Finances, 3 vols. (Washington, D.C.: Common Cause, 1976). The 1976 data are from U.S., Federal Election Commission, *FEC Disclosure Series No. 9: 1976 House of Representatives Campaigns Receipts and Expenditures* (Washington, D.C., September 1977) and *FEC Disclosure Series No. 6: 1976 Senatorial Campaigns Receipts and Expenditures* (Washington, D.C., April 1977).

15. The data source is *Congressional Districts in the 1970s*, 2nd ed. (Washington, D.C.: Congressional Quarterly, Inc., 1974). Previous vote percentages have been adjusted in these data for changes in district boundaries where redistricting has occurred.

search I repeated the analysis using registration percentages in place of CPS, and the results were essentially the same as those reported in this book, although the number of cases was halved. Both the party and party strength variables are expected to affect a candidate's ability to raise money as well as the size of the vote he receives and so must be taken into account.

Challenger and incumbent spending are entered as separate variables rather than as some composite (for example, the challenger's percentage of total expenditures by both candidates)[16] because their coefficients are expected to be quite different. The functional relationship between spending and votes is assumed to be linear. This has the advantage of simplicity but the drawback that it fails to allow for the diminishing returns that must apply to campaign spending; no candidate can get more than 100 percent of the vote no matter how much he spends. An attractive alternative is the semilog form, in which spending is entered as the natural logarithm of actual expenditures;[17] it permits diminishing returns but does not allow them to become negative as would, for instance, a quadratic model.[18]

Both the linear and semilog forms fit the data about as well; the R^2's are identical for 1972 and 1974, with the linear form showing a better fit for 1976.[19] But the semilog form has the defect of seriously underestimating the challenger's vote at higher levels of

16. Regressions that enter separate expenditure figures for Republicans and Democrats or which enter campaign spending as a ratio of the Democrat's to the Republican's expenditures, and use the vote percentage for candidates of one of the parties as the dependent variable, also ignore the strong possibility that spending does not have the same consequences for challengers and incumbents. See William P. Welch, ''The Economics of Campaign Funds,'' *Public Choice* 20 (1974): 83–97; Jonathan Silberman, ''A Comment on the Economics of Campaign Funds,'' *Public Choice* 25 (1976): 69–73.

17. See William P. Welch, ''The Effectiveness of Expenditures in State Legislative Races,'' *American Politics Quarterly* 4 (1976): 340–343.

18. See Jonathan Silberman and Gilbert Yochum, ''Campaign Funds and the Election Process'' (Paper presented to the Public Choice Society, New Orleans, March 11–13, 1977), p. 8.

19. For the semilog equations, see Gary C. Jacobson, ''Public Funds for Congressional Campaigns: Who Would Benefit?'' in *Political Finance*, ed. Herbert E. Alexander, Sage Electoral Studies Yearbook 5 (Beverly Hills, Calif.: Sage Publications, 1979). pp. 99–127.

spending. That is, its estimates exaggerate the degree to which returns diminish as spending increases. Examination of the residuals (the difference between the percent of votes actually won by the challenger and that predicted by the regression equation) showed this to be the case. The problem is illustrated by comparing the actual number of winning challengers in the three election years with the number predicted by the linear and semilog equations.

	1972	*1974*	*1976*
Winning challengers			
Actual number [20]	9	39	11
Number predicted by:			
Linear equation	5	29	8
Semilog equation	1	2	0

The linear equations exaggerate the expected vote of challengers at higher levels of spending, but inspection of the residuals indicates that this is not a significant problem until the challenger's spending exceeds $160,000, which occurs in less than 2 percent of the cases. At this level of spending, the equations are less likely to overpredict the number of winning challengers than to overstate the size of the challenger's victory. The linear form was therefore adopted for this and subsequent analyses, but the reader should be aware that a comparable analysis with semilog equations would uphold the same substantive interpretations. The regression estimates of equation 2.1 are reported in table 2.1.

According to these equations, the first hypothesis is correct. Election outcomes in all three election years were affected much more strongly by what challengers spent than by what incumbents spent. For 1972 and 1974, challengers are estimated to gain a little more than 1 percent of the vote for every $10,000 they spend. The gain is not as great in 1976, but the difference is noticeably less if the figures are adjusted for inflation. The coefficients on *CE* are

20. Actually, thirteen incumbents lost in 1972, but three of them were defeated by other incumbents they were forced to run against because of redistricting and a fourth lost a three-way race running as an independent. Forty incumbents lost in 1974, but one of these had just been elected in a special election and no separate spending figures were available for the second contest.

Table 2.1.   Effects of Campaign Spending in House Elections, 1972–76
(Estimates of Equation 2.1)

		Regression Coefficient	t Ratio[a]	Standardized Regression Coefficient	
1972	$CV = a$	20.7			
	b_1CE	.112	9.42	.51	
($N = 296$)	b_2IE	−.002	−.14	−.01	$R^2 = .49$
	b_3P	−.47	−.61	−.03	
	b_4CPS	.299	6.94	.33	
1974	$CV = a$	15.6			
	b_1CE	.121	10.45	.48	
($N = 319$)	b_2IE	−.028	−2.34	−.11	$R^2 = .65$
	b_3P	9.78	11.19	.42	
	b_4CPS	.351	7.75	.28	
1976	$CV = a$	14.8			
	b_1CE	.074	9.57	.45	
($N = 329$)	b_2IE	−.003	−.27	−.01	$R^2 = .60$
	b_3P	.26	.32	.01	
	b_4CPS	.444	10.84	.48	

[a]A t ratio of at least 1.98 is necessary for a .05 level of significance, 2.58 for .01, and 3.35 for .001.

.112, .143, and .100 across the three election years in 1972 dollars.[21]

Incumbent spending has a much weaker, although properly negative impact on the challenger's vote; only for 1974 is its effect statistically significant. Its simple relationship with the dependent variable is actually positive; the more incumbents spend, the worse they do. The respective simple correlations between incumbent spending and the challenger's vote are .39, .46, and .48 for the three elections. The explanation for this somewhat surprising result, to be defended in detail in chapter 4, is that incumbents evidently adjust their spending to the gravity of the electoral challenge posed by a specific challenger. They spend more in the face of stiff opposition (indicated by the challenger's level of spending), but this

21.   Calculated from the Consumer Price Index for October of each election year. The 1976 dollar was worth only 73.5 percent of the 19,2 dollar.

does not offset gains made by the challenger from the campaigning —and campaign spending—that inspires their reaction.

The control variables behave as we would expect. It made little difference which party a challenger belonged to in 1972 or 1976 (once the other variables are taken into account). In 1974, however, Democratic challengers typically received an additional 10 percent of the two-party vote. District party strength, as indicated by the vote for the challenger's party's candidate in the last election, had a consistent and substantial impact in all three elections; its effect was greatest in 1976. Taken together, all four independent variables explain from one-half (1972) to two-thirds (1974) of the variance in the outcomes of House elections.

The Regression Model for Senate Elections

Analysis of the data for Senate elections in these three election years also shows challenger spending to have the greater effect on the results. The regression model for estimating the effects of spending in Senate contests between incumbents and challengers is necessarily adapted to the different circumstances of these elections:

$$CV = a + b_1 \ln CEPV + b_2 \ln IEPV + b_3 P + b_4 \ln VAP + e \quad (2.2)$$

where $\ln CEPV$ = natural log of the challenger's expenditures, cents per voting-age individual[22]

$\ln IEPV$ = natural log of the incumbent's expenditures, cents per voting-age individual

$\ln VAP$ = natural log of the voting-age population of the state, thousands

and the other variables and coefficients are as defined for equation 2.1.

Expenditures were divided by the voting-age population of the states to control for the widely divergent state populations. The

22. The data are from U.S., Congress, Senate, Committee on Rules and Administration, *Federal Election Reform Proposals of 1977*, 95th Cong., 1st sess., hearings May 4–6 and 11, 1977, p. 835; and U.S., Congress, *Congressional Record*, 93rd Cong., 2d sess., October 8, 1974, p. 18542.

Table 2.2.   Effects of Campaign Spending in Senate Elections, 1972–76
(Estimates of Equation 2.2)

		Regression Coefficient	t Ratio[a]	Standardized Regression Coefficient	
1972	$CV = a$	16.5			
	$b_1 \ln CEPV$	6.29	4.79	.88	
$(N = 25)$	$b_2 \ln IEPV$	-3.98	-2.36	$-.40$	$R^2 = .55$
	$b_3 P$	2.55	.89	.14	
	$b_4 \ln VAP$	2.88	1.93	.33	
1974	$CV = a$	24.4			
	$b_1 \ln CEPV$	3.40	2.96	.70	
$(N = 22)$	$b_2 \ln IEPV$	$-.14$	$-.06$	$-.02$	$R^2 = .82$
	$b_3 P$	8.26	5.12	.55	
	$b_4 \ln VAP$	1.03	.75	.15	
1976	$CV = a$	-18.4			
	$b_1 \ln CEPV$	7.42	5.20	.97	
$(N = 23)$	$b_2 \ln IEPV$	.67	.60	.10	$R^2 = .70$
	$b_3 P$	.51	.16	.02	
	$b_4 \ln VAP$	5.37	3.57	.60	

[a]A t ratio of at least 2.08 is necessary for a .05 level of significance, 2.85 for .01, and 3.85 for .001.

semilog form was adopted because it fit the data much better than did the linear form and showed none of the defects apparent when it was applied to the House election data. The party strength variable is omitted because in none of the equations estimated was it significantly related to the dependent variable (nor did its absence affect the other coefficients).[23]

Estimates of the Senate equations are listed in table 2.2. They generally reinforce the House results, although much more variation is evident, perhaps because of the much smaller number of cases. Only for 1972 did incumbent expenditures have a substantial and statistically signficant impact on the election results, and even that year, challenger spending had a notably greater effect.

23.   The index of state party strength was computed as the smallest proportion of the total statewide House vote won in aggregate by House candidates of the Senate candidate's party in any election year from 1968 through 1976. See Warren Lee Kostroski, "Party and Incumbency in Postwar Senate Elections: Trends, Patterns, and Models," *American Political Science Review* 67 (1973): 1226.

The regression coefficients for logged variables are difficult to interpret directly from the equations. They indicate that in 1972, an increase from 0 to 6.25 in cents spent per voter would result in an estimated increase of 11.5 in the challenger's vote percentage; thereafter, each time expenditures doubled (to 12.5 cents per voter, 25 cents, 50 cents, and so on), the challenger's expected vote increases by 4.4 percentage points. Similarly, the challenger's vote is predicted to fall by 7.3 percent as the incumbent's spending goes from 0 to 6.25 cents per voter and by an additional 2.8 percentage points each time the amount doubles. The same figures for 1974 challengers are 6.2 and 2.4; for incumbents, they are .3 and .1. For 1976, they are 13.6 and 5.1 for challengers; and the challenger's vote is expected to *increase* as incumbent spending rises, 1.2 percent for the first 6.25 cents per voter, .5 percent with each doubling thereafter. In every case, the marginal return is clearly greater for challengers than it is for incumbents.

Notice once again the great disadvantage suffered by Republican challengers in 1974; Democrats could expect an additional 8.3 percent of the vote just for being Democrats.

PARTISAN DIFFERENCES IN CAMPAIGN SPENDING EFFECTS

The second proposition to be tested is that campaign spending is more important to candidates subject to any serious electoral handicaps aside from incumbency effects. At present, Republican candidates probably fall into that category; they certainly had serious problems in 1974. One piece of evidence that they do derives from separate estimates of equation 2.1 for Democrats and Republicans (with P, of course, omitted). Table 2.3 lists the partial regression coefficients on CE and IE for Republican and Democratic challengers in the three election years. Observe that Republican expenditures were substantially more effective for both challengers and incumbents in 1974; that is the only year in which incumbent expenditures had a statistically significant impact on the vote. Republican expenditures also had a somewhat greater effect in 1976, while Democratic spending made a greater difference in 1972, although the differences between the coefficients are not statistically

Table 2.3.   Regression Coefficients on Campaign Spending Variables for
Democratic and Republican Challengers and Incumbents, 1972–76

Challenger	CE[a]	IE
1972		
Democrat	.115	−.006
Republican	.101	−.028
1974		
Democrat	.105	−.031[b]
Republican	.171	−.006
1976		
Democrat	.064	−.002
Republican	.079	−.006

[a]Significant at .001.
[b]Significant at .05.

significant. Since 1972 was, by many measures, a particularly
good Republican year,[24] this latter result is understandable.

Partisan differences are even more apparent in contests for open
seats. The equation estimated for House elections was

$$DV = a + b_1DE + b_2RE + b_3DPS + e \qquad (2.3)$$

where DV = Democratic candidate's percentage of the two-party
vote

DE = Democrat's campaign expenditures, thousands of
dollars

RE = Republican's campaign expenditures, thousands of
dollars

DPS = Democrat's district party strength (measured as was
CPS in equation 2.1)

and the other variables and coefficients are as defined for equation
2.1. Estimates of this equation appear in table 2.4.

In every election year, Republican expenditures have a greater
effect on the outcome than do Democratic expenditures; the difference is most pronounced for 1974. In contests for open House

24. See Gary C. Jacobson, "Presidential Coattails in 1972," *Public Opinion
Quarterly* 40 (1976): 195.

Table 2.4. Effects of Campaign Spending in House Elections for Open Seats
(Estimates of Equation 2.3)

		Regression Coefficient	t Ratio[a]	Standardized Regression Coefficient	
1972	$DV = a$	36.0			
	b_1DE	.045	2.56	.31	
$(N = 52)$	b_2RE	$-.077$	-2.84	$-.34$	$R^2 = .46$
	b_4DPS	.308	4.15	.47	
1974	$DV = a$	51.4			
	b_1DE	$-.002$	$-.10$	$-.01$	
$(N = 53)$	b_2RE	$-.130$	-5.07	$-.54$	$R^2 = .59$
	b_3DPS	.328	3.95	.41	
1976	$DV = a$	52.1			
	b_1DE	.014	.92	.13	
$(N = 50)$	b_2RE	$-.088$	-3.70	$-.57$	$R^2 = .44$
	b_3DPS	.225	2.18	.27	

[a]A t ratio of at least 2.08 is necessary for a .05 level of significance, 2.85 for .01, and 3.85 for .001.

seats, campaign spending has greater marginal benefits for Republican candidates.

Analysis of Senate elections for open seats is complicated by the small number of such contests; the most in any of the three election years is nine. All were therefore combined into one single data set and the expenditure figures were adjusted for inflation when necessary (1976 = 100); dummy variables were used to sort out short-term trends. The equation estimated was thus

$$DV = a + b_1 \ln DEPV + b_2 \ln REPV + b_3 \ln VAP + b_4 Y_{72} + b_5 Y_{74} + e \qquad (2.4)$$

where $\ln DEPV$ = natural log of the Democrat's expenditures, cents per voting-age individual

$\ln REPV$ = natural log of the Republican's expenditures, cents per voting-age individual

Y_{72} = 1 if the year was 1972, 0 otherwise

Y_{74} = 1 if the year was 1974, 0 otherwise

and the other variables and coefficients are as defined for equations 2.2 and 2.3. The results are in table 2.5. They show that in Senate elections for open seats, too, Republican spending has the greater impact on the outcome. The expected Democratic percentage of the two-party vote increases by 7.1 as the Democrat's spending goes from nothing to 6.25 cents per voter; it subsequently increases by 2.7 percentage points each time this spending figure doubles. It decreases by 17.1 points as the Republican's spending rises from 0 to 6.25 cents per voter; and it thereafter decreases by 6.5 points each time Republican spending doubles.

The hypothesis that campaign spending is more important for candidates disadvantage for any reason is clearly supported by these findings if we accept the reasonable premise that Republicans are at a general disadvantage (one that was severely exacerbated in 1974). Certainly, the figures on party identification—and the ratio of Republican to Democratic officeholders at all levels—are strong reasons for assuming that this is indeed the case. With far fewer partisan supporters in the electorate, Republicans rely more heavily on campaigning—and thus campaign spending—to win votes. Transmitting campaign information beyond the party label is essential.

CONCLUSIONS AND CAVEATS

The preliminary regression results confirm that campaign spending does have a strong effect on congressional election outcomes and

Table 2.5.   Effects of Campaign Spending in Senate Elections for Open Seats
(Estimates of Equation 2.4)

		Regression Coefficient	t Ratio[a]	Standardized Regression Coefficient	
1972–76	$DV = a$	104.4			
	$b_1 \ln DEPV$	4.43	1.10	.32	
	$b_2 \ln REPV$	−10.94	−5.04	−1.21	
$(N = 25)$	$b_3 \ln VAP$	−3.72	−1.40	−.39	$R^2 = .62$
	$b_4 Y72$	−1.53	−.44	−.08	
	$b_5 Y74$	−5.03	−1.28	−.25	

[a]A t ratio of at least 2.08 is necessary for a .05 level of significance, 2.85 for .01, and 3.85 for .001.

that money is a particularly important campaign resource for nonincumbent candidates. Incumbents do not seem to benefit from campaign spending to anywhere near the same degree. The more they spend, the worse they do; with challenger spending controlled, their spending has little apparent effect on the vote. These findings, marginally modified by partisan effects, conform to theoretical expectations, but they cannot be accepted as definitive because they ignore one essential consideration. As Heard pointed out, "even if expenditures and success at the polls always run together, the flow of funds to a candidate might simply reflect his prior appeal rather than create it."[25] That is, money may flow to a candidate for the same reasons that votes do; both variables—expenditures and votes—might be determined by a set of external factors.

Or the relationship between expenditures and votes may be reciprocal. The expectation that a candidate will do well may bring campaign contributions. Suppose that it is possible to make a rough prediction of the outcome prior to the election; if campaign contributors prefer to contribute to candidates who are possible or even likely winners (and they do—see chapter 3), contributions to a candidate should increase with his expected vote.[26]

Alternatively, from a slightly different perspective, campaign spending may help win popular support, and thus votes, but characteristics that also help to attract votes—personal charm or "charisma," political skill and experience—should also ease the job of fund raising. Candidates who are well known and who have political experience (and thus a greater expectation of success) raise money more easily, spend it, thereby increasing their popularity even further, acquiring in consequence even more money, and so on, the ultimate payoff coming in the form of additional votes on election day.

The ordinary least-squares (OLS) regressions reported in this chapter (and in the great majority of other studies of campaign

---

25. Heard, *Costs of Democracy*, p. 16.
26. Welch, "Campaign Funds," pp. 86–88; Paul A. Dawson and James E. Zinser, "Political Finance and Participation in Congressional Elections," *American Academy of Political and Social Science Annals* 425 (1976): 63.

spending effects)[27] are inappropriate for estimating reciprocal relationships; a simultaneous equation system is required. OLS estimates of parameters when the true relationship is reciprocal are
biased and inconsistent because endogenous variables (those which
have a reciprocal affect on one another) are, when treated as explanatory variables, correlated with the error term.[28] The standard
solution to this problem is two-stage least-squares (2SLS) estimation of a simultaneous equation model. That will be undertaken in
chapter 5. The procedure requires development of a model that
treats campaign spending as a dependent as well as an independent
variable. This, in turn, demands careful exploration of what determines how much candidates spend. How is money raised? Why and
when do individuals and groups contribute to congressional campaigns? It is necessary to clarify and answer these related questions
before proceeding to estimate the full set of relationships between
campaign spending and election outcomes. This will be accomplished in the next two chapters.

27. Kristian S. Palda, "The Effect of Expenditure on Political Success," *Journal of Law and Economics* 18 (1975): 638–55, is an exception.

28. J. Johnston, *Econometric Methods* (New York: McGraw-Hill Book Company, 1972), p. 243.

3 ☆ CAMPAIGN CONTRIBUTIONS: SOURCES, MOTIVES, AND STRATEGIES

The preliminary analysis of data from the 1972, 1974, and 1976 congressional elections demonstrates a clear connection between campaign spending and election results. In contests between incumbents and challengers, the critical variable is the amount spent by the challenger. In contests for open seats, expenditures by Republican candidates appear to have the greater effect on the vote. The analysis is preliminary because the regression procedure employed assumes unidirectional causality: spending produces votes, at least for nonincumbent candidates. But if strong candidates attract campaign contributions more readily, causality may flow in both directions, or, more radically, candidates may receive money and votes for the same reasons, with the former having no true effect on the latter.

The crucial question is, then: What determines how much money congressional candidates raise and spend? The pattern of spending depends on the pattern of campaign contributions. If spending directly affects election outcomes, contributors have an important say in who wins congressional office. If, alternatively, the relationship between spending and votes is reciprocal, or even spurious, this can only be recognized through a careful examination of the behavior of contributors and of candidates who seek their support. In either case, the role of money in congressional elections cannot be understood without scrutiny of the strategies and motives of those who supply campaign funds. The present chapter analyzes campaign finance from the perspective of contributors to congressional campaigns. It establishes the basis for consideration in chapter 4 of campaign finance as a problem for candidates. The discussion in these two chapters will provide the framework for an elaborated model of money in congressional elections, which is the subject of chapter 5.

Contributions and Expenditures, 1972–1976

A broad overview of the pattern of campaign contributions and expenditures in the 1972, 1974, and 1976 congressional elections is provided by table 3.1, which lists the mean receipts and expenditures of House and Senate candidates, by party and incumbency status, in the three election years. The table makes several important points:

1. Just as incumbency status determines the (apparent) utility of campaign spending, so it directly affects total campaign contributions and expenditures in the most fundamental way. The circumstances faced by candidates seeking funds are entirely different depending on whether they are incumbents, challengers, or candidates for open seats. This crucial point will be established in much greater detail below and in chapter 4, but it is obvious even in the very general data shown here.

House incumbents typically raise and spend 60 to 80 percent more than do their opponents. Candidates for open seats usually spend even more than incumbents; the money-raising ability of nonincumbents varies enormously depending on whether or not they face incumbents. Similarly, Senate incumbents generally outspend their opponents decisively. The comparison between nonincumbents contesting open seats and challengers is less precise in these data because it does not take into account the populations of the states; spending varies directly with state populations. Still, it is evident that the former acquire money more easily than the latter.

2. The circumstances of a particular election year can affect the amount of money available to candidates dramatically. Notice the difference in total receipts by Democratic and Republican challengers in 1974, for example. The pattern of receipts and expenditures that year is very instructive; its significance is detailed in chapters 4 and 5.

3. Compare the amount spent to the amount raised by candidates according to incumbency status. Nonincumbents spend about all they can raise (sometimes more—they have campaign debts); incumbents are apparently under less pressure to spend all they get, though, as noted in chapter 4, the proportion of funds left over depends on the level of competition the incumbent faces.

4. Campaign receipts and expenditures in House races have grown over the three elections. However, the constant-dollar increase is much less than that implied by the table; the inflation rate was 36 percent between October 1972 and October 1976. The real increase in total campaign expenditures between 1972 and 1976 was not 52 percent, as the raw figures would suggest, but a much more modest 12 percent. Incumbent expenditures increased by about 20 percent, challenger spending by about 18 percent, and spending in open-seat contests actually decreased by slightly more than 1 percent.[1]

An equivalent analysis for Senate campaigns is confounded by differences in state populations. The average voting-age population of states with Senate contests in 1972 was 2.1 million; in 1976, it was 3.6 million. If we divide expenditures by population, Senate candidates spent an average of 18.6 cents per eligible voter in 1972, 17.0 cents per eligible voter in 1976. This would suggest a 33 percent constant-dollar decrease in campaign spending over the four years. However, per voter spending decreases as the voting age population of the state increases, so the figures are distorted by the races in larger states (including the two largest, California and New York) in 1976. McDevitt used a regression model based on 1972 Senate spending patterns to predict 1976 spending; he found that actual 1976 spending was 7.6 percent below that predicted by the model (in constant dollars).[2] This is a more plausible figure.

1. I compare expenditures rather than contributions because the 1972 figures on contributions are not complete; campaign contributions made prior to April 7, 1972, did not have to be reported. The apparent constant-dollar increase in campaign contributions of 25 percent between 1972 and 1976 is thus a gross overestimate.

2. Roland D. McDevitt, "Congressional Campaign Finance and the Consequences of Its Regulation" (Ph.D. diss., University of California at Santa Barbara, 1978), p. 155.

Table 3.1. Average Campaign Receipts and Expenditures in Congressional Elections, 1972–76, by Party and Incumbency Status

	Incumbents		Challengers		Open Seats	
	Democrats	Republicans	Democrats	Republicans	Democrats	Republicans
House of Representatives						
1972						
Number of cases[a]	176	142	142	176	58	58
Receipts[b]	$55,659	$61,163	$29,676	$31,419	$95,660	$88,697
Expenditures	49,249	52,263	30,176	32,340	96,762	91,352
1974						
Number of cases	160	162	162	160	52	52
Receipts	57,141	88,154	57,726	20,449	104,776	80,676
Expenditures	46,331	81,436	59,331	20,744	103,091	79,903
1976						
Number of cases	208	121	121	208	50	50
Receipts	88,706	104,846	45,284	55,079	140,292	102,277
Expenditures	79,100	90,184	44,646	55,484	144,060	97,687

Senate

1972						
Number of cases	9	16	16	9	8	8
Receipts[b]	$324,300	$464,219	$192,038	$305,311	$467,750	$431,375
Expenditures	381,066	559,744	205,719	312,400	481,175	460,225
1974						
Number of Cases	12	10	10	12	9	9
Receipts	631,458	549,480	384,520	314,550	528,722	259,800
Expenditures	562,492	600,440	390,310	284,492	531,589	273,622
1976						
Number of cases	15	8	8	15	8	8
Receipts	583,633	888,663	646,000	357,191	642,438	895,575
Expenditures	555,913	880,275	645,450	349,033	636,288	877,613

[a] Includes candidates with majority party opposition only.

[b] Some contributions received before April 7, 1972, were not reported.

Source: 1972 and 1974, Common Cause; 1976, Federal Election Commission.

Spending has clearly fallen off to some extent in Senate elections; a likely explanation is that changes in the campaign finance laws have affected these campaigns more severely than they have House contests; a fuller discussion of the effects of campaign finance reforms is presented in chapters 6 and 7.

The differing amounts of money available to incumbents, challengers, and candidates for open seats in different election years are the consequence of the behavior of those who supply campaign funds. The basic sources of campaign money are (in order of importance) individuals, interest and ideological groups, political parties, and the candidates themselves. Loans, which might be considered a fifth source, wind up either as contributions from the creditor or are repaid by funds from the first four sources. Motives and strategies vary both within and between categories of contributors, but the basic types can be specified, as can their effect on the supply of congressional campaign funds.

INDIVIDUAL CONTRIBUTIONS

Contributions from private individuals are unquestionably the most important component of campaign funds. Tables 3.2 and 3.3 list the amounts and percentages of total receipts gathered in individual contributions to House and Senate candidates, by party and incumbency status, 1972–76.[3] Generally, about two-thirds of all campaign money comes from private individuals. In House contests, the greatest proportion of individual contributions arrives in amounts of $100 or less; Senate candidates rely more heavily on larger contributions. There is a tendency, most pronounced in 1976, for Republican candidates to receive a greater portion of their fund from individuals. The tables also seem to indicate that individual contributions comprised a smaller share of campaign receipts in 1976 than in previous years, but the 1972 data include the candi-

3. The figures for 1972 do not always include contributions made prior to April 7 of that year. Individual contributions of less than $500 were not reported in a separate category in the 1974 data; they are calculated by subtracting the amounts reported for all other categories from total receipts.

date's own funds in this category, and individual gifts of less than $500 are not reported separately in the 1974 data, so no dependable comparison is really possible.

Motives for Individual Contributions

It is perhaps easiest to understand why individuals do not contribute to the candidates of their choice. For most people, the victory of any particular candidate or party is, in technical terms, a *public good*. A public good for any group is some benefit that all receive if any of them receives; it cannot by its very nature be denied to members who, for example, refuse to bear any of the cost of achieving it.[4] The victory of a candidate benefits, in some way, all those who prefer the winner to the loser. For those whose preferences are based on the candidate's party, ideology, general issue and policy orientation, good looks, ethnic affiliation, style, or any number of similar considerations, the victory is plainly a public good. It is not a purely public good only to those whose preferences stem from the hope or promise of some personal payoff not automatically available to the whole group.

It is essential to recognize this because Olson has demonstrated that, except in special circumstances, no rational, self-interested individual will voluntarily incur any of the cost of providing a public good. The special circumstances have to do with the size of the group and the way costs and benefits are divided among its members. The proposition does not hold if the benefit for at least one individual in the group outweighs the entire cost of achieving the good, for in that case that individual (rationally) pays the entire cost of providing the good. In groups which are not so fortunately situated but which are small enough that the effect of any individual's withdrawal of support is palpable (a noticeable decrease in the likelihood of the good's being provided or in the amount produced), the outcome is uncertain; at best, though, less than the optimum amount of resources will be invested in pursuit of the good.[5]

4. Mancur Olson, Jr., *The Logic of Collective Action* (Cambridge, Mass.: Harvard University Press, 1965), pp. 14–16.

5. Ibid., p. 44.

Table 3.2. Average Campaign Contributions to House Candidates by Individuals, 1972–76, by Party and Incumbency Status

	Total	Percent[a]	$100 or Less	Percent	$101– 499	Percent	$500 or More	Percent	N
1972									
Incumbents									
Democrats	$34,733	62.4	$17,304	31.1	$17,429[b]	31.1			176
Republicans	37,680	61.6	15,191	24.8	22,489	36.8			142
Challengers									
Democrats	17,219	58.0	8,753	29.5	8,466	28.5			142
Republicans	20,106	64.0	10,839	34.5	9,267	29.5			176
Open Seats									
Democrats	57,647	60.3	31,931	33.4	25,753	26.9			58
Republicans	58,748	66.2	31,367	35.4	27,381	30.9			58
1974									
Incumbents									
Democrats	40,890	71.6			34,329[c]	60.1	$ 6,652	11.5	160
Republicans	70,369	79.8			59,910	68.0	10,459	11.9	162
Challengers									
Democrats	39,822	69.0			29,368	50.9	10,436	18.1	162
Republicans	14,360	70.2			8,691	42.5	5,679	27.8	160

Open Seats									
Democrats	73,875	70.5	32,656	36.8	53,580	51.1	20,294	19.4	52
Republicans	54,749	67.9	48,450	46.2	41,844	51.9	12,865	15.9	52
1976									
Incumbents									
Democrats	53,316	59.9			11,299	12.7	9,181	10.3	208
Republicans	71,470	68.2			13,485	12.9	9,541	9.1	121
Challengers									
Democrats	21,483	47.4	13,998	30.9	3,331	7.4	4,154	9.2	121
Republicans	31,601	57.4	18,308	33.2	6,011	10.8	7,282	13.2	208
Open Seats									
Democrats	65,159	46.4	35,647	25.4	12,972	9.2	16,540	11.8	50
Republicans	62,661	61.3	36,825	36.0	12,231	12.0	13,605	13.1	50

Note: Includes candidates with major party opposition only.

[a] Percentage of all contributions.

[b] Includes all contributions of more than $100.

[c] Includes all contributions of less than $500.

Table 3.3. Average Campaign Contributions to Senate Candidates by Individuals, 1972–76, by Party and Incumbency Status

	Total	Percent[a]	$100 or Less	Percent	$101–499	Percent	$500 or More	Percent	N
1972									
Incumbents									
Democrats	$225,845	69.6	$ 81,878	25.4	$ 45,767	14.1	$ 98,200	30.3	9
Republicans	377,294	81.3	152,531	32.9	65,400	14.1	159,363	34.3	16
Challengers									
Democrats	91,863	47.8	48,100	25.0	14,788	7.7	35,275	18.4	16
Republicans	173,111	56.7	86,511	28.3	24,478	8.0	62,122	20.3	9
Open Seats									
Democrats	269,738	57.7	114,463	24.5	43,750	9.4	111,513	23.8	8
Republicans	279,726	64.8	118,188	27.4	54,200	12.6	107,338	24.9	8
1974									
Incumbents									
Democrats	457,375	72.4			287,500[b]	45.5	169,875	26.9	12
Republicans	454,580	76.5			275,890	46.4	178,690	30.1	10
Challengers									
Democrats	322,430	83.9			257,410	66.9	65,020	16.9	10
Republicans	239,333	76.1			174,900	55.6	64,433	20.5	12

Open Seats									
Democrats	406,900	77.0			217,000	41.0	189,900	35.9	9
Republicans	178,867	68.8			99,778	38.4	79,089	30.4	9
1976									
Democrats	428,680	73.4	130,733	22.4	94,227	16.1	203,720	34.9	15
Republicans	751,013	84.5	356,950	40.2	134,100	15.1	259,963	29.2	8
Challengers									
Democrats	490,063	75.9	143,050	22.1	109,388	16.9	237,625	36.8	8
Republicans	245,687	68.8	131,753	36.8	39,480	11.1	74,453	20.8	15
Open Seats									
Democrats	378,175	58.9	149,013	23.1	83,325	13.0	145,838	22.7	8
Republicans	444,205	49.6	218,700	24.4	71,963	8.0	153,613	17.1	8

Note: Includes candidates with major party opposition only.

[a] Percentage of all contributions.

[b] Includes all contributions of less than $500.

In all other circumstances—including those that obtain when a candidate or party's victory is the public good—no resources at all will be expended to achieve the good by group members whose only goal is to assure that the benefit is, in fact, provided. The basic reason is that in groups beyond a certain (quite small) size, each individual's potential contribution is so small a portion of the total needed that its presence or absence will have no perceptible effect on the provision of the good. In the case of congressional elections, this means that no rational individual will contribute a small amount of money to a candidate solely to help that candidate win the election. A gift of $100 or even $500 will not appreciably affect the outcome; hence it is irrational for anyone to bear that cost even if convinced that a sufficient amount of money would affect the outcome decisively. The pointed irony is that one of the standard goals invariably professed by all parties to the campaign finance reform debate has been to encourage greater individual participation in campaign funding through small, individual contributions. The goal can only be met by enticing people to act irrationally, to incur a cost not connected with provision of any benefit.

With unrestricted individual contributions, a person may be able to give enough money to make a perceptible difference in the vitality of the campaign (and thus its chances of success). Hence rational (and, of course, wealthy) people concerned only with the public benefits victory for the right candidate will confer may finance campaigns if they are permitted to contribute large enough sums of money. This is the only rational form of contribution intended to achieve a purely public good. Current limits on individual contributions ($1,000 per candidate per election) render this approach hypothetical.

Individuals must, then, contribute to candidates for reasons other than simply to help them win office. We need not assume that people invariably act rationally to recognize that a system of campaign finance is unlikely to function if its participants must always act contrary to self-interest. With this understanding, some of the assumptions underlying economic studies of campaign contributions are open to clarification and correction. And attention can be directed to the actual motives that inspire individual contributors.

Welch, for example, distinguishes ideological and quid pro quo contributors: "The quid pro quo contributor supplies campaign funds in exchange for political influence; he maximizes profits. The ideological contributor supplies funds to maximize the probability of electing candidates with desirable stands."[6] Quid pro quo contributors are easily understood; for them, victory by the preferred candidate is not a pure public good at all, since some particular benefit—the quid pro quo—is expected in return for the contribution. Welch recognizes that free riders—others who may benefit from the particular quid pro quo if it cannot be restricted to contributors—may take advantage of such contributors, but the contribution is still rational if the expected preferment, discounted by its probability, is worth more than the cost of the contribution.

The category of ideological contributions is more doubtful; they are made with the intention of providing a public good—success for the ideologically correct candidate. Welch apparently makes the implicit assumption that the free-rider problem can be ignored because ideological contributors are not self-interested, although they are assumed to be rational.[7] But Olson's analysis applies to selfless as well as to selfish objectives.

Zinser and Dawson's propositions about the motives of individual donors partially clarify the issue but are still subject to the same criticism. They contend that electoral participation, including giving to campaigns, "occurs because individuals derive current satisfaction intrinsic to the act of participation, a 'consumption motive,' and because they derive expected returns, such as financial rewards or a desired set of public goods, an 'investment motive.' "[8] The notion that a consumption motive underlies individual contributions is most useful and provides a basis for explaining why many individuals are willing to contribute to candidates. The investment motive, as they define it, is less helpful, because they do

6. William P. Welch, "The Economics of Campaign Funds," *Public Choice* 25 (1976): 84.

7. Ibid., p. 87.

8. James E. Zinser and Paul A. Dawson, "The Rationality of Indigenous Campaign Contributions" (Prepared for delivery at the 1977 Annual Meeting of the Public Choice Society, New Orleans, March 11–13, 1977), p. 7.

not distinguish individual quid pro quo investments from those intended to finance the pursuit of public goods. In the latter case, rational individuals would not invest.

Of course, group contributions may be large enough to make an observable difference in the vitality of campaigns, at least in House races (the current limit on contributions from political committees is $5,000 per candidate per election), and hence these may be interpreted quite differently. Part of the confusion in Welch's approach arises because group and individual contributions are treated together in the theory. Group contributions are subject to somewhat different motives and strategies, however, and are best analyzed separately.

Who Contributes?

Campaign money is supplied by a small and distinctive subsection of the politically active population, which is itself a minority segment of the adult population. This hardly need be argued for parties, groups, and candidates—but it is true of individual contributors as well. Relatively few people contribute to political campaigns of any kind in any amount. Between 1956 and 1974 no more than 12 percent of the respondents in Gallup and SRC/CPS surveys reported giving to one of the parties or its candidates in any election year. The proportion giving to congressional candidates is no doubt significantly smaller. Although the proportion of respondents who report having been solicited has increased steadily over this period, the proportion actually contributing has shown no increase at all; consequently, the proportion contributing of those solicited has fallen.[9] Most people are content to remain free riders (assuming they even care who wins).

Contributors are by no means randomly distributed in the population. They are typically much wealthier than average, as the figures in table 3.4 indicate. Wealthier individuals have more discretionary income to spend, of course, so this is scarcely surprising. These figures probably understate the extent to which individ-

9. Herbert E. Alexander, *Money in Politics* (Washington, D.C.: Public Affairs Press, 1972), p. 368.

Table 3.4.   Distribution of Campaign Contributors by Income, 1968 and 1972

	1968		*1972*	
Income Groups	*Percentage of Survey Respondents*	*Percentage of Respondents Contributing to Campaigns*	*Percentage of Survey Respondents*	*Percentage of Respondents Contributing to Campaigns*
$0–4,999	29.0	3.0	16.6	3.7
$5,000–9,999	39.1	7.6	31.4	11.5
$10,000–14,999	20.6	8.4	26.1	11.5
$15,000–19,999	6.0	14.3	14.6	19.5
$20,000–24,999	2.0	16.7	4.3	23.4
$25,000 or more	3.2	30.6	7.0	36.8
Total percentage contributing		7.6		12.4

Source: U.S., Congress, Senate, Committee on Commerce, Subcommittee on Communications, *Federal Election Campaign Act of 1973*, 93rd Cong., 1st sess., hearings March 7–9 and 13, 1973, p. 462. The 1968 data are from the 1968 SRC Survey; the 1972 data were gathered by the National Opinion Research Center for the Twentieth Century Fund. They were presented in the testimony of David W. Adamany.

ual campaign gifts come from a small and prosperous segment of the electorate, since they do not take into account the amount contributed. Berg and Eastland found in their study of donors of $500 or more to California candidates from 1968 through 1974 that the 6.2 percent of those who gave $10,000 or more accounted for 48.9 percent of the total amount given in sums this size.[10] The distribution is no doubt much less skewed in congressional elections, especially under the $1,000 limit per candidate per campaign and the $20,000 limit on total individual contributions to candidates in any election year. Still, there is no question that individual campaign contributors form a distinctive activist minority.

10.   Larry L. Berg and Larry L. Eastland, "Large Campaign Contributors in California: Personal Characteristics, Motivations, and Beliefs" (Prepared for delivery at the Conference on Political Money and Election Reform: Comparative Perspectives, at the University of Southern California, Los Angeles, December 10, 1977), p. 5.

Why Contribute?

If the public goods analysis is valid, few individual contributors give solely to help preferred candidates win elections. They would be irrational if they did so. Benefits other than the collective one of victory by the favored candidate or party (and its shared political consequences) must be forthcoming. It is easy to imagine what these might be but almost impossible to specify the frequency of any particular kind of payoff. The motives behind individual contributions surely range from the most selfless to the most venal. Even some large donors apparently have no motive other than to help the "right" candidate win (although psychological payoffs can never be ruled out), but they are not common. Keefe quotes one unnamed Senator who remarked that "the real find is someone with a lot of money who doesn't want anything. They're rare, and when you find one, you guard him like your wife."[11]

At the other extreme, individuals may give to candidates for strictly selfish reasons. They expect some direct quid pro quo in return for their help. Their most effective strategy is relatively simple. They must contribute enough to put the candidate plausibly in their debt. They will not waste money on candidates who do not have a very good chance of winning, but they will not hesitate to contribute to a sure winner even though the contribution can have no effect on the outcome. The point is not to affect the outcome but to buy influence with the winner. Before strong disclosure laws were put into effect, such contributors might freely give funds to two opposing candidates if both had a chance of winning. Some probably still do. Since incumbents are the safest investments—they are likely winners with known spheres of influence (committee assignments and so forth)—contributions of this sort are most readily available to those already in office.

Thayer's ironic rules for "fat cats" who want the most value for their investment contribution are instructive. He admonishes them to give to individual candidates rather than fund-raising com-

---

11. William J. Keefe, *Parties, Politics, and Public Policy in America*, 2d ed. (Hinsdale, Ill.: The Dryden Press, 1976), p. 83.

mittees, to focus contributions on one or a few powerful candidates, to insist on meeting with the candidate personally, and to make certain that the contribution is clearly identified as theirs.[12]

Candidates who are willing to provide direct personal benefits to contributors and who are likely to be in a position to do so after the election have this source of money available to them. Probably few can be purchased so directly; the real problem lies in the vast gray area where neither the candidate nor the contributor envision any specific quid pro quo but still recognize that the donor will have, minimally, "access" to the candidate to present his case if the occasion arises. The uncertainties and suspicions involved are reviewed more thoroughly in the chapters on campaign finance reform, but some flavor of the problem is revealed in this statement by the then Senate Republican Minority Leader, Hugh Scott:

> I think every person in the Senate . . . realizes that every time a contribution is made, some sort of obligation is implied at least by the general public, some sort of obligation is very often felt by the recipient, some sort of obligation may be in the mind of the donor. The obligation may be slight . . . some minor favor. On the other hand, the donor may expect benefits which he has no right to expect.[13]

Most candidates no doubt prefer not to accept money with explicit or implicit strings attached—if they have a choice. Challengers and other hopeless candidates rarely have a choice; they are unable to raise funds from such contributors even if they are willing to barter their souls for it, since investment in them is very likely to be fruitless. Incumbents and other candidates who do have a real shot at winning should find such money available but presumably will not tap it except under the pressure of dire necessity. Contributions of this kind are available primarily to incumbents, so the

12. George Thayer, *Who Shakes the Money Tree? American Campaign Finance Practices from 1789 to the Present* (New York: Simon and Schuster, 1973), pp. 129–32.

13. U.S., Congress, Senate, Committee on Rules and Administration, Subcommittee on Privileges and Elections, *Public Financing of Federal Elections*, 93rd Cong., 1st sess., hearings September 18–21, 1973, p. 34.

amount actually solicited and accepted will depend on how much incumbents think they need. As is shown in chapter 4, this is typical of incumbent campaign finance; incumbents can adjust how much they raise and spend according to how seriously they feel threatened by the challenger. And this, it turns out, depends on what the challenger is spending.

Individual contributions for which no quid pro quo is expected and which are not large enough to have any tangible effect on the vitality of the campaign are well characterized as "consumption" expenditures. Individuals receive benefits from the act of contributing itself; these are, of necessity, psychological. Under what conditions are people likely to receive sufficient psychological satisfaction from a political contribution to outweigh its cost? A number of plausible and empirically defensible possibilities come to mind:

1. Ideological attitudes generate one very important source of psychological payoffs. The more strongly people feel about the candidates or issues at stake, the greater the psychic satisfaction derived from contributing to the campaign (and participating in other ways as well). Campaigns with highly emotional issues (the war in Vietnam, abortion, gun control) attract more of these contributions, particularly when the candidates represent clearly dissimilar positions. Some of the best financed congressional campaigns on record were conducted by antiwar candidates during the early 1970s. They attracted both money and campaign workers in unprecedented quantities.[14]

People with strong ideological commitments may regard any campaign in which the candidates are ideologically distinct as sharply polarized and thus be willing to contribute to it. At present, such donors are found mainly among conservative ideologues. Richard Viguerie has built a fortune and a formidable reputation as a political heavyweight by raising large amounts of money in small contributions for conservative candidates and causes through direct-mail appeals to his carefully compiled list of willing conservative

14.   Examples are given in chapter 6.

donors.[15] Representative Dornan's victorious 1976 campaign for California's 27th District received an estimated $100,000 in small contributions through Viguerie's direct-mail efforts.[16] The direct-mail technique is ideal for emphasizing emotional issues because it can be tailored to receptive individuals with smaller risk of alerting and offending the rest of the electorate.

In general, then, ideologically extreme candidates or those associated with divisive emotional issues raise more money in small gifts from individual donors. It is worth recalling that the most ideologically distinctive presidential candidates of recent years —Goldwater, Wallace, and McGovern—had the most success in funding campaigns with small individual donations. Insofar as contributions to congressional campaigns are limited to small individual gifts, the more extreme ideologues are favored.

It also follows that ideologically oriented political committees that rely on individual contributions for the funds they ultimately distribute to candidates will be most successful if they abjure the political center and use emotionally charged direct-mail appeals to likely co-believers. For contributions to political groups are also costs incurred to provide public goods and thus are also subject to the free-rider problem.

2. Another kind of psychological reward to an individual contributor is personal recognition and attention from the candidate or other high-status fund raisers. At minimum, a personal "thanks" and a handshake are individualized benefits that can be expected in return for a donation. Thayer's instruction to fat cats to be sure to meet the candidate personally applies equally to contributors who anticipate no personal favor other than a few minutes of the candidate's time.

Candidates are fully aware of how important personal attention can be and also of the value of having prominent people solicit funds for them.[17] It is a commonplace among fund raisers of all

15. *Dollar Politics*, vol. 2 (Washington, D.C.: Congressional Quarterly, Inc., October 1974), p. 52.

16. *C.Q. Weekly Report* 35 (October 29, 1977): 2300.

17. David A. Leuthold, *Electioneering in a Democracy: Campaigns for Congress* (New York: John Wiley & Sons, Inc., 1968), p. 83.

kinds that personal solicitations are the most effective; it is much harder to refuse a request of a friend or acquaintance to his face than it is to ignore, say, a letter. Malbin contends that, under contribution restrictions, people who can get others to donate funds are the new financial powers in politics.[18]

The 1976 congressional candidates reported spending more time than ever raising funds because of the present limits on the size of gifts.[19] As much time and attention must be spent on contributors of $500 or $1,000 as on people who gave ten times the amount previously, so the efficiency of fund raising necessarily diminishes and the time devoted to it increases.

Rational choice models of voting frequently include a variable representing "sense of citizen duty" to explain why people go to the polls at all, since some cost is involved and the probability of any vote actually making a difference is practically zero. Voters receive sufficient satisfaction from the act of voting itself to outweigh the cost because they have internalized the value of political participation in the course of their political socialization. Some people no doubt contribute to campaigns out of a similar sense of duty. The general appeals to give to the party or candidate of one's choice are designed to tap this sentiment.

The sense of citizen duty is presumed to be more highly developed among people of higher socioeconomic status, primarily because they are better educated, and participation and education are highly correlated. Campaign contributions come even more disproportionately from higher-status individuals, and a similar explanation (along with recognition that they have more money to contribute; the real "cost" of a contribution is less) for their behavior cannot be ruled out. Thus the argument from evidence of aggregate relationships between income characteristics of districts and levels of campaign spending that political participation is essentially "economic" is not necessarily convincing.[20]

18. Michael J. Malbin, "Labor, Business, and Money—A Post Election Analysis," *National Journal* 9 (March 19, 1977): 417.

19. *A Study of the Impact of the Federal Election Campaign Act on the 1976 Election* (Prepared for the Federal Election Commission by Decision Making Information and Hart Research Associates, 1977), p. 84.

20. James E. Zinser, Paul A. Dawson, and Kurt F. Hausafus, "The Rational

4. Campaign fund raisers have found it fruitful to tap the same sources of funds repeatedly; an individual who gives once is likely to give again. The psychology of repeated donations is easily understood. The original contribution strengthens the psychological identification of the contributor with the candidate and the cause; something of his is on the line. The stronger the identification, the greater the satisfaction from contributing. If the first contribution was justified, so are subsequent ones, particularly if the candidate can argue that additional money will add to the progress already made. Even though contributors would not rationally give money only to help the preferred candidate win, the psychological benefits derived from contributions are surely enhanced if donors are able to convince themselves that their money will be put to effective use.

A variety of considerations, then, determine how much money congressional candidates can raise from individuals who expect no tangible quid pro quo from their contribution. Characteristics of the candidate—and his opponent—are obviously crucial. Candidates who are personally attractive—charismatic in the jargon—are obviously favored; more people will wish to identify with them, and their attention and gratitude will be more highly valued. The ideological and policy positions of the candidates are also relevant. Candidates can raise more money if they can attach themselves to emotional symbols and causes (although this may have a negative impact on their ability to win votes; differences between the contributing and voting constituencies can be the source of major electoral headaches). Challengers of incumbents whose votes have outraged, for example, environmentalists, benefit from individual contributions aimed at punishing the rascals; Environmental Action's "Dirty Dozen" list even furnishes a usefully small number of deserving targets.

It is also essential that the candidate convince individual contributors—as well as other suppliers of campaign funds—that he has a real chance to win. Even people who contribute for the good of the cause usually have more than one of its champions from

Analysis of Voter Participation: A Recursive Model of Household Behavior with Applications to Voter Turnout" (Presented to the 1976 Annual Meeting of the Midwest Political Science Association, Chicago, April 29–May 1, 1976), p. 21.

which to choose; once they have decided to contribute, there is no reason to suspect that they do not make a rational choice about who is to get the money.[21] The closer an election is expected to be, the more the incentive to give to this candidate rather than to another of similar views. And candidates in what seem to be tight contests are in a better position to inspire repeated donations from the same individuals.

Finally, candidates raise more money in individual gifts if they are helped by prominent and effective fund raisers, which in turn depends on the attractiveness of the candidate, his political experience (and therefore contacts), his chances of victory, and, in some cases, his ideological credentials (Viguerie only helps candidates who meet his standards of conservatism).

Generally, then, contributions of this sort go disproportionately to attractive and experienced candidates in close contests polarized by emotional issues or sharp ideological differences. Both incumbents and challengers are supported if the race looks close, but much of this money ends up in contests for open seats; these elections are much more likely to be competitive, and stronger and more experienced nonincumbents are more likely to run.

COMPETITION AND INDIVIDUAL CAMPAIGN CONTRIBUTIONS

The foregoing discussion suggests that the pattern of individual contributions should vary in a consistent and predictable way with the incumbency status of the candidate and the level of competition for the office. The data in table 3.5 indicate that it does just that. The table uses a simple trichotomous measure of competition based on the winner's share of the two-party vote in the last election for the seat (adjusted for changes in district boundaries where necessary). This measure is superior to any derived from the closeness of the actual contests for which the money is contributed because it avoids the simultaneity problem; the present election may be close because of the amount contributed (and thus spent).

---

21. See Welch, "Campaign Funds," p. 87.

Contributions to both incumbents and challengers depend on the degree of expected competition in the race. The pattern is entirely consistent across all three election years: the closer the prior contest, the more the candidate receives in individual donations. The effect is especially pronounced for challengers. Both quid pro quo and consumption contributions to challengers should increase with the expected level of competition—and probably at an increasing rate as the expected vote approaches 50.1 percent. Incumbents, on the other hand, can raise quid pro quo and, to some extent, consumption contributions independently of how close the election is expected to be. Their level of funding depends much more strongly on how actively they solicit such gifts, but this, too, is a function of how formidable the opposition appears to be.

The extent of previous competition for open seats has a much weaker effect on individual contributions to candidates in these races. Regardless of how close the last election was, candidates for open seats attract relatively large aggregate sums from individuals. They tend to collect more money if their party's candidate was the winner, but the differences are not necessarily large, and exceptions to the pattern are evident. Contributors perceive open seats as just that: open. Usually, neither candidacy is thought to be hopeless, so individual contributors of all types are inclined to give.

The evidence for Senate contests is more difficult to evaluate because neither total nor per voter spending figures permit accurate comparison across states and because relatively few observations remain in any category when cases are broken down by year, party, incumbency status, and level of competition.[22] McDevitt's regression analyses of small ($100 and under) and large ($101 and over) individual contributions did, however, show that, with population and party controlled, incumbency and competition had the expected effect on individual gifts to Senate contenders.[23]

22. The level of competition must be measured by the vote in the election under analysis, raising simultaneity problems; the six-year gap between elections makes it unwise to rely on previous vote percentages to estimate the competitiveness of Senate contests.

23. McDevitt, "Congressional Campaign Finance," p. 166.

Table 3.5. Electoral Competition and Individual Campaign Contributions to House Candidates, 1972–76, by Party and Incumbency Status

| | Winner's Share of Adjusted Two-Party Vote in Last Election[a] | | | |
	60.1% or More	55.1–60.0%	55% or Less	Percent Change[b]
1972				
Incumbents				
Democrats	$24,750 (109)[c]	$29,535 (20)	$44,600 (26)	+80.2
Republicans	30,495 (69)	43,908 (38)	46,156 (34)	+51.4
Challengers				
Democrats	9,119 (79)	22,521 (38)	36,054 (24)	+295.4
Republicans	16,358 (112)	22,129 (21)	37,136 (22)	+127.0
1974				
Incumbents				
Democrats	36,603 (102)	47,382 (28)	49,413 (30)	+35.0
Republicans	61,556 (98)	77,750 (23)	87,294 (41)	+41.8
Challengers				
Democrats	29,634 (107)	48,467 (24)	68,293 (31)	+130.5
Republicans	8,995 (108)	24,287 (26)	26,721 (26)	+197.1
1976				
Incumbents				
Democrats	43,798 (138)	66,838 (30)	75,072 (40)	+71.4
Republicans	64,366 (48)	70,572 (31)	80,043 (42)	+24.4
Challengers				
Democrats	14,914 (48)	20,573 (31)	29,660 (42)	+98.9
Republicans	15,227 (138)	52,797 (30)	72,194 (40)	+374.1

(Candidates Party	Won	Lost	Open Seats Won	Lost)		
1972						
Democrats	$67,225 (12)	$49,231 (16)	$ 41,000 (1)	$36,300 (7)	$70,312 (17)	+42.8
Republicans	58,453 (15)	38,115 (13)	68,288 (8)	62,200 (1)	76,413 (16)	+100.4
1974						
Democrats	72,785 (17)	57,247 (14)	164,870 (5)	47,690 (6)	69,218 (10)	+1.3
Republicans	66,537 (14)	36,020 (20)	61,901 (6)	72,337 (6)	64,935 (6)	+80.2
1976						
Democrats	61,786 (28)	83,206 (5)	78,951 (4)	60,596 (6)	61,584 (7)	−26.0
Republicans	53,531 (5)	43,029 (28)	75,419 (6)	61,970 (4)	98,695 (7)	+129.4

Note: Includes candidates with major party opposition only.

[a] The figures have been adjusted for redistricting where necessary; cases for which this information was not available (twenty in 1972, two in 1974) were omitted.

[b] Percentage change from least to most competitive category. For open seats, least competitive category was designated as that in which the party's candidate in the last election won less than 40 percent of the vote.

[c] Number of cases from which percentages were computed; the numbers do not match symmetrically for 1972 and 1974 because of adjustments to changes in district boundaries.

Contributions from Political Committees

The portion of political funds not supplied directly by individual donors—about one-third of the total—comes from political committees of various kinds, political parties, the candidates themselves, and loans that must be repaid from the other sources. Nonparty political action committees (PACs) supply the greatest share of these contributions, and gifts from this source grew the most between 1972 and 1976. In 1972, $8.9 million was given directly to congressional candidates by nonparty committees; in 1974, the figure was $12.5 million; and by 1976, it had jumped to $22.6 million. The constant dollar increase was 87 percent between 1972 and 1976. PAC contributions as a percentage of all contributions grew from 14.3 percent to 17.0 percent to 19.6 percent over these years.[24] The dramatic increase between 1972 and 1976 is in part a consequence of public funding of the 1976 presidential campaigns; private political funds were redirected into congressional contests. Political parties, in contrast, supply a diminished share of campaign funds. Tables 3.6 and 3.7 list the average PAC and party contributions to House and Senate candidates and the proportion of all contributions that these comprise, by party and incumbency status, in each election year.

Political action committees clearly favor incumbents and candidates for open seats. They also favor Democrats. Democrats in any category typically receive larger average PAC contributions than their Republican counterparts, and these form a larger portion of their total campaign funds. Republicans, on the other hand, receive substantially more from party sources. If PAC and party contributions are combined, Democrats and Republicans receive much more similar totals and proportions from these sources.

PACs, like individuals, vary in their objectives and strategies for funding campaigns. They must cope with the additional problem of

24. The 1972 figure is calculated from "Common Cause Releases Study of 1972 Congressional Campaign Finances" (News release from Common Cause, September 13, 1973), table 1; the 1974 and 1976 figures are from Common Cause data reported in Malbin, "Labor, Business and Money," p. 416.

raising the money they eventually distribute to candidates and are equally liable to the free-rider problem because they, too, are organized to produce collective benefits for those they purport to represent. The simplest analysis treats interest group PACs as rational, self-interested utility maximizers, but their actual behavior is complicated by the internal dynamics of particular organizations and the disparate goals of the people who operate them.

The assumption that most PACs operate as rational, profit-seeking actors—the dominant view among proponents of campaign finance reform—is supported by examples of groups that openly contribute most heavily to politicians who are in a position to do them the most good—or harm. The notorious dairy industry committees, the American Medical Association's AMPAC, the banking industry committees, and the maritime unions are good illustrations. They give overwhelmingly to incumbents of both parties who sit on committees that handle matters directly affecting their financial interests, although if an election is in doubt, they may contribute to both candidates. Dairy industry committees, for instance, fund incumbents of both parties, with special attention to members who sit on congressional committees dealing with agriculture. They contribute seven dollars to incumbents for every dollar to challengers but do not hesitate to supply money to both an incumbent and challenger if it appears that the latter might win.[25] And they are entirely indifferent to whether or not an incumbent actually needs the money. Although their avowed intention is ''to keep our friends in office and elect those who are our friends,''[26] it is perhaps more accurate to say that they aim to ensure that those in office remain their friends.

Similarly, AMPAC money goes disproportionately to sponsors of the AMA's national health proposals and to members of committees dealing with health policy, regardless of party, although this group otherwise favors Republican candidates.[27] The banking industry's BankPAC supports members of committees

25. *C.Q.* *Weekly Report* 31 (March 17, 1973): 569.
26. Ibid.
27. Ibid. 30 (October 21, 1972): 2720–21; ibid. 31 (March 17, 1973): 570.

Table 3.6. Average Party and PAC Campaign Contributions to House Candidates, 1972–76

	Party Contributions	Percent[a]	PAC Contributions	Percent	Cumulative Percent
1972					
Incumbents					
Democrats	$ 4,581	8.2	$12,043	21.6	29.9
Republicans	7,933	13.0	7,135	11.7	24.6
Challengers					
Democrats	1,833	6.1	5,827	19.6	25.8
Republicans	6,130	19.5	1,712	5.4	25.0
Open seats					
Democrats	4,064	4.2	12,059	12.6	16.9
Republicans	12,003	13.5	8,176	9.2	22.8
All candidates					
Democrats		6.7		19.5	26.2
Republicans		16.1		8.4	24.5
1974					
Incumbents					
Democrats	1,076	1.9	14,523	25.4	26.4
Republicans	4,565	5.2	12,737	14.4	19.6
Challengers					
Democrats	588	1.0	10,897	18.9	19.9
Republicans	1,636	8.0	1,017	5.0	13.0
Open seats					
Democrats	1,277	1.2	20,590	19.7	20.9
Republicans	9,890	12.3	9,087	11.3	23.6

All candidates					
Democrats		1.4		21.8	23.2
Republicans		7.4		9.9	17.3
1976					
Incumbents					
Democrats	3,952	4.5	29,488	33.2	37.7
Republicans	8,897	8.4	22,774	21.7	30.1
Challengers					
Democrats	3,053	6.7	9,435	20.8	27.5
Republicans	8,459	15.3	7,391	13.4	28.7
Open seats					
Democrats	4,109	2.9	24,626	17.6	20.5
Republicans	14,320	14.0	17,176	16.8	30.8
All candidates					
Democrats		5.0		27.2	32.2
Republicans		12.9		16.5	29.4

Note: Includes candidates with major party opposition only.
[a] Percentage of all contributions.

Table 3.7. Average Party and PAC Campaign Contributions to Senate Candidates, 1972–76

	Party Contributions	Percent[a]	PAC Contributions	Percent	Cumulative Percent
1972					
Incumbents					
Democrats	$35,244	10.9	$ 51,167	15.7	26.6
Republicans	44,950	9.7	41,308	8.9	18.6
Challengers					
Democrats	26,481	13.8	43,288	22.5	36.3
Republicans	66,722	21.9	12,722	4.2	26.1
Open seats					
Democrats	64,275	13.7	76,313	16.3	30.0
Republicans	78,750	18.2	31,575	7.3	25.5
All candidates					
Democrats		13.0		19.1	32.1
Republicans		15.1		7.2	22.3
1974					
Incumbents					
Democrats	10,267	1.6	91,583	14.5	16.1
Republicans	44,090	7.4	59,930	10.1	17.5
Challengers					
Democrats	5,700	1.5	38,840	10.1	11.6
Republicans	55,542	17.7	13,992	4.4	22.1

Open seats					
Democrats	8,844	1.7	78,133	14.8	16.5
Republicans	37,356	14.4	17,600	6.8	21.2
All candidates					
Democrats		1.6		13.2	14.8
Republicans		13.4		6.9	20.3
1976					
Incumbents					
Democrats	8,980	1.5	129,820	22.2	23.7
Republicans	26,850	3.0	107,775	12.1	15.1
Challengers					
Democrats	27,275	4.2	99,513	15.4	19.6
Republicans	25,769	7.3	37,640	10.5	17.8
Open seats					
Democrats	15,713	2.4	114,625	17.8	20.2
Republicans	39,563	4.4	80,588	9.0	13.4
All candidates					
Democrats		2.4		19.3	21.7
Republicans		5.4		10.5	15.9

Note: Includes candidates with major party opposition only.
[a] Percentage of all contributions.

which write banking legislation.[28] And "the Maritime Engineer's Beneficial Association channeled its contributions mainly to members of Congress who supported a bill requiring that a great proportion of oil imports be shipped in U.S. tankers manned by U.S. crews" in 1974.[29]

Contributions of this sort are easily interpreted as "investments" in the most immediate sense. As Welch points out, the greater the discretionary regulation of an industry, the greater the incentive for those in it to invest in political influence.[30] When congressional decisions have a direct and substantial impact on the balance sheet, it is a sound business decision to use financial resources to promote the friendliest possible relations with congressmen. Campaign contributions are one approach among many. It is no surprise that business associations contribute almost as much to Democrats as to Republicans, despite the ideological differences that continue to exist. In 1976, for example, 46.5 percent of the more than $10.7 million given by business and professional committees went to Democratic congressional candidates.[31] And this is no recent development; Heard observed the same phenomenon in the 1950s.[32] It should continue as long as the Democrats control Congress.

Under current campaign finance regulations, business firms may set up and administer PACs to solicit voluntary contributions from employees and stockholders to be eventually passed on to political candidates. Analysis of the business PACs that were operating by the 1976 election confirms that the degree of regulation strongly affects political involvement. Forty-two percent of the fifty largest utilities had organized PACs; 36 percent of the top one hundred military contractors, 32 percent of the fifty largest transportation companies, but only 18 percent of the fifty largest retail corporations had done likewise.[33] In general, the larger the firm,

28.   C.Q. Weekly Report 31 (March 17, 1973): 570.
29.   Dollar Politics, vol. 2, p. 54.
30.   Welch, "Campaign Funds," pp. 86–87.
31.   C.Q. Weekly Report 36 (January 21, 1978): 119.
32.   Alexander Heard, The Costs of Democracy (Chapel Hill, N.C.: The University of North Carolina Press, 1960), p. 129.
33.   Victoria Louise Radd, "Business in Electoral Politics: The Corporate Politi-

the more likely it is to have a PAC. Sixty-nine percent of the one hundred largest corporations, 28 percent of the top five hundred, but only 4 percent of the next largest five hundred had PACs.[34]

These figures also indicate that a majority of corporations have *not* taken the opportunity offered by present regulations to set up PACs. Simple theories of corporate self-interest cannot explain this surprising reticence (unless we assume that most corporations are content to remain free riders; it is impossible to specify the mix of collective and individual goods corporations anticipate as a consequence of PAC contributions). Radd's careful study of business PACs revealed that the individual motives and attitudes of corporate officers are crucial in determining both the degree of political involvement and the form it takes. A typical hindrance in 1976 was explained by a former treasurer of the Democratic National Committee: "Companies are still recovering from the trauma of Watergate. The 'old man'—the President or Chairman of the Board—is still rattled by what happened to his friends in 1972. You can't get him to understand that a PAC is different from corporate bribery."[35] Presumably, this will change as memories of Watergate fade.

Once organized, PACs face the problem of raising money. Although they are legally permitted to solicit all stockholders and employees, in practice few attempt to do so; most concentrate their efforts on upper-level management personnel. Like candidates and campaign fund raisers, PAC officials find that personal face-to-face appeals produce the best results.[36] The law explicitly prohibits companies from threatening "physical force, job discrimination, or financial reprisal" for failure to contribute; participation may not be made a "condition of employment." Still, in the corporate world, the most subtle pressures can be effective. Radd quotes an

---

cal Action Committee" (Honors thesis, Department of Government, Radcliffe College, March 1978), pp. 22–23.

34. Ibid., pp. 23–24; Olson argues that when it comes to paying the cost of achieving a collective benefit, there is a tendency toward the exploitation of the great by the small. See *Collective Action*, pp. 35–42.

35. Radd, "Business in Politics," p. 37.

36. Ibid., p. 53.

unnamed attorney for several PACs: "The major business corpora-
tion is an intensely competitive place. In order to help himself
'climb the ladder,' the cautious guy will go along with anything
management suggests. So he ends up giving to the PAC."[37] Indeed, to avoid even the suspicion of illegal pressure, many corporate PACs deliberately abjure personal solicitation—and forgo its
recognized advantages. Only 31 percent reported using face-to-face
solicitation in a 1976 survey.[38] Other than personal advancement,
the most common motives for contributions to PACs are ideological
attitudes and the sense of civic duty—the same motives underlying
other individual political contributions.[39]

The contribution strategies pursued by PAC officials explain
why so much business money goes to incumbents, including Democrats. Most focus on the short run, necessarily forfeiting the potential long-term advantages of consistently supporting pro-business
candidates, nonincumbents as well as incumbents. The incumbent
is a known quantity; his challenger is frequently a mystery. PACs
often contribute defensively; even if they decline to fund campaigns
of uncongenial incumbents, they may also refrain from giving anything to preferred challengers for fear of retaliation if, as is usual,
the incumbent wins. They avoid contributing against powerful congressmen.[40]

PAC officials also feel pressure to support winners. They suspect that their own performance is evaluated by their win-loss record, so they are reluctant to fund candidates who do not have a
good chance to win, and they may be tempted to fund sure winners
to improve their record. Naturally, incumbents benefit once
again.[41]

PACs tend to concentrate their resources on a few highly visible
races. Radd suggests that a kind of bandwagon psychology is at
work. "PAC officials seem to *want* to spend in these races often

37.   Ibid., p. 67.
38.   Ibid., pp. 51–61.
39.   Ibid., p. 64.
40.   Ibid., pp. 72–74.
41.   Ibid., p. 31.

because their colleagues are doing so or because their superiors and contributors would expect them to.''[42] Going along with what other groups are doing also reduces the vexing sense of uncertainty about what candidates are electable. Some important consequences of this phenomenon are discussed in chapter 4.

Labor Committees

Organized labor's involvement in congressional campaigns is the most multifaceted and complex. Labor PACs contribute for a variety of motives and therefore follow a variety of strategies; indeed, within the universe of labor committees are found representatives of all types of political committees, including, in practice, political parties.

Traditionally, the leaders of organized labor have professed to abjure direct support of any political party, preferring to "reward friends and punish enemies" wherever they are found. In fact, labor has become a major source of financial and organizational support for Democrats. In 1976, for example, national and state Committees on Political Education (COPE) of the AFL-CIO contributed to 250 Democratic House candidates but to only four Republicans—one of whom switched to the Democratic party shortly after the election.[43] More than 95 percent of labor contributions went to Democrats in the 1972, 1974, and 1976 congressional elections.[44] Friendly Republicans are helped more often by labor's lack of support for their Democratic opponents than from any direct assistance. Labor contributions account for the Democrats' overall advantage in PAC money.

In 1976, labor PACs concentrated on helping freshman Democrats retain the seats they had won in 1974. In doing so, they operated as would a political party attempting to maximize its represen-

42. Ibid., p. 107.
43. *C.Q. Weekly Report* 36 (January 21, 1978): 119.
44. Ibid.; Common Cause Campaign Monitoring Project, *1974 Congressional Campaign Finances*, vol. 1 (Washington, D.C.: Common Cause, 1976), p. ix; I calculated the 1972 figure from data in Common Cause Campaign Monitoring Project, *1972 Congressional Campaign Finances*, 10 vols. (Washington, D.C.: Common Cause, 1974).

tation in Congress. Indeed, one clear labor goal is maintaining a strongly Democratic Congress. The money that consequently flows to Democrats from organized labor more than makes up the difference between what Democratic and Republican candidates can expect from their respective parties.

Labor committees also operate like other economic groups whose interests are decisively affected by congressional decisions—and for the same reasons. Organized labor's strength and status depend in large measure on federal legislation, and labor leaders are keenly interested in maintaining strategically located friends in Congress. Representative Rodino, about to become chairman of the House Judiciary Committee, received $19,300 from union sources in 1972; Representative Madden, about to become chairman of the Rules Committee, received $17,700; neither faced serious opposition. Labor groups also target specific enemies in Congress, contributing substantial amounts to candidates opposing prominent labor foes. For example, labor contributed $42,199 to an unsuccessful attempt to unseat Senator McClellan, a frequent investigator of labor corruption, in a 1972 primary election.[45]

Labor committees also support candidates for more broadly ideological reasons; not just Democrats, but the right kind of liberal Democrats (supporters of labor's economic policies) are favored.

The multiplicity of labor goals and contribution strategies derives from the structure and ideology of the labor movement itself. The pursuit of direct economic interests is easily understood; specific unions focus on congressmen and committees that write legislation regulating their sectors. The broader interest in Democrats and economic liberals stems from organized labor's traditional concern for redistributing wealth downward, protecting the general interests of the working man (and the movement), and pursuing generally liberal economic policies (maintaining full employment, increasing health and pension benefits, and so forth).

Olson traces labor's success in mobilizing resources for political action to its ability to enforce closed shops. Control of a selective incentive—the job—permits unions to circumvent the free-rider

45. *C.Q. Weekly Report* 30 (October 14, 1972): 2643.

problem; compulsory unionism gives labor the resources to pursue public goods in politics as in negotiations with management. Although union dues cannot legally be used for campaign contributions (a restriction generally ignored until the reforms of the 1970s),[46] they may be used to finance the administration of PACs funded by voluntary contributions. Present campaign finance regulations have yet to dampen labor's financial participation in congressional elections. Labor gifts amounted to $6.3 million in 1974; the 1976 total was $8.2 million.[47]

It should not be forgotten that labor unions also provide a great deal of assistance to favored candidates that does not show up in any campaign contribution records. The cost of internal communications with members and of registration and get-out-the-vote drives does not fall under campaign spending restrictions, and labor groups use these activities to help many Democratic candidates.[48] Alexander thinks they are of greater value to Democrats than are the direct money contributions.[49]

Ironically, labor has found it easier to elect candidates than to influence their votes once elected. It has failed to win desired reforms in legislation regulating union activities (common site picketing, the labor reform package) and has endured other legislative frustrations in recent years. One possible explanation is the willingness of business PACs to fund incumbent Democrats. If Democrats whose records are not flagrantly objectionable can count on money from business PACs, they are free to ignore labor's demands without suffering serious financial consequences.

Ideological Committees

Not all PACs can be suspected of having narrow and selfish objectives; at the opposite end of the continuum lie groups that contribute to candidates for purely ideological reasons. Ideological

46. Edwin M. Epstein, "Labor and Federal Elections: The New Legal Framework," Institute of Industrial Relations Reprint no. 408 (Berkeley, Calif.: University of California, 1976), p. 259.
47. *C.Q. Weekly Report* 35 (April 16, 1977): 710.
48. Malbin, "Labor, Business, and Money," p. 414.
49. Alexander, *Money in Politics*, p. 170.

groups are unique in contributing more money to challengers than to incumbents; they favored challengers two to one in 1974 and three to two in 1976.[50] One reason is that ideological money is currently supplied disproportionately by conservative organizations bent on replacing incumbents of the large Democratic majority. Since these groups aim to maximize the number of congressmen who are ideologically congenial, they tend to concentrate their resources on close races where money is most likely to make some difference.[51]

COMPETITION AND PAC CONTRIBUTIONS

PACs, like individuals, vary their contributions with the level of electoral competition. Table 3.8 lists the pertinent data. Again, contributions to challengers are most decisively affected by the expected degree of competition; the average PAC contribution total increases as much as nine times across the three competition categories. At most, donations to incumbents only double. In two of the three elections, Democratic challengers in the most competitive category actually enjoyed higher average PAC funds than did their Republican opponents. Still, the overall pattern reveals a clear incumbent advantage.

Again, the pattern of PAC contributions to candidates for open seats indicates that previous vote percentages have much less effect on current expectations about the outcomes of these contests. Once an incumbent is no longer involved, almost all races are perceived as potentially competitive—and PAC contributions are made accordingly.

PAC gifts to Senate candidates also vary with the incumbency status of the candidate and the degree of electoral competition; incumbents are favored and more money is supplied to candidates in competitive contests.[52]

50. Common Cause, *1974 Campaign Finances*, vol. 1, p. ix; Common Cause, *1976 Federal Campaign Finances*, vol. 2 (Washington, D.C.: Common Cause, 1977), p. viii.
51. *C.Q. Weekly Report* 34 (November 6, 1976): 3138.
52. McDevitt, "Congressional Campaign Finance," p. 172.

Political Parties

Congressional candidates normally find the political parties of surprisingly little help in their efforts to get elected. Not only are the parties organizationally feeble in most congressional districts, but they provide little in the way of financial assistance to their nominees. Fishel reports that "Even in those counties where candidate recruitment is tightly controlled by organizations which approximate the stereotype 'machine,' candidates are normally expected to develop much of their own resource base." He quotes one challenger as saying, "If I hadn't been able to guarantee that I could gain financial backing, I would have been passed over."[53] Neither national nor local parties can be relied upon for much financial help, although some money is usually forthcoming from these sources, and substantial amounts are occasionally contributed to a few fortunates designated "marginal." Republicans receive much more money from party sources than do Democrats, but another look at tables 3.6 and 3.7 indicates that party money never accounts for as much as 20 percent of receipts in any year or category, and usually it accounts for a good deal less.

The proportion of campaign funds contributed directly to candidates by political parties has declined sharply in recent years. It fell from 12.2 percent to 6.2 percent of the total between 1972 and 1976. The reasons for this drop are not entirely clear. It may reflect the continuing trend toward more personalized campaigning, with contributions increasingly directed to individual candidates rather than parties—another facet of the atrophy of partisan institutions. It may also stem from changes in campaign finance laws. The amount of money spent by parties on House races actually increased between 1972 and 1976, but the entire increase was in direct spending on the election by national party committees rather than in transfers of party money to candidates. The relevant figures are in table 3.9. Transfers declined in real dollars between 1972 and 1976 for both parties; direct spending increased, very

---

53. Jeff Fishel, *Party and Opposition: Congressional Challengers in American Politics* (New York: David McKay Company, Inc., 1973), p. 100.

Table 3.8. Electoral Competition and PAC Campaign Contributions to House Candidates, 1972–76, by Party and Incumbency Status

	Winner's Share of Adjusted Two-Party Vote in Last Election [a]						
	60.1% or More		55.1–60.0%		55% or Less		Percent Change [b]
1972							
Incumbents							
Democrats	$10,218	(109)[c]	$12,900	(20)	$19,100	(26)	+86.9
Republicans	5,258	(69)	7,386	(38)	10,759	(34)	+104.6
Challengers							
Democrats	2,969	(79)	7,626	(38)	12,492	(24)	+320.7
Republicans	1,073	(112)	2,114	(21)	4,932	(22)	+359.6
1974							
Incumbents							
Democrats	12,192	(102)	16,907	(28)	20,223	(30)	+65.9
Republicans	9,747	(98)	15,870	(23)	18,127	(41)	+86.0
Challengers							
Democrats	7,747	(107)	15,125	(24)	19,438	(31)	+160.1
Republicans	541	(108)	1,365	(26)	2,646	(26)	+389.1
1976							
Incumbents							
Democrats	22,670	(138)	40,205	(30)	44,971	(40)	+98.4
Republicans	16,190	(48)	21,669	(31)	30,092	(42)	+85.9
Challengers							
Democrats	3,081	(48)	7,490	(31)	18,132	(42)	+488.5
Republicans	2,377	(138)	10,475	(30)	22,397	(40)	+842.2

(Candidate's Party)	Won	Lost	Open Seats Won	Lost		
1972						
Democrats	$12,175	$ 4,040	$10,650	$12,972	$18,164	+349.6
	(12)	(16)	(1)	(7)	(17)	
Republicans	9,260	3,146	7,237	8,800	12,894	+309.9
	(15)	(13)	(8)	(1)	(16)	
1974						
Democrats	21,535	15,557	18,700	25,183	24,220	+55.7
	(17)	(14)	(5)	(6)	(10)	
Republicans	8,915	7,055	14,100	9,683	10,650	+49.7
	(14)	(20)	(6)	(6)	(6)	
1976						
Democrats	24,652	28,872	15,224	22,654	28,549	−1.1
	(28)	(5)	(4)	(6)	(7)	
Republicans	32,571	9,511	24,964	11,513	31,973	+236.2
	(5)	(28)	(6)	(4)	(7)	

Note: Includes candidates with major party opposition only.

[a] See table 3.5.
[b] See table 3.5.
[c] See table 3.5.

Table 3.9. Direct Spending and Transfers to House Candidates by
National Congressional Campaign Committees, 1972 and 1976

Type of Spending	Democratic Committees	Republican Committees
Direct spending		
1972	$ 304,000	$1,997,000
1976	806,504	7,171,670
Transfers to candidates		
1972	1,004,374	1,968,935
1976	449,300	2,071,525

Source: Roland McDevitt, "Congressional Campaign Finance and Consequences of Its Regulation" (Ph.D. diss., University of California at Santa Barbara, 1978), p. 121.

substantially in the case of Republicans. Under the FECA's 1976 Amendments, national party congressional campaign committees are allowed to transfer a maximum of $10,000 to each House candidate. Theoretically, Republicans could have transferred a total of $3.9 million to the 390 Republican House candidates. But if we assume that the real need for funds is in the more competitive races, the present transfer restrictions severely limit the potential help Republican congressional candidates might receive from this source.[54] Money spent on their behalf independently of the campaign may also be helpful, but no doubt the great majority of candidates would prefer to spend it themselves.

Republican House campaign committees run much more effective money-raising operations. In 1976, 97.4 percent of the $12.4 million they raised came from individuals, 70.5 percent of the total in sums of $100 or less; PACs accounted for only 2 percent of the total. Democratic House committees received 45.5 percent of their $1.7 million from PACs, 54.1 percent from individuals, and only 3.9 percent in amounts of $100 or less. Republicans have developed an efficient direct-mail operation which the Democrats have been slow to imitate.[55] But the difference is also a consequence of

54.   McDevitt, "Congressional Campaign Finance," p. 27.
55.   Ibid., pp. 122–23.

the different demographic and organizational foundations of the two parties. Democratic supporters among organized labor, for example, channel their funds through their unions, which in turn prefer to supply money directly to individual candidates rather than through party committees. Republican supporters are more willing to channel funds through the party.

Rational parties would presumably distribute the funds at their disposal to maximize party membership in Congress (and, perhaps, to encourage party loyalty); they would concentrate resources on close campaigns, ignoring safe or hopeless candidacies. McKeough observed two Democratic national-level committees which operated in this fashion in 1964:

> PCJC (President's Club for Johnson Committee) and JHC (Johnson-Humphrey Committee) contributions in particular went to candidates in contests which appeared to become close as election day drew near. Thus some non-incumbents whose efforts had originally been considered futile received last minute aid as they demonstrated chances for victory. Similarly, some incumbents originally thought to be safe found themselves hard pressed for funds in the closing days of the campaign. The overriding impression drawn from these allocations, therefore, is that the Democrats made every effort to extend the sweep of the Johnson landslide by redirecting funds not needed for the Presidential contest to Congressional aspirants.[56]

Normally, however, national party committees do not appear to follow a strategy aimed at maximizing the number of their partisans in Congress. They do contribute more to candidates in what are expected to be close contests; national committees maintain secret lists of supposedly marginal contests and provide more funds to candidates in these races.[57] But they also give a significant amount

56. Kevin L. McKeough, *Financing Campaigns for Congress: Contribution Patterns of National-Level Party and Non-party Committees, 1964* (Princeton, N.J.: Citizens' Research Foundation, 1970), p. 46.

57. Robert J. Huckshorn and Robert C. Spencer, *The Politics of Defeat* (Amherst, Mass.: University of Massachusetts Press, 1971), pp. 10–11.

of money to incumbents who are, by their own criteria, quite safe. The obvious explanation is that sitting congressmen have a direct voice in determining how party funds are to be distributed; national campaign committees have offices conveniently located on Capitol Hill.[58]

The pattern of contributions by national party organizations to 1964 House and Senate candidates is shown in table 3.10. The data were gathered by McKeough. He used *Congressional Quarterly*'s preelection analysis to classify seats as marginal or otherwise. Both parties made contributions more frequently, and in larger sums, to safe incumbents than they did to hopeless challengers, although the money is "wasted" in either case. Marginal incumbents also received money more frequently and in larger amounts than did marginal challengers; marginal candidates for open seats also enjoyed relatively generous funding.

Almost all Senate candidates got some money from their party's national committees; the significant difference lies in the amount. Even safe incumbents were given relatively large contributions, although marginal incumbents typically received even more. Hopeless challengers were given much less than their safe incumbent opponents.

Party contributions to House candidates in 1972, 1974, and 1976 also reflect the level of anticipated competition. Table 3.11 lists the mean party contributions to candidates by year, party, incumbency status, and the winner's share of the vote in the previous election. The pattern of party contributions is similar to that of individual and PAC contributions in one obvious respect; parties give significantly more when competition is tighter. But there are some noteworthy differences. Republican party committees in 1972 and 1976 gave more to challengers than to incumbents in the two more competitive categories. They also clearly favor candidates for open seats. Once again it is apparent that contribution decisions are more strongly influenced by the absence of an incumbent than by past electoral history. And observe also that in every category in every

58. McKeough, *Financing Campaigns*, p. 14.

Table 3.10. Contributions to Congressional Candidates by National Party Campaign Committees, 1964

		Democrats			Republicans	
	N	Percentage Receiving Contributions	Mean Contribution	N	Percentage Receiving Contributions	Mean Contribution
House of Representatives						
Incumbents						
Safe	189	49.7	$ 1,025	86	91.9	$ 2,414
Marginal	40	90.0	1,742	74	100.0	3,317
Challengers						
Marginal	74	73.0	1,498	40	95.0	2,389
Hopeless	85	16.5	768	149	31.6	1,159
Open seats						
Safe	14	28.6	1,250	4	100.0	2,000
Marginal	28	82.1	2,061	28	92.9	2,673
Hopeless	4	25.0	1,000	13	53.8	1,529
Senate						
Incumbents						
Safe	11	81.8	$ 8,732	1	100.0	$ 7,200
Marginal	13	100.0	11,533	7	100.0	11,482
Challengers						
Marginal	7	100.0	10,357	13	100.0	6,458
Hopeless	1	100.0	1,500	10	80.0	4,462
Open seats						
Marginal	3	100.0	11,833	3	100.0	5,000

Source: Kevin L. McKeough, *Financing Campaigns for Congress: Contribution Patterns of National-Level Party and Non-party Committees, 1964* (Princeton, N.J.: Citizens' Research Foundation, 1970), pp. 27, 32, 49, 53.

year, Republican party committees supply more funds to their candidates than do their Democratic counterparts.

National party contributions in particular may be more important than the actual amount contributed would imply. Relatively large contributions to a candidate—particularly a nonincumbent—may act as a cue to other potential contributors; they see it as a sign that the candidate has a chance to win and distribute their own funds accordingly. Radd found that some business PACs use information from the national parties to learn which contests are marginal.[59] National party contributions thus multiply themselves and so may have a greater impact than would appear at first glance.

A Statistical Analysis of Party and PAC Contributions

Welch[60] has done a sophisticated tobit study of the contribution patterns of twelve political committees, including the nine most generous, the national committees of both parties, and some representative ideological groups in 1974. His findings nicely summarize the different strategies of interest PACs, ideological groups, and parties. As part of the analysis, he determined the mode and distribution of the vote percentage won by the recipients of campaign contributions from each type of committee. Economic interest group contributions consistently went to likely winners, with the modal recipient's vote ranging from 55 to 71 percent, depending on the group. These contributions were also the most highly dispersed, indicating that no effort was made to target close races; money was given to candidates regardless of how much they really needed it.

Ideological groups, in contrast, contributed to candidates whose modal vote was much closer to 50 percent, and the distribution of vote percentages was much less dispersed, indicating that these groups focused on close races where the contribution might do the most to assure that the right candidate won: a maximizing strategy. Parties, which Welch had expected to do likewise, were found to

---

59.   Radd, "Business in Politics," p. 108.

60.   William P. Welch, "The Allocation of Political Monies: Parties, Ideological Groups, and Economic Interest Groups" (Working Paper no. 72, Department of Economics, University of Pittsburgh, September 1977).

contribute disproportionately to likely winners. His quite plausible explanation is that congressmen control these committees, and "while congressmen would like their party to control the Congress, they also want themselves to be reelected. Thus we are not surprised that they give money to themselves."[61] Even the safest incumbents feel they need some money; it is no doubt less unpleasant to take advantage of party funds than it is to solicit other sources.

CANDIDATES' CONTRIBUTIONS TO THEMSELVES

A final source of campaign funds for many candidates is their own pockets. A little more than 10 percent of the money collected by congressional candidates in 1976 was supplied by loans or direct gifts from the candidates themselves; in 1974 the figure was about 6 percent. The distribution of candidate contributions by party and incumbency status in these two election years is found in table 3.12. Nonincumbents obviously bear a much greater share of campaign costs than do incumbents. This is one source of funds for which a candidate does not depend on others' assessments of his personal qualities or chances for victory. Still, even candidates themselves appear to be more willing to invest their own resources in a contest if it appears that they have a chance to win. Table 3.13 lists the relevant figures. Challengers in competitive districts and candidates for open seats are generally most willing to spend their own money—perhaps because they realize that funds from other sources are likely to be forthcoming if they do win, allowing them to at least repay themselves for loans made to the campaign. But candidate contributions in general show a much weaker relationship to electoral competition. Candidate contributions as a *proportion* of all receipts are greatest for challengers in the least competitive category; hopeless candidates rely disproportionately on their own resources because they find others so much less accessible.

Personal wealth is obviously a useful asset, especially for candidates not blessed with the advantages of incumbency. Under pres-

61. Ibid., p. 14.

Table 3.11. Electoral Competition and Party Campaign Contributions
to House Candidates, 1972–76, by Party and Incumbency Status

Winner's Share of Adjusted Two-Party Vote in Last Election[a]

	60.1% or More	55.1–60.0%	55% or Less	Percent Change[b]
1972				
Incumbents				
Democrats	$3,575 (109)[c]	$6,125 (20)	$8,342 (26)	+133.3
Republicans	6,193 (69)	7,313 (38)	12,247 (34)	+97.8
Challengers				
Democrats	1,129 (79)	1,732 (38)	4,358 (34)	+286.0
Republicans	2,968 (112)	8,505 (21)	21,432 (22)	+621.8
1974				
Incumbents				
Democrats	905 (102)	850 (28)	1,870 (30)	+106.6
Republicans	3,285 (98)	4,109 (23)	7,883 (41)	+140.0
Challengers				
Democrats	384 (107)	775 (24)	1,145 (31)	+198.2
Republicans	830 (108)	2,108 (26)	4,515 (26)	+444.0
1976				
Incumbents				
Democrats	1,781 (138)	7,054 (30)	9,114 (40)	+411.7
Republicans	6,112 (48)	8,005 (31)	12,627 (42)	+106.6
Challengers				
Democrats	1,660 (48)	3,090 (31)	4,617 (42)	+178.1
Republicans	4,396 (138)	13,581 (30)	18,633 (40)	+323.9

(Candidate's Party)	Won	Lost	Open Seats Won	Open Seats Lost)	Won	
1972						
Democrats	$ 3,658 (12)	$ 2,894 (16)	$ 8,900 (1)	$ 5,071 (7)	$ 5,088 (17)	+75.8
Republicans	14,700 (15)	7,969 (13)	11,663 (8)	11,300 (1)	14,819 (16)	+86.0
1974						
Democrats	1,288 (17)	1,014 (14)	1,420 (5)	1,333 (6)	1,520 (10)	+49.9
Republicans	10,614 (14)	7,855 (20)	14,000 (6)	10,633 (6)	10,133 (6)	+29.0
1976						
Democrats	3,408 (28)	5,241 (5)	1,929 (4)	4,707 (6)	6,837 (7)	+30.5
Republicans	18,651 (5)	11,421 (28)	15,576 (6)	14,380 (4)	21,565 (7)	+88.8

Note: Includes candidates with major party opposition only.

[a] See table 3.5.
[b] See table 3.5.
[c] See table 3.5.

Table 3.12.   Average Contributions by Congressional Candidates to Their Own Campaigns, 1974 and 1976, by Party and Incumbency Status

	House of Representatives		*Senate*	
	Contribution	*Percent*[a]	*Contribution*	*Percent*
1974				
Incumbents				
Democrats	$ 651	1.1	$ 417	0.0
Republicans	483	0.5	2,820	0.5
Challengers				
Democrats	6,417	11.1	5,500	1.4
Republicans	3,436	16.8	2,942	0.1
Open seats				
Democrats	9,035	8.6	9,267	1.8
Republicans	6,950	8.6	11,589	4.5
1976				
Incumbents				
Democrats	842	0.9	11,400	2.0
Republicans	860	1.8	800	0.1
Challengers				
Democrats	10,276	27.7	24,538	4.0
Republicans	6,778	12.3	44,100	12.3
Open Seats				
Democrats	41,440	29.5	113,025	17.6
Republicans	7,501	7.3	325,363	36.3

Note: Includes candidates with major party opposition only. Loans made by candidates to the campaign unrepaid when data were published are treated as candidate contributions.

[a] Percentage of all contributions.

ent regulations, candidates may spend all they wish of their own money on the campaign, and with the limits on other kinds of contributions, wealthy candidates occupy a privileged position. A notorious example from 1976 is Senator Heinz, who loaned himself $2,465,500 to finance his successful campaign to succeed the retiring Hugh Scott in Pennsylvania. His finances account for the very high average and proportionate candidate contributions to Republican candidates for open Senate seats. Otherwise, Senate candidates appear to supply a smaller proportion of their own campaign funds, no doubt because their campaigns are usually so much more expensive than those for the House.

Candidates who contribute heavily to their own campaigns are by no means uniformly successful. For one thing, they are usually nonincumbents and so often face incumbents who have resources of their own to tap if need be. But beyond that, candidates who are able to rely on their own money need not cultivate any strong political support to develop a broader political appeal in order to fund the campaign, so the campaign process itself may be less effective. Crotty lists six Senate and six House candidates who spent more than $25,000 of their own money on their campaigns in 1970.[62] Five of each lost, four of the total in primary elections. Wealthy candidates did somewhat better in 1976 but still did not sweep the field. Half of ten House candidates who spent more than $100,000 of their own money were defeated; four of nine Senate candidates who did the same also failed to win.[63]

CONCLUDING COMMENTS

An overview of the data presented in this chapter shows that money from every source, excepting only candidates themselves, arrives in varying quantities depending on the incumbency status of the candidate and the competitiveness of the election. The pattern of distribution according to these variables is rather consistent across sources. The contribution "mix" is thus relatively stable for candidates across incumbency and competition categories (again excepting candidate contributions). Challengers in hopeless races receive the smallest amount of money from all sources (excepting themselves); incumbents in close elections and nonincumbents contesting open seats receive the largest aggregate contributions from all sources (except themselves). In particular, it is important to note that incumbents do not enjoy more lavish campaigns simply be-

62. William J. Crotty, *Political Reform and the American Experiment* (New York: Thomas Y. Crowell Company, Inc., 1977), pp. 127–28.

63. *C.Q. Weekly Report* 35 (June 25, 1977): 1292; ibid. (October 29, 1977): 2305.

Table 3.13. Electoral Competition and Candidate Contributions
to House Campaigns, 1974 and 1976, by Party and Incumbency Status

| | Winner's Share of Adjusted Two-Party Vote in Last Election[a] | | | |
	60.1% or More	55.1–60.0%	55% or Less	Percent Change[b]
1974				
Incumbents				
Democrats	$ 533 (102)[c]	$ 342 (28)	$ 1,337 (30)	+60.1
Republicans	409 (98)	1,143 (23)	288 (41)	−29.5
Challengers				
Democrats	6,832 (107)	4,088 (24)	6,800 (31)	−0.0
Republicans	2,441 (108)	4,346 (26)	6,658 (26)	+172.8
1976				
Incumbents				
Democrats	514 (138)	382 (30)	2,317 (40)	+350.8
Republicans	843 (48)	741 (31)	961 (42)	+14.0
Challengers				
Democrats	9,232 (48)	4,385 (31)	15,819 (42)	+71.3
Republicans	5,168 (138)	7,929 (30)	11,467 (40)	+120.9

	Open Seats		Won	Lost)		
(Candidate's Party	Won	Lost				
1974						
Democrats	$13,994	$ 4,664	$ 7,960	$ 5,600	$ 9,320	+99.8
	(17)	(14)	(5)	(6)	(10)	
Republicans	7,442	6,255	9,050	4,817	8,150	+30.3
	(14)	(20)	(6)	(6)	(6)	
1976						
Democrats	29,227	79,145	134,516	26,590	22,899	−71.6
	(28)	(5)	(4)	(6)	(7)	
Republicans	8,786	6,923	10,643	10,689	4,383	−36.7
	(5)	(28)	(6)	(4)	(7)	

Note: Includes candidates with major party opposition only. Candidate contributions were not recorded separately in the 1972 data.

[a] See table 3.5.
[b] See table 3.5.
[c] See table 3.5.

cause of their appeal to ''special interests.'' Their advantage is just as strong among individual contributors who supply money for less obviously ''selfish'' motives. They have, in fact, increased their take from individual contributors of $100 or less more successfully than have nonincumbents.

Chapter 4 extends the analysis of campaign contributions by shifting from the perspective of potential contributors to that of candidates seeking funds.

4 ☆ CAMPAIGN FUND RAISING: CANDIDATES' PERSPECTIVES

The strategies and objectives of the elites who finance congressional campaigns structure the problems faced by candidates seeking campaign funds. The ability of candidates to raise money depends on a set of well-defined variables as well as on a variety of more obscure and idiosyncratic factors. Clarification of these variables will lay the groundwork for the elaborated statistical model of money in congressional elections which is developed in chapter 5. This is undertaken in the first part of the present chapter. The second part puts some empirical flesh on the abstract bones of several important arguments made in this and the previous chapter through a brief look at some case studies from the 1974 election.

Incumbency is without question the most critical variable affecting a candidate's ability to raise money for a campaign; the entire fund-raising environment is fundamentally different for incumbents and nonincumbents. Leuthold mentions the exemplary case of a House incumbent who "said that he had had great difficulty raising money when he first ran for Congress, but . . . now, after nine terms, he did not need to solicit at all. In fact, he found that he got larger contributions if he just waited for people to send them than if he asked for them."[1]

CAMPAIGN FUNDS FOR NONINCUMBENTS

The most important factor affecting how much money nonincumbents can raise is their perceived probability of winning. Sure

1. David A. Leuthold, *Electioneering in a Democracy: Campaigns for Congress* (New York: John Wiley & Sons, Inc., 1968), p. 84.

losers do not attract campaign contributions, and except in rare circumstances, nonincumbents who cannot attract a substantial amount
of money are sure losers. Candidates must convince the elites who
provide campaign funds that they have a chance to win—otherwise, they have no chance to win.

A crucial consideration is whether or not the nonincumbent candidate's opponent is an incumbent. Elections for open seats are typically much more competitive than those between incumbents and
challengers.[2] Indeed, these elections may now be more competitive
than ever. The same weakening of partisanship that has helped elevate incumbency to electoral dominance should also make it easier
for candidates of the locally weaker party to win open seats.
Erikson's and Cover's measures of the "retirement slump" mentioned in chapter 1 indicate that seats which are quite safe when
held by an incumbent often become strongly competitive once he is
gone from the scene. Consequences for fundraising are unmistakable: as the data in chapter 3 show, candidates for open seats tend to
raise and spend more money than do other candidates.

Another important variable, one that interacts strongly with the
probability of election (as well as the availability of funds), is the
quality of the candidate. In general, the greater the chances of winning, the easier it is to recruit good candidates. Good candidates attract financial support; the availability of money attracts good
candidates. The consequence is a triad of mutually reinforcing
variables:

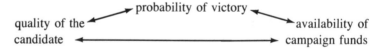

A "good" candidate cannot be precisely defined, of course. The
quality of a candidate depends on a variety of characteristics, many
of which cannot be specified in objectively measurable terms. I
therefore adopted, for purposes of analysis, the simple expedient of
measuring the candidate's quality by previous electoral experience.

Candidates who have successfully competed for an elective office are assumed to have valuable experience and contacts as well as some minimal skill in dealing with an electorate. Evidence is presented in chapter 5 that nonincumbent congressional candidates who have previously won elective office do indeed raise significantly more money than those who have not. At this point I only wish to show that these "good" candidates run selectively; that is, they are more likely to run when conditions suggest that their chances of winning are better.

This is immediately apparent from the data in table 4.1. Table 4.1 lists the percentages of nonincumbent candidates for the House who had won elective office at some time prior to their try for Congress. About half the candidates for open seats are good candidates by the criterion of experience. This is about twice the proportion typical among candidates challenging incumbents. And it is evident that expectations about national tides favoring one party or the other also encourage (or deter) potentially good candidates; notice for 1974 the abnormally large proportion of experienced Democrats and the abnormally small proportion of experienced Republicans. Observe also that the highest proportion of experienced Republicans in either category ran in 1972.

Table 4.1. Percentage of Nonincumbent House Candidates Who Had Won
Elective Office Previously

	Democrats		Republicans		Total	
Challengers						
1972	21.5	(144)[a]	21.7	(175)	21.6	(319)
1974	38.3	(162)	12.6	(159)	25.5	(321)
1976	29.5	(122)	16.9	(207)	21.6	(329)
Candidates for open seats						
1972	41.4	(58)	51.7	(58)	46.6	(116)
1974	54.7	(53)	49.1	(53)	51.9	(106)
1976	60.0	(50)	38.1	(50)	59.0	(100)

Note: Includes candidates with major party opposition only.

[a] Number of cases from which percentages were computed.

Source: *C.Q. Weekly Reports*, Special Pre-election Editions, 1972, 1974, and 1976.

National political trends also affect the amount of money available to nonincumbent candidates. If, as in 1974, political tides appear to be flowing strongly in one direction, nonincumbents of the favored party will find it easier to raise money (and, again, the money available will attract stronger candidates). Of the three elections for which usable data have been gathered, only 1974 shows evidence of a significant national tide. Nonincumbent Democrats obviously benefited (see chapters 3 and 5).

National tides are scarcely influenced by individual congressmen; they are a function of the general state of the economy, presidential popularity, or the presidential candidates' coattails. Members of Congress are in a position to influence most other factors which affect their vulnerability; some are entirely under their control. The behavior of individual incumbents normally has a pronounced effect on the capacity of their challengers to raise campaign funds. Incumbents are likely to face a strong, well-financed challenge when they have let themselves seem vulnerable. This they may do in a number of ways.

One is simply to reveal weakness at the polls in any election. In general, the smaller the incumbent's winning margin in the last election, the easier it is for the next challenger to raise money. An incumbent considered "safe" who is surprised by an unexpectedly close contest will inspire even more serious competition the next time around.[3] First-term incumbents often face stiff opposition for the same reason; the typically narrow margin of their first victory make them likely targets for formidable opposition. Party and PAC officials pay careful attention to voting statistics to determine which seats are competitive and thus which candidates are most worthy of campaign contributions. Incumbents, then, have a long-term interest in winning by wide margins.

Incumbents may also make themselves tempting targets for opponents and their financial backers by their behavior in office. District voters rarely know anything about specific votes or policy

3. Lewis A. Froman, Jr., "A Realistic Approach to Campaign Strategies and Tactics," in *The Electoral Process*, ed. M. Kent Jennings and L. Harmon Zeigler (Englewood Cliffs, N.J.: Prentice-Hall, Inc., 1966), p. 2.

stands taken by their legislators, but attentive elites within or outside the constituency may be very knowledgeable indeed.[4] A member who flagrantly violates district sentiment or who conspicuously successfully promotes policies that offend active groups with a national constituency invites serious opposition. Recall that Environmental Action's "Dirty Dozen" list attempts to funnel contributions from environmentalists into campaigns challenging incumbents who are, from their perspective, worst on environmental issues. Organized labor also targets specific "enemies" to be most heavily opposed, financially and organizationally. The National Rifle Association concentrates its financial firepower against active proponents of gun control legislation. Republican members of the House Judiciary Committee who defended President Nixon longest and loudest similarly attracted the attention of opponents and their contributors.

Indeed, consider the unwelcome dilemma forced upon most Judiciary Committee Republicans: by supporting the impeachment of a Republican president, they risked arousing the wrath of local and national Republican activists who could finance strong primary challengers (who would themselves be encouraged to run by the promise of support). If they opposed impeachment, they made themselves prominent targets for anti-Nixon forces which could underwrite their opponents' general election campaigns. Nixon's resignation several months before the election prevented the full impact of the dilemma from being felt, but even so, not all escaped. More will be said about these particular incumbents in chapter 5.

Incumbents also invite opposition if they fail to take advantage of the resources of office to serve and communicate with constituents. Mayhew points out that "When we say that 'Congressman Smith is unbeatable,' we do not mean that there is nothing he could do that would lose him his seat. Rather, we mean, 'Congressman Smith is unbeatable as long as he continues to do the things he is doing.' "[5]

4. Thomas Edward Mann, "Candidate Saliency and Congressional Elections" (Ph.D. diss., University of Michigan, 1977), p. 62.

5. David R. Mayhew, *Congress: The Electoral Connection* (New Haven, Conn.: Yale University Press, 1974), p. 37.

An incumbent who ignores his district, who does not use his communication and travel allowances, who does not spend much of his own or his staff's time handling constituent problems, makes the task of defeating him appear less formidable, and so it may become. As Mann's research clearly shows, incumbency is a variable rather than a constant asset in congressional elections; how valuable it is depends on the use incumbents make of the resources they have.[6]

Finally, a host of other signals may indicate that an incumbent is vulnerable. Publicized lapses in personal morality, advanced age, or signs of ill-health or senility can suggest that the incumbent is losing his grip on the district and is ripe for defeat. Under such circumstances, many incumbents no doubt simply retire, but if they do not, they can expect serious competition.

Unlike election results, the quality (or at least experience) of challengers, and national political trends, incumbent behavior cannot be quantified with sufficient precision to be included in equations that estimate the effects of a set of variables on how much money is contributed to nonincumbent candidates. Anecdotal evidence for its importance abounds, however. Its effects show up in the unexplained variance.

Try, Try Again

One strategy occasionally followed by challengers deserves comment at this point. Challengers sometimes enter a contest knowing that their candidacy is hopeless in order to build momentum for a second, more formidable try in the following election. The first campaign is used to gain recognition, experience, and supporters for the second. Some evidence indicates that this strategy is effective, although other factors clearly intervene, and it is not very frequently pursued. Table 4.2 displays data on the spending patterns of challengers in 1972, 1974, and 1976 who had opposed the same incumbent in the immediately preceding election. The resources available to these challengers the second time around depends decisively on how well they did in the first contest. Those who

6. Mann, "Candidate Saliency," p. 18.

Table 4.2. Campaign Expenditures by House Candidates Who Challenged the Same Incumbent in Two Successive Elections

Vote Won in First Election	Expenditures in First Election	Expenditures in Second Election	Difference	Number of Winners	Number of Cases
1970–72					
Democrats					
40% or more	a	$ 70,132	a	1	9
Less than 40%	a	13,296	a	0	9
Republicans					
40% or more	a	24,734	a	0	2
Less than 40% or more	a	4,612	a	0	8
1972–74					
Democrats					
40% or more	$52,332	111,122	$58,790	6	8
Less than 40%	15,721	25,607	9,886	1	9
Republicans					
40% or more	8,910	33,064	24,154	1	1
Less than 40%	5,170	1,623	−3,547	0	5
1974–76					
Democrats					
40% or more	60,142	55,944	−4,198	0	10
Less than 40%	11,937	24,469	12,532	0	4
Republicans					
40% or more	69,588	158,474	88,886	1	4
Less than 40%	9,506	5,815	−3,691	0	12

a Data not available.

won 40 percent or more of the major party vote in the first attempt enjoyed relatively well financed second campaigns. Compare these figures to the averages for challengers in table 3.1. Challengers who failed to win at least 40 percent of the vote in the first election remained seriously underfinanced in the second race; they appear to be inordinately willing sacrificial lambs enduring another drubbing for the sake of the party.

The strategy apparently worked best for Democrats who were fortuitously able to take advantage of Republic problems in 1974; six of the eight repeaters who had received more than 40 percent in 1972 won that year; even one whose vote had been less than 40 percent managed to win. The effects of 1974 political trends are also obvious in the change in spending between the first and second campaigns. Notice specifically the great jump in funds available to Democrats running in 1974 who had proved their "viability" in 1972. Observe the still larger increase in funds supplied to those Republican challengers who won more than 40 percent of the vote against the strong 1974 Democratic tide. Democrats who were not able to win in 1974, even if they got more than 40 percent of the vote, experienced a slight decline in financial support when they made a second run in 1976; they had *not* shown themselves to be particularly strong candidates.

Evidently, candidates can prove themselves viable by making a good, though losing effort the first time out against sitting congressmen, but the proportion of candidates who actually follow this strategy is so small that it has little effect on the overall pattern of campaign contributions and expenditures. No more than 4 percent of the challengers in any of these election years can be interpreted as exploiting this approach.

To recapitulate: the ability of nonincumbent candidates to raise money depends on the extent to which they can convince the elites who finance campaigns that they have a chance to win. Circumstances of the particular election year, recent electoral history, and the behavior (or even presence) of specific incumbents are factors considered by both potential candidates and potential contributors. If the auspices are favorable, experienced and skillful candidates and shrewd political contributors are likely to join forces. Each is attracted by the other. Together they may be able to provide real competition even against apparently entrenched incumbents.

It goes without saying, however, that most of the time incumbents appear anything but vulnerable, and serious, well-financed challenges are the exception. Challengers normally have a great deal of difficulty raising money. Two-thirds of the losing candidates in 1976—the great majority of them challengers—reported finding fundraising very difficult; only 14 percent of the winners had similar complaints.[7] The source of difficulty mentioned most frequently by challengers (66 percent noted it) was being considered a sure loser.[8] Such reactions are hardly surprising in light of the behavior of contributors as analyzed in chapter 3.

CAMPAIGN FUNDS FOR INCUMBENTS

For incumbents, campaign finance involves an entirely different set of problems. Recall from chapter 2 that, in simple terms, the more incumbents spend, the worse they do in the election. This implies that incumbents adjust their level of campaign spending—and hence their money-raising efforts—to the magnitude of the challenge they face. But to a large degree, the strength of that challenge depends on the behavior of the incumbents themselves, for they are able to control many of the factors that encourage or discourage good candidates who might mobilize resources against them. Michael J. Kirwin, while Chairman of the Democratic National Committee, argued that "No Congressman who gets elected and who minds his business should ever be beaten. Everything is there for him to use if he'll only keep his nose to the grindstone and use what is offered."[9] Kirwin overstates his case—strong

---

7. *A Study of the Impact of the Federal Election Campaign Act on the 1976 Election* (Prepared for the Federal Election Commission by Decision Making Information and Hart Research Associates, 1977), p. 70.

8. Ibid., p. 79.

9. H. Douglas Price, "The Electoral Arena," in *Congress and America's Future*, ed. David B. Truman (Englewood Cliffs, N.J.: Prentice-Hall, Inc., 1965), p. 49.

national tides may take the matter out of an incumbent's hands —but incumbents clearly do have a great deal of control over their own electoral fortunes.

The argument that incumbents are able to adjust their fund-raising, and thus spending, to the gravity of the challenge is obviously crucial both for understanding how money works in congressional elections and for evaluating the effects of "reforming" congressional campaign finance regulations. I therefore defend it in some detail. First, regression of incumbent spending on a variety of explanatory variables demonstrates that the challenger's level of spending has the most explanatory power by far. The equation estimated is

$$IE = a + b_1 CE + b_2 P + b_3 CPS + b_4 IP + b_5 YRS + b_6 PO \\ + b_7 L + e \qquad (4.1)$$

where

IE = incumbent's expenditures, thousands of dollars

CE = challenger's expenditures, thousands of dollars

P = challenger's party (1 if Democrat, 0 if Republican)

CPS = challenger's party's strength (the proportion of votes won by the challenger's party's candidate in the last election for this seat)

IP = 1 if the incumbent ran in a primary election, 0 otherwise

YRS = number of consecutive years the incumbent has been in the House

PO = 1 if the challenger has previously held elective office, 0 otherwise

L = 1 if the incumbent is chairman or ranking member of a subcommittee or holds a higher leadership position in the House, 0 otherwise

a = intercept

b = regression coefficient

e = error term[10]

10.   Data are from the sources indicated in notes 14 and 15 of chapter 2, with

The first four independent variables are familiar from equation 2.1. Here, an incumbent's level of spending is hypothesized to be a function of his opponent's spending, his opponent's party (a measure of national tides), the results of the last election for the seat, his opponent's political experience, his seniority, his position as a leader, and whether or not he had to contest a primary election.

The results for 1972, 1974, and 1976 appear in table 4.3. Plainly, the challenger's spending is the most important explanatory variable in these equations. The other variables work as expected given the premise that incumbents raise and spend money in response to the gravity of the electoral challenge. For example, incumbent spending increases with the challenger's party's vote in the last election; incumbents spend more if the challenger has held elective office or, in 1974, if the challenger was a Democrat; they spend less, other things being equal, the longer they have been in office. But all of these variables would be expected to show opposite signs if the equations estimated the incumbent's capacity to raise money according to his political assets and likelihood of winning.

It might be argued that these equations merely show that expenditures by incumbents and challengers vary together rather than that the latter generate the former, but additional analysis renders this interpretation unacceptable. The difference in spending between any two of these elections by incumbents who ran and were opposed in both is clearly a function of the difference in spending by their opponents between the two contests. This is evident from estimates of

$$IE_{74} - IE_{72} = a + b_1(CE_{74} - CE_{72}) + b_2 IE_{72} + b_3 CE_{72}$$
$$+ b_4 IP_{72} + b_5 IP_{74} + b_6 P + e \qquad (4.2)$$

these additions: data for *IP*, *YRS*, and *L* are from Michael Barone, Grant Ujifusa, and Douglas Matthews, *The Almanac of American Politics: The Senators, The Representatives—Their Records, States and District, 1974* (Boston: Gambit, 1973), *passim*, and the same publication for *1976* and *1978* (New York: E. P. Dutton & Co., Inc., 1975 and 1977), passim; the data for *PO* are from the special preelection issues of *C.Q. Weekly Report* 30 (October 7, 1972): 2485–2588; 32 (October 12, 1974): 2715–2815; and 34 (October 9, 1976): 2751–2869.

Table 4.3. Determinants of Campaign Spending by House Incumbents, 1972–76
(Estimates of Equation 4.1)

			Regression Coefficient	t Ratio[a]	Standardized Regression Coefficient	
1972	IE =	a	28.08			
		$b_1 CE$	.522	10.33	.54	
		$b_2 P$	3.31	.87	.04	
		$b_3 CPS$	.224	1.05	.06	
(N = 296)		$b_4 IP$	10.50	2.69	.13	$R^2 = .39$
		$b_5 YRS$	−.79	−2.69	−.15	
		$b_6 PO$	3.10	.69	.03	
		$b_7 L$	.89	.14	.01	
1974	IE =	a	14.11			
		$b_1 CE$	.495	10.30	.51	
		$b_2 P$	12.69	2.88	.14	
		$b_3 CPS$	.673	3.05	.14	
(N = 319)		$b_4 IP$	.10	.02	.00	$R^2 = .47$
		$b_5 YRS$	−.04	−.11	−.01	
		$b_6 PO$	6.79	1.45	.07	
		$b_7 L$	−12.50	−2.00	−.10	
1976	IE =	a	32.22			
		$b_1 CE$	.395	9.89	.48	
		$b_2 P$	8.31	1.67	.08	
		$b_3 CPS$	.797	3.14	.17	
(N = 329)		$b_4 IP$	5.75	1.22	.05	$R^2 = .44$
		$b_5 YRS$	−.69	−1.93	−.10	
		$b_6 PO$	13.29	2.47	.11	
		$b_7 L$	7.38	.92	.05	

[a] A t ratio of at least 1.98 is necessary for a .05 level of significance, 2.58 for .01, and 3.35 for .001.

and equivalent equations for 1974–76 and 1972–76, where the subscripts refer to the election year and the variables and coefficients are as defined for equation 4.1. The results appear in table 4.4. Controlling for party, primary elections, and expenditures in the last election, the change in spending by incumbents is a positive function of the change in spending by challengers. The change is

Table 4.4. Determinants of Changes in Campaign Spending by House Incumbents (Estimates of Equation 4.2)

		Regression Coefficient	t Ratio[a]	Standardized Regression Coefficient	
1972–74	$IE_{74} - IE_{72} =$				
	a	29.00			
	$b_1(CE_{74} - CE_{72})$	.490	11.74	.60	
	b_2IE_{72}	−.546	−12.00	−.58	
(N = 296)	b_3CE_{72}	.399	7.78	.43	$R^2 = .63$
	b_4IP_{72}	−8.33	−2.38	−.09	
	b_5IP_{74}	−1.44	−.41	−.02	
	b_6P	−13.06	−3.52	−.15	
1974–76	$IE_{76} - IE_{74} =$				
	a	39.26			
	$b_1(CE_{76} - CE_{74})$	.409	11.70	.54	
	b_2IE_{74}	−.594	−11.64	−.62	
(N = 290)	b_3CE_{74}	.448	8.07	.46	$R^2 = .52$
	b_4IP_{74}	−12.81	−3.02	−.13	
	b_5IP_{76}	11.34	2.49	.11	
	b_6P	−7.25	−1.65	−.07	
1972–76	$IE_{76} - IE_{72} =$				
	a	55.02			
	$b_1(CE_{76} - CE_{72})$	.369	7.18	.40	
	b_2IE_{72}	−.766	−10.38	−.63	
(N = 204)	b_3CE_{72}	.427	5.29	.33	$R^2 = .59$
	b_4IP_{72}	−6.86	−1.20	−.06	
	b_5IP_{76}	17.96	2.92	.15	
	b_6P	−25.69	−4.58	−.23	

[a] A t ratio of at least 1.98 is necessary for a .05 level of significance, 2.58 for .01, and 3.35 for .001.

also negatively related to what the incumbent spent in the first election, which makes intuitive sense; the more spent the first time, the smaller the increase, other things equal. But the degree of change is positively related to what the challenger spent in the previous election, suggesting that a more formidable challenge in one campaign spurs incumbents to greater efforts in the next.

If the control variables are omitted, the basic relationship scarcely changes. The 1972–74 regression coeffficient becomes .50, its t ratio 13.18, its standardized regression coefficient .61; the same figures for 1974–76 and 1972–76 are .39, 10.12, and .51, and .47, 8.33, and .51, respectively.

Incumbents clearly increase or decrease their spending in reaction to changes in the amount spent by opponents. Any increase, however, does not counterbalance benefits to challengers from the expenditures that inspire it. The difference in the incumbent's vote between two election years is negatively associated with differences in spending by both the incumbent and challenger, as shown by estimates of

$$
\begin{aligned}
IV_{74} - IV_{72} = \quad & a + b_1 \, (IE_{74} - IE_{72}) + \\
& b_2(CE_{74} - CE_{72}) + b_3P + e
\end{aligned}
\tag{4.3}
$$

and equivalent equations for 1974–76 and 1972–76, where IV is the incumbent's percentage share of the two-party vote and the other variables and coefficients are as defined for equations 4.1 and 4.2. The estimates are given in table 4.5. Incumbents spend more when they are in trouble because of a serious challenge, but their greater spending does not offset the effects of greater spending by the opposition, so the more they spend, the worse they do in the election.

Some additional data speaking to this critical point are found in table 4.6, which lists the average amount spent by incumbents who ran in two successive election years broken down by whether or not they won the second election. Incumbents spend much more in losing than in winning. The future losers also spend a slightly more than average in winning the last election before their defeat, which implies that they are more insecure to begin with. But their increase in spending between the two elections is much greater. Most of the 1974 losers were, of course, Republicans. But in a year disastrous for Republicans electorally (and for Republican challengers, financially as well—see table 3.1), Republican incumbents actually outspent Democratic incumbents by, on the average, about $35,000. Despite the extraordinarily hostile political environment,

Table 4.5. Change in Incumbent's Vote as a Function of Change in Campaign
Spending
(Estimates of Equation 4.3)

		Regression Coefficient	t Ratio[a]	Standardized Regression Coefficient	
1972–74	$IV_{74} - IV_{72} =$				
	a	−5.00			
	$b_1(IE_{74} - IE_{72})$	−.065	−5.13	−.25	
($N = 296$)	$b_2(CE_{74} - CE_{72})$	−.070	−6.61	−.33	$R^2 = .57$
	b_3P	8.83	9.17	.38	
1974–76	$IV_{76} - IV_{74} =$				
	a	5.28			
	$b_1(IE_{76} - IE_{74})$	−.015	−1.57	−.09	
($N = 290$)	$b_2(CE_{76} - CE_{74})$	−.055	−7.75	−.44	$R^2 = .34$
	b_3P	−4.43	−5.51	−.27	
1972–76	$IV_{76} - IV_{72} =$				
	a	2.12			
	$b_1(IE_{76} - IE_{72})$	−.064	−5.70	−.36	
($N = 204$)	$b_2(CE_{76} - CE_{72})$	−.058	−5.64	−.35	$R^2 = .41$
	b_3P	1.78	1.59	.09	

[a] A *t* ratio of at least 1.98 is necessary for a .05 level of significance, 2.58 for .01, and 3.35 for .001.

Republican incumbents were able to increase their spending by almost 55 percent over the previous election; spending by Democrats actually decreased.

Recognition that incumbents are able to adjust their campaign finances to the demands of the electoral challenge they face implies several other things. First, campaign resources are available to be tapped if the need arises. That is, incumbents can raise more money when they think they need it, even though they need it most when the prospects for victory are most uncertain. This is quite understandable in light of the contribution strategies pursued by those who control campaign funds. Economic interest groups are always ready to contribute to incumbents in return for either tangible favors

Table 4.6.   Average Change in Campaign Spending by Winning and
Losing Incumbents

	Average Campaign Spending			
	Winning Incum-bents	*N*	*Losing Incum-bents*	*N*
1972 Election[a]				
1970	$ 4,591	323	$ 8,696	12
1972	5,721		16,220	
Percent				
change	+25		+87	
1974 Election				
1972	$60,679	257	$ 69,218	39
1974	57,837		101,645	
Percent				
change	−5		+46	
1976 Election				
1974	$70,219	280	$ 76,287	10
1976	81,494		130,293	
Percent				
change	+16		+71	

[a] Television and radio expenditures only; total spending figures are not available for 1970. These data are from U.S., Congress, Senate, Committee on Commerce, Subcommittee on Communications. *Federal Election Campaign Act of 1971: Appendix A*, 92nd Cong., 1st sess., hearings March 2–5 and 31, and April 1, 1971 and the same Subcommittee, *Federal Election Campaign Act of 1973: Appendix A*, 93rd Cong., 1st sess., hearings March 7–9 and 13, 1973.

or a backlog of good will; when funds are most needed, they are likely to be most appreciated. Party and ideological groups will come to the aid of favored incumbents readily when the need arises, since it is more efficient to maximize the party or ideological cohort by attending to seats threatened but already held than by trying to take them from the opposition. Incumbents may resist tapping these sources—particularly those involving a suggestion of quid pro quo—when they feel no great need for the money. Most find fund raising thoroughly distasteful. But it is not usually as distasteful as the thought of losing, so members do use their capacity to raise a substantial campaign kitty when they think it necessary.

And they think it necessary more readily than would less involved observers. Despite the well-known statistics on the reelection rates of incumbent members, they are a surprisingly insecure lot. Insecurity is born of uncertainty, and congressmen "see electoral uncertainity where outsiders would fail to unearth a single objective indicator of it."[11] Although in any given election year relatively few incumbents are defeated (and not very many are evenly seriously threatened), over the course of a career most members have had close calls at one time or another. From the perspective of a long-term career, it may seem necessary to engage in some electoral "overkill" in one election to discourage opposition in the future. Important elements of electoral politics over which they have little control—redistricting, demographic change, national tides—provide additional grounds for anxiety.

The instinctive tendency, then, is for incumbents to react—or, more precisely, overreact—to what their challengers are doing. It is remarkable that before 1972, when the first solid data showed incumbents outspending challengers nearly two to one, congressmen invariably claimed that they were outspent by their opponents. Clapp observed in his discussions with anonymous congressmen from both parties in 1959 that "Virtually every congressman with whom campaign expenditures was discussed emphasized that, whatever the cost of his campaign, his opponent had exceeded them."[12] This inclination to exaggerate the opposition's spending is also apparent in the survey taken for the Federal Election Commission following the 1976 elections. By now, incumbents are quite aware that they do, in fact, spend more than challengers; 68 percent thought they spent more, 20 percent thought the challenger spent more. But challengers view it somewhat differently; only 12 percent thought they outspent the incumbent, 80 percent thought they were outspent. Even more revealing, only 16 percent of the candidates for open seats thought they spent more than the other

11. Richard F. Fenno, Jr.; *Home Style: House Members in Their Districts* (Boston: Little, Brown and Company, 1978), pp. 10–11.

12. Charles L. Clapp, *The Congressman: His Work As He Sees It* (Washington, D.C.: The Brookings Institution, 1963), pp. 387–88.

candidate; 76 percent though the opponent spent more; accurate estimates would have produced a fifty–fifty split.[13]

Incumbent members admit to reactive spending. Senator Dole once said, "You see your opponent spending, and you buy equal or comparable time. And he runs an ad, and you run an ad. It is reaction and reaction and reaction."[14] But since uncertainty exaggerates perceptions of the opponent's level of campaigning, the response is likely to be exaggerated as well. Uncertainty also promotes a strategy of minimizing regret;[15] no candidate wants to wake up Wednesday morning a loser with unexploited resources. not only do incumbents raise more money in closer elections; they also spend a greater proportion of the money they do raise.

For incumbents, then, campaign finance represents a paradoxical problem. They are able to raise campaign money with comparative ease; they may not enjoy doing it, but they can get the funds they think they need. But the money is apparently of limited value to them in the election; the more they spend, the worse they do. The preliminary analysis presented in chapter 2, which will be largely confirmed by some additional work in chapter 5, indicates that if the challenger's spending is taken into account, the incumbent's spending has relatively little effect on the outcome. What matters to incumbents is the amount spent by challengers. Money *is* very important to challengers, but they have much less control over how much they can raise. The behavior of incumbents (along with some other factors already mentioned) is more important in this regard. So the most effective strategy for incumbents is to deny campaign resources to potential challengers (thereby also discouraging the more experienced and effective candidates). They serve themselves best by attending to their opponents' resources rather than their own.

The key is to avoid being singled out for special attention by the

13. *Impact of the FECA*, p. 74.

14. U.S., Congress, Senate, Committee on Commerce, Subcommittee on Communications, *Federal Election Campaign Act of 1971*, 92nd Cong. 1st sess., hearings March 2–5 and 31, and April 1, 1971, p. 465.

15. Charles O. Jones, "The Role of the Campaign in Congressional Politics," in *The Electoral Process*, p. 29.

individuals and committees that are potential contributors to their challengers' campaigns. The problem faced by contributors wanting to make the most effective electoral use of their donations is coordinating their decisions with other sharing similar views and intentions. The capacity of campaign contributions to augment the number of successful challenges by preferred candidates (those with desirable ideological, partisan, or policy orientations) depends on what additional contributions are forthcoming. Especially with the current limits on both committee and individual political contributions, contributors can expect their gifts to have some effect only if they are confident that others will be adding to them. Their aim must be to fund candidates others will also choose to fund; and of course the others are trying to do the same thing.

Schelling has examined some of the ways people can coordinate their expectations and actions when each knows that the others are trying to do the same thing without any direct communication between them being necessary. His conclusion is that "People *can* often concert their intentions or expectations with others if each knows that the other is trying to do the same. Most situations . . . provide some clue for coordinating behavior, some focal point for each person's expectation of what others expect him to expect to be expected to do."[16] The focal point is provided by the particular situation. The definitive characteristic of a focal point is its conspicuousness; something that is unusual and prominent provides the focal point solution to the problem of coordinating mutual expectations and thus actions. The incumbent's wisest course, then, is to keep the district from becoming a focal point for the mobilization of campaign resources, and the most effective way to achieve this is to avoid becoming a focal object himself.

SOME EXAMPLES FROM CASE STUDIES

A collection of articles covering seven specific House contests in 1974 provides some excellent illustrations of the points made in this

16.   Thomas C. Schelling, *The Strategy of Conflict* (New York: Oxford University Press, 1963), p. 57.

and the previous chapter. Only one of the seven contests was for an open seat—the 21st District of Texas—and, as expected, both candidates were amply financed and the election was close. The winner, Democrat Robert Krueger, spent $311,953 and won 53.8 percent of the two-party vote. The Republican loser, Douglas Harlan, spent $164,675. One revealing observation made about this campaign touches on the value of a primary election race to a nonincumbent candidate. The authors note that Harlan suffered from

> the absence of a vigorous and hotly contested primary campaign. In an undercontested Republic Primary where Harlan needed to spend only $12,000, he won so handily that the race was not a vehicle for galvanizing voter attention. His Democratic opponent, on the other hand, faced a tough primary and closely fought runoff election, and was thus able to spend up to the edges of the legal financial expenditure limits for the primary, the primary runoff, and the general election.[17]

The limits referred to are those on mass media spending in force until October 15 under the Federal Election Campaign Act of 1971.

The other six cases involved incumbents and challengers. Perhaps most typical was the race in Ohio's 13th District between veteran Republican incumbent Charles Mosher and Fred Ritenauer, a Democratic county commissioner. Neither candidate did much campaigning; Mosher spent $17,253, Ritenauer, $14,889. The challenger's campaign never got off the ground and he remained largely unknown; the incumbent therefore got by with a minimal campaign. As it was, his winning share of the two-party vote was only 57.5 percent, the lowest since 1964, but this was basically a consequence of the strong post-Watergate trend against Republicans.[18] The incumbent need do little to win when everyone is convinced he is going to win anyway.

17. Robert L. Lineberry, John E. Sinclair, Lawrence C. Dodd, and Alan M. Sager, "The Case of the Wrangling Professors: The Twenty-first District of Texas," in *The Making of Congressmen: Seven Campaigns of 1974*, ed. Alan L. Clem (Belmont, Calif.: Wadsworth Publishing Company, Inc., 1976), p. 177.

18. Thomas A. Flinn, "The Case of the Quiescent Campaign: The Thirteenth District of Ohio," in ibid, p. 109.

A similar contest took place in the 6th District of Wisconsin, where William A. Steiger, the Republican incumbent, easily defeated Democratic challenger Nancy Simenz. The district was considered hopeless even in a very good Democratic year, and the Democrats' problem was to find someone willing to run. Simenz was the district party chairman whose job it was to round up a nominee; when she could not, she took on the duty herself. Steiger had made the cause appear hopeless because of his consistently strong showing in earlier campaigns. Among other things, he had in the past made judicious appeals to district labor organizations, paying sufficient attention to their interests to keep them from endorsing and funding his opponents.[19] Steiger's aim in 1974 was to avoid a narrow margin of victory in that difficult Republican year that might lead to strong challenges in the future. "Like other resourceful congressmen with long-term commitments to their profession, Steiger has constantly sought to avoid the appearance of weakness or vulnerability for fear that hostile forces will allocate their maximum resources against him in future elections."[20]

His strategy worked. In addition to making full use of communications resources available to him as an incumbent, he raised a substantial campaign war chest early in the campaign; he had no trouble raising as much as he felt necessary.[21] Simenz, with only token support from labor ($2,000), raised very little money; she suspected that, as a woman, it was harder to convince contributors she was a serious candidate.[22] Ultimately, she spent only $6,128 to Steiger's $51,495, and she lost decisively. The incumbent in this instance drew on his past record of success and the full range of resources open to incumbents to assure his continued success in the future, denying the opposing party both strong candidates and the financial backing they would need for a serious challenge.

The race in the 4th District of Massachusetts between Robert Drinan, Democrat and Jesuit Priest, and two opponents, Alvin

19. John F. Bibby and Roger H. Davidson, *On Capitol Hill: Studies in the Legislative Process* (Hinsdale, Ill.: The Dryden Press, Inc., 1972), p. 64.

20. John F. Bibby, "The Case of the Young Old Pro: The Sixth District of Wisconsin," in *Making of Congressmen*, p. 217.

21. Ibid., p. 219.

22. Ibid., p. 224.

Mandell, the Republican, and Jon Rotenberg, a Democrat running as an Independent, illustrates another aspect of campaign finance. Drinan faced split opposition, almost guaranteeing victory. Mandell was an archetypal "sure loser"; he was not well known, his political experience was limited, and he only ran after the original nominee backed out, apparently because he thought the cause hopeless. He spent only $14,322 and won only 14.4 percent of the vote. Rotenberg had more experience (two terms in the state legislature; before that, he had been an aide to Representative O'Neill) and a stronger financial backing (he spent $76,576), but had little chance in a three-candidate race.

The most interesting aspect of campaign finance in this contest is the way Drinan raised the $178,871 he spent. Drinan is a classic example of a candidate whose appeal is strongly ideological. He was among the most vehement critics of the Vietnam war and was among the first to suggest that Nixon should be impeached. His militant liberalism won him the support of like-minded contributors across the country, and an inordinate amount of money—and many campaign workers—arrived from outside the district.[23] This caused him some local problems, as did his radical stances; both provided targets for his opponents and probably helped Rotenberg financially. But the divided opposition provided a safe cushion.

Drinan's relatively radical political image has brought him well-financed challenges in the other two election years he has run as an incumbent. In 1972 he spent $199,703 to hold off two challengers, the most formidable of whom spent $148,285. He faced stiff competition again in 1976, this time from only one candidate, and wound up spending $219,297 to win only 52.1 percent of the vote against a Republican who had spent $186,262. It is unusual for an incumbent to be challenged so strongly election after election; Drinan's militant liberalism, however, makes him stand out as an obvious focal target for opposition activities. But it also makes him a focal object for those supporting his positions so that he is able to mobilize extensive campaign resources in response to these challenges.

23. John H. Fenton and Donald M. Austern, "The Case of the Priestly Zealot: The Fourth District of Massachusetts," in *Making of Congressmen*, pp. 96–97.

California's 16th District provides an example of the challenger who uses a good showing in one election as the basis for a stronger run in the next election. Julian Camacho, the Democratic challenger, had won 44.4 percent of the two-party vote in 1972; that year he spent $57,865 against the $61,828 spent by the incumbent Republican, Burt Talcott. With that showing, and with Watergate, a slow economy, and Ford's pardon of Nixon in the background, Camacho became one of the fortunate designated marginal challengers and thus a focal point for the converging expectations of potential contributors. Cavala reports that

> the loose coalition of people that make up the Democratic party in California had come, by June of 1974, to a rough consensus to target the Sixteenth District as one of their key races for November. Various national liberal endorsing groups listed the race as one of the top fifteen in the nation. The National Committee for an Effective Congress called the race one of the three most important in the country. Environmental Action, a Washington watchdog group, listed Talcott as one of its "dirty dozen." The ADA and the AFL-CIO both listed the race as one of the top ten of the year.[24]

Camacho had valuable attributes besides his performance in 1972 and his strong victory against two other candidates in the 1974 primary. He was a Chicano, and therefore an important symbolic candidate, but at the same time, "he had acquired a mode of dress and demeanor which made him look and sound very little like an ethnic candidate;"[25] he was, therefore, "electable" as well as symbolically attractive.

Talcott's behavior as an incumbent had also invited attention. He was rated zero by ADA and only 10 percent by COPE. He vociferously supported the Vietnam war and Richard Nixon and was considered by environmentalists to be among the very worst congressmen.

24. William Cavala, "The Case of the Chicano Challenger: The Sixteenth District of California," in *Making of Congressmen*, p. 27.

25. Ibid., p. 31

Thus to many of the Democratic Party's elite constituency in California and in the nation, the opportunity to beat Talcott was more than simply the chance of increasing the Democratic margin in the House or even replacing a conservative Republican with a liberal Chicano—it was the possibility of inflicting a defeat on a man who personified leadership on those issues which they considered to be the paramount issues of American politics.[26]

Cavala argues that, in fact, Talcott was not, by objective standards, one of the more vulnerable Republicans. But he was considered so objectionable to many liberal groups that they convinced themselves he could be beaten, and the various group endorsements reinforced one another. "There was a tendency, in sum, for the endorsement of one national group to be perceived by others as increasing the potential 'winnability' of the race. Or as one of Talcott's campaign people put it, 'Like vultures, one endorsement seems to attract others.' Several of these endorsements seemed to indicate a weak candidate."[27] The interaction of such convergent expectations operates as a self-fulfilling prophecy; candidates who are expected to do well get the resources that help them to do well.

The effect of these endorsements was twofold. "The various endorsements brought him substantial outside money (over $40,000) and publicity." But in addition, and "More importantly, they aided in the effort to galvanize workers and contributors within the district. Convinced that Camacho had a realistic chance to win, many local contributors went far beyond their previous levels of support in 1974. The fundraising efforts of the Camacho campaign became almost a social existence for those involved."[28]

The fund raisers took advantage of the growing conviction that victory was possible by successfully tapping the same individuals repeatedly. One supporter is quoted as saying, "I didn't really mean to give as much as I did, but it always seemed to be going so

26.   Ibid.
27.   Ibid., p. 32.
28.   Ibid., p. 35.

well with only a little bit more needed here and there that I couldn't
say no; they got it out of me by dribs and drabs.''[29]

As a result, Camacho nearly tripled his spending over 1972, the
total amounting to $156,084; even his campaign manager admitted
that ''Resources were not a problem. Oh, we always had cash flow
problems and we always seemed to be scrambling, but *we had
enough to do all we planned to do*.''[30]

Talcott also increased his expenditures to match those of his
challenger; he ended up spending $152,455 on the campaign. He
had failed to discourage a serious challenge and had not made full
use of the perquisites of office, but he was capable of mounting a
strong counterattack. He went far beyond his usual campaign activities, hiring an outside firm of professional campaign managers for
the first time. Ultimately, Talcott won a very close race with 50.7
percent of the two-party vote. According to Cavala, the race was
decided on the quality of the campaigns, not on the difference in
resources or advantages and disadvantages usually attaching
to incumbents and challengers.[31] Talcott was not so fortunate in
1976; his evident vulnerability attracted another strong challenge,
this time from Leon Panetta, who spent $181,410 to Talcott's
$217,053, and won with 53.4 percent of the vote.

Not all incumbents were able to starve off defeat in 1974; the
two in this collection who did lose did so largely through their own
fault. Incumbent John Davis lost the primary election for the Democratic nomination in the 7th District of Georgia to Dr. Larry
McDonald, a member of the National Council of the John Birch
Society. Davis had ''basically lost touch with his district.''[32] He
did not exploit the resources available to him to communicate with
or serve his constituents. When seriously challenged, his response
was uninspired; he relied on friendships with local courthouse elites
that had proved sufficient in the past, did little personal cam-

29. Ibid.
30. Ibid.; emphasis in the original.
31. Ibid., p. 49.
32. Charles S. Bullock III and Catherine Rudder, ''The Case of the Right-Wing
Urologist: The Seventh District of Georgia,'' in *Making of Congressmen*, p. 72.

paigning, and did not use television in its place. He was also thought to have a drinking problem.[33]

McDonald, on the other hand, waged a well-financed media-oriented campaign. He was able to raise $115,000 in contributions between January 1 and the August 13 primary, added $30,000 to this in bank loans, and so spent three times as much as the $45,000 Davis spent in the primary. Bullock and Rudder feel that "McDonald's greater total resources may have been a decisive factor. McDonald barraged the Seventh District with advertising, successfully translating money into exposure."[34] He raised another $60,000 for the general election. His funds did not come from parties or political groups, but rather in "relatively large contributions from people who evidently believed in what he said. . . . While it cannot be traced, he probably received contributions from John Birch Society members in response to a full-page ad soliciting funds which he ran in the Society's *American Opinion* magazine."[35] His extreme ideological stance was, then, the basis of his financial support.

McDonald defeated Davis by 2,625 votes, a margin that should have been easily overcome by some harder campaigning and more careful attention to the district by the incumbent. McDonald went on to win the general election against Quincy Collins, a former air force colonel who had spent seven and a half years in a North Vietnamese prison, by 543 votes. Collins, who is almost as conservative as McDonald, mounted another campaign against him in 1976; McDonald won again with 55.1 percent of the vote, spending $157,651 to Collins' $72,638. McDonald's extreme positions, like Drinan's, attract the attention of political opponents, but these same positions provide him with a kind of national constituency that is ready to supply campaign resources when the need arises.

Another incumbent who lost in 1974 was Frank Denholm of the 1st District of South Dakota. He pulled the unlikely trick of losing to a little-known Republican in that strongly anti-Republican year. And he did it by almost total failure to take any advantage of his in-

33.   Ibid., pp. 66–72.
34.   Ibid., pp. 67–68.
35.   Ibid., p. 82.

cumbency. He "was one of that rare breed of congressional incumbent who approached the November election with no clear advantage in terms of the quality or quantity of campaign staff or organization."[36] He had no campaign staff; he relied on bumper stickers and billboards, spending only $20,583 on the entire campaign. He did not exploit his generally favorable image in the district and "did not effectively use his campaign resources because he did not seem to understand what they were or how they could be employed to withstand a serious challenge."[37] The value of incumbency is not a constant; it depends on what the incumbent does with what he has.[38] And if he does nothing with it, his incumbency is worth very little.

The Republican challenger, Larry Pressler, waged an aggressive, vigorous campaign. He outspent Denholm decisively (his total expenditure was $58,106), spending more than twice as much on advertising as the incumbent, less on printing, billboards, and campaign novelties. Worth noting is that "much of the 'big' money was contributed very late in the campaign, and perhaps would not have been given had it not been apparent that Pressler was running a strong race for Denholm's seat." Pressler himself thought that "he had the campaign won on the $35,000 he had collected by mid-October in donations of less than $100. Certainly the money received in the last two weeks of the campaign was difficult to put to good use."[39] Pressler won with 55.3 percent of the vote.

Each of these case studies nicely illustrates one or more aspects of how and why money flows—or fails to flow—into House campaigns. They all reveal the decisive importance of incumbency —and what the incumbent does with it—in determining both the magnitude of the challenge and the ability of the incumbent to surmount a strong challenge if one arises. Clearly, incumbents cannot abjure campaigning entirely in the face of a formidable challenge,

36. Alan L. Clem, "The Case of the Upstart Republican: The First District of South Dakota," in *Making of Congressmen*, p. 141.

37. Ibid., p. 161.

38. Mann presents the best evidence for this point. See "Candidate Saliency," p. 146.

39. Clem. "First District of South Dakota," p. 139.

especially if they have been lax in using those perquisites of office that normally make formal campaigning less crucial. If they do not exploit their potential resources, they can be defeated. But it is clear from the overall data on congressional elections that this does not happen very often. Incumbents who do not work consistently at re-election are selected out, as it were, and replaced by ones who do.

These case studies reiterate one other central point: it is the vigor of the challenge that determines whether or not a race is competitive.

Fund Raising in Senate Campaigns

The evidence and examples supporting the points made so far in this chapter have been drawn from House elections. The same arguments apply to Senate fund raising, although the distinctive circumstances of these contests alter the relative weights of the various factors involved. They also prohibit the kind of precise empirical analysis possible for House races.

In general, Senate contests are distinguished by closer competition, more experienced (and, presumably, skillful) candidates, and greater media attention. A large majority of nonincumbent Senate candidates have held elective office, not a few of them in the House; 63 percent of all Senate challengers, 1972–76, had previously won at least one election. Those without this kind of electoral experience are frequently well known from other sectors of public life. Two former astronauts (John Glenn and Harrison Schmitt) currently sit in the Senate; Senator Hayakawa made his mark on the public consciousness as President of San Francisco State College in confrontations with student radicals; Senator Moynihan advanced to the Senate through a series of appointive national offices, including advisor to President Nixon, Ambassador to India, and Ambassador to the United Nations.

It is not difficult to imagine why more experienced and prominent candidates are attracted to Senate races. The higher status of the Senate is certainly not irrelevant; neither is the greater attention paid to members of that body by the media and the public. Fewer Senate seats are "safe" by any of the usual criteria; states are evidently harder to represent in a way that discourages opposition. The results of the last election—normally six years earlier—are less relevant to current judgments about how vulnerable a Senator really is.

Contributors are also attracted to Senate races, and by many of the same considerations: more competitive contests, the greater power of individual Senators (each is, in a sense, worth 4.35 Representatives), the greater saliency of Senate campaigns. They are also attracted by the more experienced and prominent candidates. Contributions (and expenditures) in Senate races are, of course, also larger because of the greater size of all but a few Senate constituencies, but differences in House and Senate campaign funding are not fully explained by differences in constituency size. In 1974, for example, Senate candidates spent an average of $185 for every thousand people in the state; House candidates spent an average of $103 per thousand in the district.[40]

Still, a few Senators are able to discourage all significant opposition and are therefore able to run minimal campaigns. Senator Proxmire of Wisconsin established something of a benchmark by spending only $697 to win 73 percent of the vote in 1976. He had received 71 percent in 1970; his opponent in 1976, who had held party but not elective office, raised only $66,321 to challenge him. Senator Jackson of Washington had won even more handily in 1970 (84 percent of the vote); his obscure 1976 opponent raised and spent only $10,841, assuring Jackson of an easy victory despite the energy and other resources diverted into his unsuccessful run for the Democratic presidential nomination.

Senator Williams of New Jersey also won an easy victory against weak opposition in 1976; his opponent spent only $73,499 to win 38 percent of the vote. The interesting aspect of this contest was that back in 1970, Williams had looked very vulnerable indeed. At that time he was known to have a drinking problem and was re-

40. William P. Welch, "The Effectiveness of Expenditures in State Legislative Races," *American Politics Quarterly* 4 (1976): 344.

puted to be a less than outstanding Senator. But he was also lucky. The defeat of Senator Yarborough in a Texas primary in May 1970 "meant that Williams, if reelected, would become Chairman of the Senate Labor and Public Welfare Committee (since renamed the Human Resources Committee). Suddenly, Williams became the nation's number one recipient of union political action committee funds and other assistance. Williams won that term with 56%."[41] The record he made as committee chairman and as chairman of the subcommittee dealing with securities legislation inspired generous contributions from labor and securities interests for his next campaign; by December 1975, he had raised a total of $442,893, evidently enough to discourage any but the most intrepid—or naive—opponent. A month before the election a statewide poll of New Jersey voters found that only 1 percent could identify the Republican nominee.[42]

Normally, however, Senators face stiff opposition when they run for reelection and feel compelled to raise and spend money accordingly. The available evidence suggests that Senate incumbents, too, adjust their level of spending to the strength of the challenge. The simple correlations between per voter expenditures of incumbents and challengers, 1972–76, are .38, .94, and .65, respectively.[43] Unfortunately, data are not yet at hand to study the change in spending by an incumbent between two election years. There is reason to believe that fund raising is more onerous for Senate candidates, at least those from larger states, than it is for House candidates. The same restrictions on individual and PAC contributions apply to both, but Senators may find it necessary to raise much larger total funds. This point will be elaborated during the discussion of the effects of campaign finance reform in chapter 7.

41. Barone, Ujifusa, and Matthews, *Almanac of American Politics—1978*, p. 518.

42. Roland D. McDevitt, "Congressional Campaign Finance and the Consequences of Its Regulation" (Ph.D. diss., University of California at Santa Barbara, 1978), p. 162.

43. The correlations between untransformed expenditures, which tend to be exaggerated because spending varies with the population of the state, are .61, .77, and .80, respectively, for 1972, 1974, and 1976.

CONCLUDING COMMENTS

Many of the arguments and interpretations of cases presented in this chapter rest implicitly on the regression findings from chapter 2, indicating that challengers gain much more from their campaign expenditures than do incumbents. As spending by both candidates increases, so does the vote for the challenger. In chapter 5, this proposition is given a more thorough test, one that acknowledges the possibility of a reciprocal relationship between campaign funds and votes. Evidence is also adduced for an explanation of why campaign expenditures have different consequences for incumbents and nonincumbents. The full account of the flow of money in congressional elections is then used to account for some puzzling findings produced by studies of the 1974 congressional elections.

5 ☆ THE EFFECTS OF CAMPAIGN SPENDING: THE FULL MODEL

Chapter 2 presented tentative evidence that campaign spending has an important impact on the outcomes of congressional elections. In particular, the amount spent by nonincumbents strongly affects how well they do. The marginal gains in political support from a given expenditure are much greater for challengers and other disadvantaged candidates (for example, Republicans in contests for open seats in 1974) than for incumbents. The evidence is only tentative because the actual structure of the relationship between spending and election outcomes could not be confidently taken directly from estimates of these equations, since the connection between spending and votes may be reciprocal. That is, votes and expenditures may vary together because more money is contributed to candidates who are expected to do well or because candidates attract money and votes for the same reasons.

The motives and strategies of contributors and candidates analyzed in chapters 3 and 4 certainly support the thesis that (expected) votes affect campaign contributions, and hence expenditures. If the money–votes connection is indeed reciprocal, the coefficients calculated for the equations in chapter 2 are biased and inconsistent estimates of the true structural relationship between what congressional candidates spend and how well they do on election day. The true coefficients must be estimated from a simultaneous equation system.

A Simultaneous Equation Model of Campaign Spending Effects

The variables identified as important determinants of campaign

136

contributions to both incumbents and challengers provide the basis for a more complete model of the money–votes relationship:

$$CE = f(P, CPS, PO, YRS, CP, EV) \qquad (5.1)$$
$$IE = f(P, CPS, PO, YRS, IP, EV, CE) \qquad (5.2)$$
$$CV = f(CE, IE, P, CPS) \qquad (5.3)$$
$$EV \simeq CV \qquad (5.4)$$

The variables are as defined for the equations in chapters 2 and 4, with the addition of CP (1 if the challenger ran in a primary election, 0 if not), and EV, the challenger's expected share of the two-party vote.

The interpretation of these equations is straightforward. Challengers are assumed to spend all they can raise. Equation 5.1 proposes that the challenger's ability to attract campaign funds depends primarily on his likelihood of victory, which is in turn a function of several other variables; those which can be measured are included in the equation. The first of these is the challenger's party (P), which is important in any year, such as 1974, when strong national tides are running. The second is the vote in the last election for the seat (CPS), which was interpreted as indicating the challenger's district party strength in the equations in chapter 2, but which may also be considered a measure of the incumbent's vulnerability.

The third is the challenger's prior political experience (PO). It is measured as a simple dichotomous variable indicating whether or not the candidates has ever won elective public office. It is intuitively plausible that not all offices are equal, that there are important differences, for example, between being mayor of a city coterminous with the congressional district and sitting on the city council of one small town in the district. However, a variable taking this possibility into account by weighing the office according to the ratio of the population of the constituency it served to the population of the congressional district added nothing to the explanatory power of any of the equations and so was dropped from the analysis.

The number of years the incumbent has held office (YRS) is another indicator of potential vulnerability—first-term incumbents seem to make the most tempting targets—which once again should affect the attractiveness of the challenger as an "investment" of any kind.

Since the data do not include separate figures for primary and general elections, *CP* (like *IP* in equation 5.2) is included to pick up any differences in spending brought about by the demands of a primary contest. There is no way to determine accurately how much of the campaign's money was spent in the primary. This is not as troublesome as it may appear. Challengers usually spend as much money as they can raise anyway. Their basic need is to get the attention of voters, and this can be done as effectively in a primary as in a general election campaign.[1] Primary election campaigning no doubt has general election payoffs. Recall that the absence of tough primary competition was considered a handicap for the Republican candidate in the 1974 contest for the 21st District of Texas. On the average, challengers who have had primary campaigns do better in the general election than those who have not, but then this may only mean that more candidates choose to compete for nominations to oppose weaker incumbents.

Incumbents will spend more money, in general, if they face primary opposition, but their spending is much more strongly affected by the severity of the general election challenge, as the analysis in chapter 4 has shown.

Finally, challengers are assumed to attract contributions in proportion to their likely share of the vote (*EV*), which is itself assumed to be associated to some significant degree with the actual share of the vote they receive (equation 5.4). Obviously, this variable interacts with all of the other conditioning variables in this equation, but it also represents additional components (e.g., the behavior of the incumbent in office) which are not measured by the other variables.

Interpretation of the equation for incumbent spending (5.2) is quite different. Incumbent spending is not a positive function of the likelihood of victory at all; rather, the more certain they are of

1. See Gary C. Jacobson, "Practical Consequences of Campaign Finance Reform: An Incumbent Protection Act?" *Public Policy* 24 (1976): 22–23.

reelection, the less incumbents spend. This does not mean that contributors deliberately ignore them—what rational quid pro quo investor would overlook a sure thing?—or that they could not raise much more money if they wished. The explanation is simply that incumbents sure of victory feel no need to gather and spend the funds that are available. Soliciting and accepting contributions is hardly something politicians relish (see chapter 6).

Incumbents, then, acquire and spend funds only in proportion to the perceived necessity to do so. And they can usually get all they feel they need, although they may not enjoy doing it. The variables that determine incumbent spending, therefore, are those which indicate how much the candidate is likely to need. This, in turn, is primarily a function of the strength of the challenger. Since the challenger's strength is best indicated by his financial resources, CE belongs in equation 5.2 as a conditioning variable. The measure of incumbent expenditures, IE, does not similarly belong in the challenger's expenditure equation; challengers are not able to raise money at will to contest an incumbent who may be spending a great deal. Rather, they spend all they can (at least up to very large amounts) independently of what the incumbent is spending.

The other variables in equation 5.2 are to be interpreted in the same way; they determine how threatened the incumbent is likely to feel and therefore how much he finds it prudent to raise and spend.

The third equation (5.3) is of course the one originally estimated in chapter 2 by ordinary least-squares (OLS) regression. The other exogenous variables (those determined entirely outside the system of equations) are left out on the theoretical premise that they affect CV only indirectly, through their effect on spending; empirically, these variables had no statistically significant connection with election outcomes with the other variables controlled. Candidates who have held elective office, for example, do no better than those who have not once differences in campaign spending are taken into account. Furthermore, they are no more likely to be recalled by voters if spending is controlled. Experienced challengers are more successful than inexperienced ones only insofar as their experience generates a larger campaign kitty. Party (the measure of national trends) and *CPS*, interpreted as the challenger's district party strength, on the other hand, can affect the outcome quite apart from any special characteristics of the candidates.

Since the challenger's vote (*CV*) is approximated with some significant degree of accuracy by *EV*, the ordinary least-squares estimates are liable to bias and inconsistency and thus are unreliable estimates of the structural parameters (those of the true casual relationships in equation 5.3). The two-stage least-squares (2SLS) procedure is a standard solution to this problem. The first step is to regress challenger and incumbent spending on all the exogenous variables in the system. The equations are

$$CE^* = a + b_1P + b_2CPS + b_3PO + b_4YRS + b_5CP \\ + b_6IP + e \qquad (5.5)$$
$$IE^* = a + b_1P + b_2CPS + b_3PO + b_4YRS + b_5CP \\ + b_6IP + e \qquad (5.6)$$

The estimated parameters are then used to compute CE^* and IE^* for each observation, and these instrumental variables replace *CE* and *IE* in the second-stage equation,

$$CV = a + b_1CE^* + b_2IE^* + b_3P + b_4CPS + e \qquad (5.7)$$

The 2SLS procedure "purges" the explanatory variables *CE* and *IE* of the component associated with the error term. The resulting estimates are still biased estimates of the true structural parameters but are now consistent; the bias decreases as the sample size increases, approaching zero in the limit.[2] The estimates of equations 5.5, 5.6, and 5.7 appear in table 5.1.

The 2SLS results recapitulate the OLS findings in some important respects, but there are predictable difficulties, clearest in the estimates for 1976, which will require further attention. These equations confirm that a given amount of campaign spending does not have the same consequences for challengers and incumbents. Spending by challengers has a much more substantial effect on the

---

2. Potluri Rao and Roger L. Miller, *Applied Econometrics* (Belmont, Calif.: Wadsworth Publishing Company, Inc., 1971), p. 214; J. Johnston, *Econometric Methods*, 2d ed. (New York: McGraw-Hill Book Company, 1972) pp. 380–84.

1972 and 1974 outcomes even with simultaneity bias purged from the equation. Indeed, the regression coefficients on CE^* for these years are larger than those for CE. However, the standardized regression coefficients for CE^* are smaller than those for CE (.31 compared to .51 for 1972, .38 compared to .48 for 1974); the steeper slopes are evidently an artifact of the much smaller range of the instrumental variable CE^*, less than half that of CE in both election sets. Even so, OLS does not appear to greatly exaggerate the effects of the challenger's spending, nor does it substantially underestimate the effects of incumbent spending, for these elections.

The parameters estimated in the second-stage equations for 1972 and 1974 indicate that challengers receive 1.63 to 1.79 percent of the vote for each $10,000 they spend; they are expected to lose between .51 and .22 percent for each $10,000 the incumbent spends; thus if spending by both candidates increases by this amount, the net gain for challengers should approximate 1 percent of the vote. The net gain for challengers under the same condition in 1976 is similar—0.8 percent—indeed, almost identical if the decline in the purchasing power of the dollar is taken into account. But the second-stage equation for 1976 generates highly questionable estimates for the coefficients on all variables.

The problem here, which is present to a smaller degree in the two other election sets, is multicollinearity. In particular, CE^* and IE^* are very highly correlated, at greater than .9 in every case. The reason for this is clear from the first-stage equations: the variables have very similar effects on the spending levels of both incumbents and challengers. *This is exactly what should happen if, as I contend, incumbent spending is a direct reaction to challenger spending*; the same variables should affect expenditures by both candidates in the same way. But the multicollinearity this engenders destroys the precision of the estimates; a very large positive correlation between two explanatory variables is likely to produce large and opposite errors in the estimates of regression coefficients.[3] The recommended way to cope with multicollinearity is to get more

3. Johnston, *Econometric Methods*, p. 163.

			Regression Coefficient	t Ratio[a]	Standardized Regression Coefficient	
1972	$CE^* = a$		-17.56			
		$b_1 P$	-11.34	-2.60	$-.14$	
		$b_2 CPS$	1.39	5.92	$.34$	
$(N = 296)$		$b_3 PO$	21.20	4.18	$.23$	$R^2 = .23$
		$b_4 YRS$	$-.40$	-1.36	$-.07$	
		$b_5 CP$	8.28	1.96	$.10$	
		$b_6 IP$	1.92	$.42$	$.02$	
First-stage						
equations	$IE^* = a$		18.23			
		$b_1 P$	-2.86	$-.66$	$-.04$	
		$b_2 CPS$	$.93$	3.95	$.23$	
		$b_3 PO$	13.40	2.64	$.15$	$R^2 = .18$
		$b_4 YRS$	$-.99$	-3.36	$-.19$	
		$b_5 CP$	8.85	2.10	$.12$	
		$b_6 IP$	10.73	2.34	$.13$	
	$CV = a$		22.3			
Second-stage		$b_1 CE^*$	$.163$	2.59^b	$.36$	
equation		$b_2 IE^*$	$-.051$	$-.89$	$-.10$	$R^2 = .46^b$
		$b_3 P$	$-.01$	$-.01$	$-.00$	
		$b_4 CPS$	$.269$	3.55	$.30$	
1974	$CE^* = a$		-16.03			
		$b_1 P$	28.15	5.40	$.31$	
		$b_2 CPS$	1.07	4.25	$.22$	
$(N = 319)$		$b_3 PO$	21.00	3.89	$.20$	$R^2 = .29$
		$b_4 YRS$	$-.19$	$-.58$	$-.03$	
		$b_5 CP$	3.77	$.77$	$.04$	
		$b_6 IP$	-3.16	$-.66$	$-.03$	
First-stage						
equations	$IE^* = a$		6.15			
		$b_1 P$	22.55	4.40	$.25$	
		$b_2 CPS$	1.23	4.94	$.26$	
		$b_3 PO$	17.00	3.19	$.17$	$R^2 = .28$
		$b_4 YRS$	$-.42$	-1.31	$-.07$	
		$b_5 CP$	7.37	1.53	$.08$	
		$b_6 IP$	-2.30	$-.49$	$-.02$	

Table 5.1. Effects of Campaign Spending in House Elections, 1972–76 (2SLS Estimates)

Second-stage	$CV = a$	17.1			
equation	$b_1 CE^*$	.179	1.21^b	.38	
	$b_2 IE^*$	−.022	−.14	−.05	$R^2 = .63^b$
	$b_3 P$	7.51	4.20	.32	
	$b_4 CPS$	.264	2.94	.21	
1976	$CE^* = a$	−33.82			
	$b_1 P$	−31.58	−4.78	−.25	
	$b_2 CPS$	2.56	7.78	.45	
$(N = 329)$	$b_3 PO$	25.84	3.50	.17	$R^2 = .27$
	$b_4 YRS$	−.29	−.67	−.03	
	$b_5 CP$	1.62	.27	.01	
	$b_6 IP$	8.62	1.32	.07	
First-stage					
equations	$IE^* = a$	16.95			
	$b_1 P$	−3.66	−.67	−.04	
	$b_2 CPS$	1.79	6.67	.39	
	$b_3 PO$	23.12	3.83	.19	$R^2 = .27$
	$b_4 YRS$	−.64	−1.81	−.09	
	$b_5 CP$	4.00	.80	.04	
	$b_6 IP$	9.42	1.77	.09	
	$CV = a$	39.81			
Second-stage	$b_1 CE^*$	.628	3.35^b	2.00	
equation	$b_2 IE^*$	−.548	−2.96	−1.42	$R^2 = .18^b$
	$b_3 P$	15.52	2.93	.75	
	$b_4 CPS$	.053	.33	.06	

[a] A t ratio of at least 1.98 is necessary for a .05 level of significance, 2.58 for .01, and 3.35 for .001.

[b] The R^2's and t ratios for the second-stage equations are not taken directly from the statistics produced by estimating these equations. Rather, they are found by replacing the standard error of the estimate for the equation as computed by the standard error computed from a combination of the 2SLS parameters with the actual spending variables CE and IE replacing CE^* and IE^*. I am obliged to John Ferejohn for explaining this procedure to me.

data; that is not possible in this instance, and by the theory advanced here, more data would not reduce multicollinearity in any case.

Given these circumstances, it is appropriate to run the second-stage equations excluding one of the correlated variables. Estimates of equation 5.7 omitting IE^* are found in table 5.2. The coefficients on CE^* are reduced very substantially in the 1976 equation, as anticipated. If, instead, IE^* were left in the equation, its connection with the challenger's share of the vote would also be positive and statistically significant.

In general, these findings indicate that simultaneity bias did not distort the regression coefficients estimated in chapter 2 in any major way. An explanation for this rather surprising conclusion (which was reinforced by analysis of several alternative versions of the first-stage equations, not reported here) will be offered once some other pertinent findings have been presented.

These equations also reiterate that it was very helpful to be a Democrat in 1974 (it was worth an additional 7.5 percent of the vote), but that national tides did not appear to be a factor in 1972 or 1976. And they indicate that the challenger's district party strength also contributes significantly to his share of the vote, even apart from its effect on his capacity to raise funds.

Table 5.2.   Effects of Challengers' Campaign Spending in House Elections,
1972–76 (Second-Stage Equations Omitting IE^*)

			Regression Coefficient	t Ratio[a]	Standardized Regression Coefficient	
1972	$CV =$	a	20.8			
		b_1CE^*	.117	3.42[b]	.26	
	$(N = 296)$	b_3P	−.41	−.48	−.02	$R_2 = .49^b$
		b_4CPS	.289	4.07	.32	
1974	$CV =$	a	16.7			
		b_1CE^*	.160	3.60	.34	
	$(N = 319)$	b_3P	7.53	4.21	.32	$R_2 = .62^b$
		b_4CPS	.257	3.49	.21	
1976	$CV =$	a	15.4			
		b_1CE^*	.089	2.96	.29	
	$(N = 329)$	b_3P	.85	.66	.04	$R_2 = .59^b$
		b_4CPS	.392	4.17	.42	

[a] A t ratio of at least 1.98 is necessary for a .05 level of significance, 2.58 for .01, and 3.35 for .001.
[b] See table 5.1.

The first-stage equations also merit some discussion. A difference of 1 percent in the vote of the challenger's party's candidate in the last election alters the challenger's spending by from $1,070 to $2,557, the incumbent's by from $939 to $1,792, depending on the election year. Challengers who have held elective office spend substantially more (between $21,000 and $26,836, on the average, depending on the election year) than those who have not. Incumbents naturally also spend more against these candidates (the mean difference ranges from $13,400 to $23,120). These two variables make the most difference. The advantages of incumbency are plain; notice the intercepts. So are the advantages of being a Democrat in 1974 and, interestingly, a Republican challenger in 1976. The R^2's for these equations are not as large as would be desirable; a number of additional explanatory variables were tested at earlier stages of the research, but none of them improved any of the equations significantly. The criterion for inclusion, other than theoretical plausibility, was that a variable had to have a regression coefficient at least twice its standard error in at least one of the equations.

The 2SLS technique was also attempted with the Senate data. For 1972, the first-stage equations explained so little of the variance that even remotely trustworthy estimates of the instrumental variables were out of the question. Estimates were obtained for 1974; the 2SLS coefficients were nearly identical to those estimated by OLS. For 1976, the 2SLS estimates were again similar to the OLS estimates, but they were very imprecise. There is, in sum, no clear evidence that simultaneity bias seriously distorted the estimates of the relationship between campaign spending and the outcomes of Senate elections presented in chapter 2, but the evidence is, at best, incomplete.

Campaign Spending and Candidate Familiarity

In chapter 2, I offered a simple explanation of why campaign spending is more important to challengers (and other nonincumbents) than it is to congressional incumbents. The more information voters have about a candidate, the more likely they are to vote for him. Incumbents do most of their "campaigning" before the formal campaign period, using the resources of office to publicize themselves and their services to the district on a regular basis. The extra increment of information provided by the campaign has relatively little additional impact on how well they are known by their constituents. Nonincumbents, in contrast, usually begin the race in obscurity; the campaign is crucial because it is the only means for grabbing the attention of voters. An effective campaign costs money; the more nonincumbents spend, the better they are known, and the better they do on election day.

This explanation is only valid if a connection exists between campaign spending and candidate familiarity. A simple test is produced by combining data on campaign expenditures with the CPS survey data on candidate name recall; these are jointly available for the 1972 and 1974 House elections and the 1974 Senate elections. We know from Mann's research and from other findings reported in chapter 1 that much more is actually involved than simple candidate recall. Voters who are aware of candidates are also likely to have opinions about them; these opinions are by no means uniformly favorable, and they clearly affect voting behavior. But the bare connection between candidate recall and the vote is well documented; candidates who cannot get the attention of a substantial proportion of the electorate will certainly not do well in any case.[4]

The relationship between campaign spending and candidate saliency may, of course, also involve reciprocal causation. Candidates who are well known are able to raise more money, which, spent judiciously, increases their reknown even further. If so, a model of these relationships should consist of two simultaneous equations with two endogenous variables. Theoretically, candidate saliency is considered a function of campaign spending plus some exogenous variables, while campaign spending is, in turn, a function of candidate saliency and some exogenous variables. Identification of these equations (and thus the possibility of estimating their parameters)

4. Thomas Edward Mann, "Candidate Saliency and Congressional Elections" (Ph.D. diss., University of Michigan, 1977), p. 82.

depends on the available exogenous variables and the assumptions that can be made about them. Consider a preliminary specification:

$$CR = a + b_1E + b_2PO + c_1 \cdots _5X_1 \cdots _5 + e \qquad (5.8)$$
$$E = a + b_1CR + b_2PO + b_3NPS + b_4NI + e \qquad (5.9)$$

where CR = candidate recall, measured as 1 if the respondent remembers the candidate's name, 0 otherwise[5]

E = nonincumbent candidate's campaign expenditures, thousands of dollars

PO = 1 if the candidate has previously held elective office, 0 otherwise

NPS = strength of the nonincumbent candidate's party in his constituency (measured as was CPS in earlier equations)

NI = 1 if the nonincumbent is running against another nonincumbent, 0 if he opposes an incumbent

$X_1 \cdots _5$ = respondent variables: social class, education, attentiveness to the mass media, political interest, and whether or not the respondent shares the candidate's partisan affiliation[6]

a = intercept

b and c = regression coefficients

e = error term

The reasoning underlying this specification should be apparent. Observations on all nonincumbents, not merely challengers, can be included because, theoretically, spending should affect popular awareness of all nonincumbent candidates in about the same way. The small quantity of empirical evidence available suggests that it does.[7] This also augments the number of observations, particularly

5. The data are from the CPS surveys for 1972 and 1974; the 1974 sample is weighted.
6. The construction of these variables is reported in Jacobson, "Campaign Finance Reform," p. 32.
7. Ibid., p. 19.

at the upper end of the expenditure scale. Whether or not the respondent remembers a candidate's name depends on how much the candidate spends, his prior political exposure, and characteristics of the respondent himself.

The candidate's level of spending depends on how well he is known, his prior political experience, which party he belongs to, the strength of his party in his district, and whether or not he is running against an incumbent. The variables P, NPS, and NI are expected to affect the candidate's ability to raise money—primarily because they are closely related to his presumed chance of victory—but should not, in theory, affect the likelihood that a voter will recognize the candidate independently of the voter's individual partisan orientation. Equation 5.9 is similar to equation 5.1; NI replaces YRS as one measure off the effects of ʾncumbency (necessary because not all nonincumbents are challengers), and the primary election variables are dropped because they had no statistically significant effect in any of the regressions examined.

Both equations are identified (overidentified, in fact), but this specification is unsatisfactory. The first equation involves a categorical dependent variable and therefore raises some difficulties to be addressed shortly. Before proceeding to that, it will be helpful to simplify the equation. The first simplification is to ignore the respondent variables $X_1 \cdots {}_5$. Although some of these variables are indeed related to the likelihood that the respondent will remember a candidate's name,[8] none is correlated with the other independent variables as high as .1, so their omission should not affect the regression coefficients of those variables.[9] Furthermore, we can assume that $b_2 = 0$ in equation 5.8. Although on theoretical grounds we might expect that candidates who have held elective office would have a greater probability of being known by voters, empir-

8. The only respondent variable that has a consistent and significant impact on candidate recall is attentiveness to the mass media; voters who follow the election regularly in at least one mass medium are significantly more likely to remember candidates' names. See ibid., p. 19.

9. Jan Kmenta, *Elements of Econometrics* (New York: Macmillan Publishing Co., Inc., 1971), pp. 392–95.

ically this does not seem to be true. If spending is taken into account, the relationship between this variable and candidate recognition, weak to begin with, disappears.[10]

Even though the dependent variable in equation 5.8 actually takes only two values, 1 and 0, the equation can be interpreted as estimating the conditional probability that a respondent remembers a candidate's name. A problem is that least-squares estimates of the parameters may predict values of more than 1.0 or less than 0.0 for this probability for some observations. In addition, the error term cannot have a zero expectation, invalidating one of the assumptions required for unbiased least-squares estimation.[11] Logit analysis avoids these difficulties. The odds on a voter's knowing a candidate are defined as $P_{cr}/(1 - P_{cr})$, where P_{cr} is the probability that a voter knows the candidate. This term can take any value from zero to infinity; a logarithmic transformation of the term, $\ln [P_{cr}/(1 - P_{cr})]$, restricts the possible values of P_{cr} to a range of from 0 to 1 as the transformed term varies from minus infinity to plus infinity.[12] The transformed term, designated L_{cr}, replaces CR in equation 5.8.

To get observations for P_{cr}, it is necessary to group the survey observations and estimate P_{cr} as F_{cr}, the proportionate frequency with which respondents in each group remember the candidate's name. The standard procedure, followed in this instance, is to group observations on intervals of the independent variables. For each group the average expenditure (in thousands of dollars) is calculated along with the recognition frequency. The equation is now

$$L_{cr} = a + b_1 \bar{E}^* + e \qquad (5.10)$$

Since the groups providing observations for this equation are of different sizes, the errors are heteroscedastic, so weighted least

10.   The simple correlations between a candidate's having held elective office (*PO*) and respondents' recall of the candidate's name (*CR*) for 1974 Senate and 1972 and 1974 House voters are, respectively, .11, .09, and .13; with campaign spending controlled, the corresponding partial correlations are .01, .03, and −.01.

11.   Henri Theil, *Principles of Econometrics* (New York: John Wiley & Sons, Inc., 1971), pp. 632–33.

12.   Ibid., p. 632.

squares are used to compute the estimates.[13]

Ordinary (weighted) least-squares estimates of equation 5.10 would still be biased and inconsistent because it is part of a simultaneous equation system in which $\bar{E}$ is assumed to be endogenous and therefore not independent of the error term. The 2SLS procedure is again in order. First E is regressed on the exogenous variables,

$$E^* = a + b_2 PO + b_3 P + b_4 NPS + b_5 NI + e \qquad (5.11)$$

and the results are used to compute expected values, E^*, for each observation. Grouping these observations on intervals of values of E^* and taking the recognition frequency and mean value of E^* ($\bar{E}^*$) for each group, the second-stage equation,

$$L_{cr} = a + b_1 \bar{E}^* + e \qquad (5.12)$$

may be estimated using OLS.

This was the procedure followed for the two House election sets. For the Senate elections, the grouping was done by states, and the observations on expenditures and the 2SLS instruments for spending are therefore not averages but rather figures for the separate contests in each individual state. Because the states vary widely in populations and hence presumably in the cost of conducting an equivalent campaign, expenditures were divided by the voting-age population in each state and were entered as cents per voting-age individual (EPV). But per voter spending declines as the size of the population increases (campaign spending enjoys economies of scale); therefore, the equation estimating Senate campaign spending includes as a conditioning variable the natural logarithm of the voting-age population (in thousands). It replaces NPS, which was

13. Grouping observations on interval values of the independent variable minimizes the loss of efficiency engendered by grouping. The groups are of different sizes because fixed intervals of the explanatory variable were employed in their formulation. For this reason, equations using the grouped observations were estimated by weighted least squares, the weights being proportional to the reciprocal of the approximate standard deviation of the error term, e, where the variance of e is estimated as $1/[NF_{cr}(1 - F_{cr})]$, N being the number of observations in a group and F_{cr} the proportionate frequency a candidate is recalled for that group. The procedure is from ibid., p. 635. The number of observations (groups) in the several logit equations varies from 13 to 29. The mean number of cases in the Senate groups is 34; that in the House groups, 61.

dropped because it had no effect whatever on spending when the other variables were controlled.[14] The first-stage equation for Senate elections is thus

$$EPV^* = a + b_2PO + b_3P + b_4 \ln VAP + b_5NI + e \qquad (5.13)$$

where EPV is spending in cents per voting age individual, $\ln VAP$ is the natural log of the voting-age population (in thousands), and the other variables and coefficients are as defined previously.

The regression estimates for equation 5.11, 5.12, 5.13, and, for comparison, 5.10 are listed in table 5.3. Equation 5.10 was also used to estimate the equivalent parameters for incumbents in the three election sets, and these also appear in the table. Results in this form are not easy to interpret, so they are displayed graphically in figures 1 through 3. The estimated curve for 1972 House candidates is shown for spending up to $160,000, that for 1974 up to $200,000, and the scales are adjusted to assure comparability; inflation must be acknowledged.

The coefficients of determination (R^2's) and the standard errors are not listed for the logit equations because they are rendered meaningless by the grouping. Estimates based on individual rather than grouped data (from OLS and reduced-form versions of equation 5.8) indicate that the relationship between spending and candidate saliency is significant at .001 for nonincumbents in all election sets and for incumbents in the 1974 elections. The relationship for 1972 House incumbents is not statistically significant even when the data are grouped for the logit analysis.

---

14. *NPS* for Senate elections was measured as the smallest proportion of the total statewide House vote won in aggregate by House candidates of the Senate candidate's party in any election year from 1968 through 1974. The idea is from Warren Lee Kostroski, "Party and Incumbency in Postwar Senate Elections: Trends, Patterns, and Models," *American Political Science Review* 67 (1973): 1226. This variable, when included, was not significantly associated with spending and had a perverse sign. One extreme case had to be dropped from both the incumbent and nonincumbent Senate groups. This was South Dakota, where the challenger spent twice as much per voting-age individual as any other nonincumbent and the incumbent more than four times as much as any other incumbent in the states covered by the survey (a total of twenty-four). Both candidates were known by all the voters surveyed in the state ($N = 26$).

Table 5.3. Effects of Campaign Spending on Voter Recall of House and Senate
            Candidates (OLS and 2SLS Regression Estimates)

Equation 5.11: House elections

1972 $E^* = 2.28 + 17.11PO + 5.19P + .682NPS + 60.97NI$
                 $(4.10)^a$ (1.45) (5.33) (14.73)

         $N = 718$ $R^2 = .36$

1974 $E^* = -46.34 + 26.37PO + 33.27P + 1.77NPS + 21.62NI$
                       (8.19) (12.14) (12.73) (5.81)

         $N = 976$ $R^2 = .47$

Equation 5.13: Senate elections

1974 $EPV^* = 205 + 41.8PO + 12.6P + .04NI - 24.6 \ln VAP$
                   (14.46) (5.02) $(.02)$ (-21.56)

         $N = 997$ $R^2 = .46$

Equation 5.12: 2SLS

House elections	1972	$L_{cr} = -1.25 + .0087\bar{E}^*$
	1974	$L_{cr} = -1.20 + .0104\bar{E}^*$
Senate elections	1974	$L_{cr} = -.615 + .0178E\bar{P}V^*$

Equation 5.10: OLS

Nonincumbents

House elections	1972	$L_{cr} = -1.22 + .0076\bar{E}$
	1974	$L_{cr} = -1.10 + .0094\bar{E}$
Senate elections	1974	$L_{cr} = -.750 + .0444E\bar{P}V$

Incumbents

House elections	1972	$L_{cr} = -.036 + .0005\bar{E}$
	1974	$L_{cr} = -.129 + .0078\bar{E}$
Senate elections	1974	$L_{cr} = .521 + .0209E\bar{P}V$

[a] t ratio of regression coefficient.

The hypothesis that campaign spending is more useful to
nonincumbents than to incumbents because of its greater effect on
how frequently they are remembered by voters is, in general, well
supported by these data. The evidence is strongest for the 1972
House elections; the amount spent by incumbents had little apparent
effect on the probability they would be remembered; the expected
gain is only .02 as spending increases from $0 to $160,000,
whereas awareness of nonincumbents more than doubles over the

FIGURE 1: U.S. HOUSE OF REPRESENTATIVES 1972 ELECTIONS

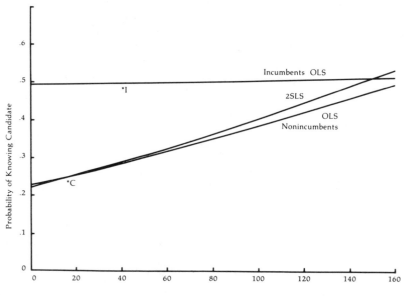

Spending in Thousands of Dollars

*Median expenditures
I--incumbents
C--challengers

same range of expenditures. Those few nonincumbents fortunate enough to spend over $150,000 were as likely as incumbents to be remembered.

In 1974, spending by both incumbents and nonincumbents had a positive effect on the probability voters would remember them. Nonincumbents did benefit more than incumbents from the same amount of spending, but the difference is not so great as it was in 1972; they gain about .13 more than incumbents as spending increases from $0 to $200,000. We are reminded that 1974 was an unusual year for Republican incumbents. Four whose districts were covered in the survey spent in excess of $200,000; three of them had also spent more than $100,000 in 1972; their collective frequency of recall by voters was .93 ($N = 29$). Very high levels of

FIGURE 2: U.S. HOUSE OF REPRESENTATIVES 1974 ELECTIONS

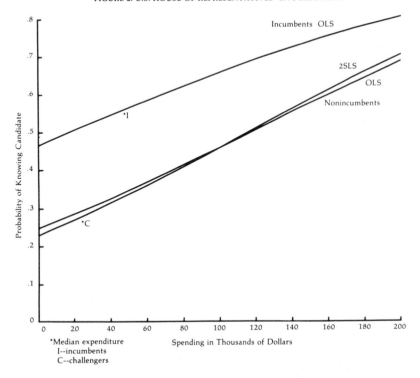

*Median expenditure
I--incumbents
C--challengers

Spending in Thousands of Dollars

spending evidently do make a difference, even for incumbents. Parenthetically, three of them lost and the fourth squeaked by with 51.1 percent of the vote.[15] Saliency is obviously not the only important factor determining candidate success.

Spending was notably more effective in increasing the awareness of House candidates of all kinds in 1974 as compared to 1972. An obvious inference is that in presidential election years, messages

15. The candidates were Samuel Young, Illinois 10th, spending $251,200 in 1974 and $206,166 in 1972; William Hudnut III, Indiana 11th, with $201,700 in 1974 and $163,442 in 1972; Joel T. Broyhill, Virginia 10th, with $248,700 in 1974 and $141,290 in 1972; and Sam Steiger, Arizona 3rd, who spent $203,900 in 1974, but only $37,691 in 1972. Steiger was the only winner.

FIGURE 3: U.S. SENATE 1974 ELECTIONS

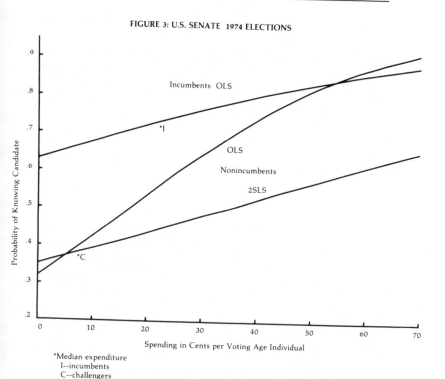

*Median expenditure
I--incumbents
C--challengers

from congressional candidates are crowded out by those coming from the presidential campaigns; at midterm, with less competition, congressional campaigns reach the intended audience more consistently. Information on future elections will be necessary to test this interpretation.

For both the 1972 and 1974 House elections, the 2SLS and OLS estimates are almost identical; by this evidence, simultaneity bias was not a problem in the OLS estimates of the relationship. These findings suggest that the structure here is actually recursive; spending affects saliency, but saliency has little effect on spending.

The results for Senate elections, however, indicate that simultaneity bias was present in the OLS estimate. The slope of the 2SLS regression coefficient for nonincumbents is much less steep than the OLS slope; comparing the 2SLS estimate to the OLS estimate for incumbents, the conclusion must be that spending affects both groups similarly. But even if spending has the same marginal effects on recall of challengers and incumbents, incumbents begin with such a great advantage in saliency that an equal increase in spending may still benefit the challenger. For one thing, it will decrease the proportionate advantage in awareness enjoyed by the incumbent. For example, incumbent senators are remembered 1.8 times as frequently as are nonincumbents (by the 2SLS estimates) if no money is spent; the ratio drops to 1.4 at 70 cents per eligible voter, even though the absolute gain in saliency is about the same for both groups. Very few voters recall a challenger without also remembering the incumbent (about 1 percent in these surveys), while more than one-fourth of the respondents recall the incumbent's name without remembering the challenger's. Greater spending may therefore help challengers more than incumbents by increasing the instances in which both candidates are familiar.

These surveys measure candidate recall at a single point in time (after the election) and so cannot be used to indicate changes in candidate familiarity over the course of a campaign; this is one reason the 2SLS procedure was required. Not much evidence is available on changes in candidate familiarity during a campaign, but Mann's research produced some suggestive findings. His surveys showed that "Most incumbents amass an early lead over their challengers based on an overwhelming advantage in public visibility; this lead then narrows as the challenger's candidacy begins to penetrate the electorate's consciousness, but is usually sufficiently large to insure victory in November."[16] He argues that the degree to which that lead narrows, especially if the incumbent is vulnerable on other grounds, "depends in large part on the ability of the challenger to present a publically visible and attractive alternative."[17] This, in turn, should depend in large part on the campaign resources of the challenger and how they are used. Mann

16. Mann, "Candidate Saliency," p. 107.
17. Ibid.

mentions the example of a 1976 challenger with only local school board experience whose recall index rose from 26 percent to 63 percent between August and October surveys; he eventually won with slightly more than 50 percent of the vote,[18] spending more than $100,000 in the process.

The preponderance of evidence, then, supports the original explanation that challengers and other nonincumbents do better the more they spend because their campaign expenditures purchase the attention of voters. A sufficiently lavish campaign will make the challenger as familiar to voters as the incumbent, at which point the outcome of the contest will be decided by the quality of the candidates and the campaigns, not the difference in resources between them. Incumbents do not derive the same value from campaign expenditures (that is, from campaigning) because they are much better known to voters at the outset of the campaign. Diminishing returns applies much more drastically to their expenditures. The content of the campaign is not irrelevant, however, and incumbents may well have to send out a different set of messages during the campaign in order to deal with a specific challenge.[19] And this takes money. But normally it is the strength (or, more typically, weakness) of the challenge that is decisive.

THE 1974 ELECTIONS: SOLVING A PUZZLE

At this point it is possible to make some sense out of the intriguing finding from survey research on the 1974 election that, with other variables controlled, respondents' attitudes toward Watergate, Nixon, or Ford's pardon of his predecessor had little independent impact on the individual vote. Recall from chapter 1 that Miller and Glass concluded from their analysis of the CPS survey for 1974 that *"Watergate and the distrust of government it fostered was not the most important factor in the Democratic landslide of 1974"*[20] be-

18.   Ibid., p. 111.
19.   For an example, see ibid., p. 112.
20.   Arthur H. Miller and Richard Glass, "Economic Dissatisfaction and Electoral Choice" (Unpublished paper, Center for Political Studies, The University of Michigan, 1977), p. 38.

cause cynical or distrusting voters were no more likely to vote for Democrats for Congress than were more sanguine voters. Neither did Watergate-related attitudes affect voter turnout.[21] Conway and Wyckoff, using the same data but quite different analytic methods, reach the same conclusion: Watergate and the fall of Nixon had little independent effect on individual voting.[22]

But the aggregate evidence, some of which has been presented in this book, shows that 1974 was disastrous for Republicans. House Republicans suffered a net loss of 48 seats between the 93rd and 94th Congresses. Watergate and its consequences are widely considered to be the source of the disaster. Indeed, the heaviest toll of congressional Republicans was taken among those identified as friends of Richard Nixon.[23] Coefficients on the party variable, P, in the regressions reported here, imply that the average Republican could expect to lose about 8 percent of the vote in 1974 just because of his party affiliation; party made very little difference in the more "normal" years of 1972 and 1976 (with the other variables controlled). It is difficult to comprehend how the effects of a debacle of Watergate's magnitude could fail to show up at the individual level; it is even harder to accept that there were no effects.

Miller and Glass's normal vote analysis of voting in 1974 provides a clue for solving the puzzle. It shows that respondents report voting Democratic more frequently than "normal" no matter what their level of cynicism or distrust or, for that matter, their more general attitudes about the government's handling of the economy. The most important determinant of voting in congressional elections, aside from party identification (and usually not contrary to it),[24] is the voter's knowledge and evaluation of the candidates. Re-

---

21. Ibid.

22. M. Margaret Conway and Mikel L. Wyckoff, "Vote Choice in the 1974 Congressional Elections: A Test of Competing Explanations" (Prepared for delivery at the Annual Meeting of the Midwest Political Science Association, Chicago, April 21–23, 1977). p. 20.

23. Gerald C. Wright, Jr., "Constituency Response to Congressional Behavior: The Impact of the House Judiciary Committee Impeachment Votes," *Western Political Quarterly* 30 (1977): 406.

24. Mann, "Candidate Saliency," p. 47.

call that 38.3 percent of the 1974 Democratic challengers had previously held elective office, compared to only 12.6 percent of the Republican challengers; 29.6 percent of the Democrats held elective office at the time of the election, compared to only 7.9 percent of the Republicans. Recall also that Democratic challengers spent an average of $59,331, Republican challengers $20,744. Since the quality of the challenger and the dimensions of his campaign (and thus his impact on the consciousness of voters) make the most difference, it is hardly surprising that Republicans did worse than usual, both as challengers and as incumbents. The general increase in support for Democratic candidates quite apart from individual attitudes toward Watergate or Nixon or Ford can be attributed to the high quality (and visibility) of the Democratic challengers and their unusually well financed campaigns and, conversely, to the low quality of Republican challengers and their abnormally inadequate campaign resources.

Further evidence to this point can be gleaned from the fates of Republicans on the House Judiciary Committee. Wright has shown that pro-impeachment Republicans did better than expected; only one of the six who sought reelection lost. Committee Republicans who supported Nixon and opposed impeachment did worse than expected; four of the nine were defeated. Wright reasonably concludes that the Nixon loyalists were punished for that virtue by disaffected constituents.[25] By analysis of the campaign spending patterns in these elections offers a supplementary explanation, one that explains why some loyalists were punished and others were not.

Democratic opponents of the pro-impeachment Republicans spent an average of $53,025—below the average for Democratic challengers as a whole; the incumbents spent an average of $57,473 to retain their seats. Opponents of the four antiimpeachment Republicans who lost spent an average of $113,523; none spent less than $70,000. Opponents of the five loyalists who won spent an average of $22,515; none spent more than $70,000. The losing Repub-

25. Wright, "Constituency Response," p. 409.

licans spent an average of $85,874; the winners spent $34,261. The losers' mean vote share was 7.9 percentage points lower than expected; the winners' mean share was 7.9 percentage points higher than expected; if one very deviant case is omitted, they did .1 percentage point better than expected.

In other words, the electoral fates of Republican members of the Judiciary Committee are in good part explained by the strength of the opposition they faced. Of course, it may well have been their loyalty to Nixon that generated strong, well-financed opposition to the four losers; but without such opposition, loyalty to Nixon was not translated into defeat at the polls.

This suggests a theory of how aggregate national political events and conditions—scandals such as Watergate, unpopular wars, presidential evaluations, the state of the economy—are translated into individual voting decisions (and, of course, back again into aggregate election results). Voters need not respond to events and conditions at all; they need only to respond to the electoral choice they face in the particular election. But that electoral choice is structured by political circumstances because these affect the expectations and strategies of the elites who run for office or who help recruit and finance those who do.

In a year such as 1974, these elites sense, from their attentive reading of the political climate, that a strong national tide is in the offing and adjust their behavior accordingly. Potential Democratic congressional candidates see a favorable opportunity to pursue their ambitions; the shrewder and more skillful of them determine that this is the year to make their move, and they use their skills and resources to pursue effective primary and general election campaigns. One inspiration to do so is the availability of money for the campaign; the elites who fund campaigns perceive it as a good year to invest in challenges to Republican incumbents (especially the prominent defenders of the disgraced ex-president); they are also attracted by the quality of the challengers.

From the other side, it looks to be a very bad year indeed. Potentially strong candidates (particularly those already in office) decide not to waste their energy and other resources in an apparently hopeless cause, leaving the field to weaker candidates who may reluctantly agree to run merely out of loyalty to the party. People who control campaign funds assume that challenges are futile and invest instead in the campaigns of congenial incumbents who may be hard-pressed by challengers of the advantaged party.

National political circumstances, then, are reflected in the quality of the candidates and the vitality of their campaigns. These, in turn, affect voters' perceptions and evaluations of the candidates, which determine (along with party identification) their votes. The process by which events such as Watergate or phenomena such as presidential popularity are translated into aggregate congressional election results consists of multiple steps. The ambiguous results of individual-level studies intended to complement the robust findings of aggregate studies (the best example being Tufte's)[26] are not so mysterious if the effect of the aggregate variables is mostly indirect.

Political elites—candidates and their active supporters—are an essential link in this sequence. Their expectations and decisions determine the ultimate choices presented to voters. These are based on their readings of the national political pulse. If an event like Watergate is perceived by them to be a national trauma and is expected by them to have drastic electoral consequences, they will adjust their behavior accordingly, and by doing so, will act to fulfill their own expectations. They will do the things that tend to bring about the very result they expect. Now clearly, their expectations must be based on some specific facts and events that probably would have some independent electoral effect, but the action they take on the assumption that circumstances will have particular electoral consequences may multiply these effects several times over.

From this perspective it is possible to understand why simultaneity bias does not seriously distort estimates of the relationship between campaign expenditures and election outcomes. The ability of

26. Edward R. Tufte, "Determinants of the Outcomes of Midterm Congressional Elections," *American Political Science Review* 69 (1975): 812–26.

a challenger to raise funds depends less on his popular appeal than on the expectations of a relatively small set of elite contributors about his potential appeal. Not voters in general, but a much smaller number of individuals and groups fund campaigns. Candidates who make a convincing case that they have a real chance to win will receive funds, which they can then put to use pursuing popular recognition and, presumably, affection and regard. Candidates do no doubt need some means to convince contributors that they can, indeed, win, and surely part of this is their potential for attracting popular support once their campaigns are funded. But in the absence of adequate financial support, this potential is rarely fulfilled; money is almost always required to get the message across, no matter how good the candidate.

By this interpretation, candidates are given money according to how well they are expected to do, but campaign expenditures have an independent effect on how well they actually do, because without them, the expectation would not be realized. The process is largely recursive because elite perceptions and strategies determine how much is spent in campaigns, and the level of campaign spending in turn determines how much is known about candidates and therefore how much support they actually recieve from voters. Elite expectations about how the vote will go are only fulfilled if they do, in fact, supply enough money to the candidate.

CONCLUDING REMARKS

The final two chapters of this book deal with congressional campaign finance as a political issue. Congress has thoroughly rewritten the laws regulating money in federal elections during this decade; the consequences of these changes have yet to be clarified. The understanding of money in congressional elections developed in these first five chapters establishes a solid background for analyzing both the politics of campaign finance reform and the actual (and potential) effects of enacted (and proposed) changes in congressional campaign finance policy. We now turn to this analysis.

6 ☆ CAMPAIGN FINANCE REGULATION: A DECADE OF REFORM

Analysis of the kind undertaken in chapters 2 through 5 could not have been done at all only a few years ago. The necessary data were simply lacking. Before 1972, it was impossible to find out even how much most campaigns cost, let alone who supplied the money and in what quantities. Since then, new campaign finance regulations have generated the data exploited in this book for a detailed statistical analysis of money in congressional elections. Financial disclosure rules were not, to be sure, the only changes in campaign finance policy. Nearly a decade of legislative innovation, administrative rule making, and court intervention has transformed all aspects of federal election campaign finance. The transformation has been radical; its consequences have yet to be fully realized. And there is no indication that the cycle of campaign finance reform is now complete.

This and the following chapter focus on the politics of campaign finance reform. Most attention is directed to changes in congressional campaign finance policy, although pertinent comparisons to the even more extensive changes in presidential campaign finance practices are not ignored. Evaluation of the motives for reforms, both enacted and proposed, and assessment of their consequences, actual and potential, are based directly on the interpretation of money in elections developed in previous chapters.

PREVIEW: A BASIC DILEMMA

The form currently taken by campaign finance policy issues inevitably raises a basic dilemma. On the one hand, the plainest point made by the evidence presented in this book is that congressional elections are not likely to be competitive unless candidates (particularly nonincumbents) are adequately financed. What constitutes "adequate" financing varies, of course, but it is clearly more than most congressional challengers manage; a conservative figure would be, at present, in the neighborhood of $200,000 for a full-scale House campaign. If competitive elections are an essential element of democracy—and it would be odd to argue that they are not—the extent of democratic competition depends on candidates' financial resources. Competitive elections are expensive.

But the quality of democracy also depends on how the money is raised, who supplies it, what they expect and receive in return, and how the money is spent. Apart from any other defects—or any virtues—they may have, privately financed elections are open to a fundamental criticism. Political equality is the democratic ideal: one person, one vote. But the distribution of financial assets is anything but equal; money, used effectively as a political resource, inevitably violates democratic equality. Many of the central issues involved in campaign finance reform arise from variations in how this dilemma is perceived and how serious it is taken to be. They will be considered in due course. First, however, a prior question must be addressed: Why did Congress finally take campaign finance reform seriously?

Why Change the Game When You're Winning?

What led Congress to consider revising campaign finance regulations in the first place? Members had, after all, been elected and reelected under the old financial rules of the game. That the laws on the books did not actually regulate campaign finance at all is scarcely an answer; this had been true for more than forty years.

The principal instrument of campaign finance regulation before 1970 had been the Federal Corrupt Practices Act of 1925 (with some minor amendments in the Hatch Act of 1940). It was neither enforced nor enforceable. It set impossibly low limits on campaign expenditures ($10,000 to $25,000 for Senate candidates, $2,000 to $5,000 for House candidates), then allowed them to be ignored through the fiction that candidates were officially ignorant of, and thus not legally responsible for, most of the money spent in their campaigns. Its $5,000 individual contribution limit was no more effective; it applied only to gifts to a single committee, so campaigns merely spawned a sufficient number of committees to accept as much as anyone was willing to give. The Act did not apply to primary elections at all. And even open violations were not prosecuted.

The Corrupt Practices Act was universally considered a failure and never lacked critics, but no broad support for reform emerged before the 1960s. During that decade, however, the atmosphere changed radically, and in the early 1970s substantial and far-reaching changes in campaign finance regulation were enacted. Reasons for this development are not hard to discern. The most important was the startling rise in the cost of major political campaigns.

When the amount of money thought adequate to finance a competitive campaign was relatively small, the questionable financial transactions the Act both permitted and required were tolerable. Although the subterfuges necessary to finance campaigns may have disquieted many candidates, they were easier to tolerate when money did not seem so crucially important. The corrupting influence of the system was more easily perceived as petty when the amounts involved were relatively small.

Once campaign costs began to rise steeply, however, the demand for ever larger campaign war chests exaggerated all the problems and potential for abuse inherent in the old system, bringing the issue of campaign finance reform forcefully to the attention of both "good government" or "public interest" groups and elected officials themselves. Once called into question, the old regulations found hardly a defender; the issue was not whether campaign finance policy should be changed, but how it should be changed.

THE GROWING COST OF POLITICAL CAMPAIGNS

There is no doubt that campaign spending grew rapidly during the 1960s. The details of that growth are much more difficult to specify. Prior to 1972, few reliable figures on campaign spending exist, so an overall picture of the growth cannot be put together easily. A plausible and widely quoted set of figures compiled by the Citizens' Research Foundation, a nonprofit organization specializing in campaign finance research, provide a general indication of the increase in total spending for all elective offices. Estimates of total campaign expenditures in presidential election years between 1952 and 1972 were as follows:

1952	$140 million[1]
1956	155 million
1960	175 million
1964	200 million
1968	300 million
1972	425 million

These aggregate figures hide some important differences among elections, however. The constant-dollar increase of more than 200 percent between 1952 and 1972 was not distributed proportionately among all kinds of elections. Presidential election expenses rose much more steeply than did those for other offices. General election expenditures for presidential candidates grew about 400 percent (in constant dollars) over this period; total expenses, including primaries, increased by more than 360 percent.[2] In contrast, expenditures for all other federal offices increased by less than 50 percent over the same period. The Citizens' Research Foundation estimated that $138 million was spent on the presidential campaigns in 1972; the entire cost of electing all 435 U.S. Representatives and a third of the Senate was put at only $98 million.[3]

Presidential campaign costs grew much more rapidly because the basic causes of increased spending acted most directly on presidential campaigning. The development of television as a campaign medium is usually accorded the most blame, but the use of television

---

1. Herbert E. Alexander, *Financing Elections: Money, Elections, and Political Reform* (Washington, D.C.: Congressional Quarterly Press, Inc., 1976), p. 17.
2. Ibid.
3. Ibid., p. 20.

was actually only one element in a more general transformation of campaign technology—and political conditions—that drove up campaign expenses. This was touched on briefly in chapter 2. The decline of parties and partisanship, the parallel and related growth of professionalized campaign management, and the subsequent adaption of modern techniques of research, organization, and mass persuasion for use in political campaigns inevitably increased the cost of campaigning. The entire package of new technology—not just television—is costly.

Because it is so expensive, modern campaign technology is not accessible to every candidate; it is only practical in large campaigns. This is particularly evident of television, which requires candidates to pay for the audience reached regardless of whether or not its members are potential constituents. Only presidential campaigns can use network television efficiently. Even local television is of limited utility to most House candidates; it is much better suited to Senate and other statewide campaigns.

It is no coincidence, then, that presidential campaign costs have grown most rapidly; it also follows that the cost of Senate campaigns should have risen faster than those for the House. Data that speak to this point are not easy to find. The most complete set covering the period is from California. Owens's estimates of expenditures for House and Senate seats in that state from 1958 to 1970 are as follows:

	House	*Senate*
1958	$1.0 million[4]	$1.3 million
1960	1.6 million	
1962	2.4 million	.8 million
1964	2.4 million	3.2 million
1966	2.6 million	
1968	3.7 million	5.3 million
1970	3.6 million	6.7 million

4. John R. Owens, *Trends in Campaign Spending in California, 1958–1970: Tests of Factors Influencing Costs* (Princeton, N.J.: Citizens' Research Foundation, n.d.), p. 57.

Controlling for inflation, expenditures for California's seats in the U.S. House (which increased from thirty to thirty-eight after the 1960 census) grew about 178 percent between 1958 and 1970; Senate campaign costs grew 279 percent.

Data to judge whether or not California is typical are simply not available. If television costs are the major component of the growth in campaign expenses, Senate campaigns would certainly feel the effects most strongly. A survey taken after the 1968 elections of a sample of twenty-three senators and ninety-one representatives found that 72.7 percent of the senators had used television heavily, another 18.2 percent used some television, and the remaining 9.1 percent used none at all. The comparable figures for House respondents were 25.5 percent, 27.7 percent, and 46.8 percent. More than 80 percent of the U.S. Representatives from urban areas reported using no television at all in their campaigns.[5]

Perhaps the strongest indication that campaign costs rose more steeply in Senate campaigns comes from the legislative process itself. The Senate has consistently taken the lead in campaign finance reform and has shown particular interest in measures designed to restrict campaign costs. More will be said about this below.

Technological and political changes are not the only sources of increased campaign spending. Economic growth over the same period made more money available; until 1972, campaign spending was not growing any faster than the gross national product. Nor was it growing any faster than the federal budget. Both the growth in federal spending and the extension of federal regulatory activity raised the political stakes enormously; decisions made by federal officials could have drastic effects on the prosperity of whole industries. The dairy industry's pledge of $2 million to Nixon's reelection campaign and other smaller gifts to key members of Congress helped to win an increase in price supports for milk worth "at

5. U.S., Congress, House, Committee on Interstate and Foreign Commerce, Subcommittee on Communications and Power, *Political Broadcasting—1970*, 91st Cong., 2d sess., hearings June 2–4, 1970, p. 43.

least tens of millions of dollars to the milk producers.''[6] Campaign contributions that could assure favorable action—or even simple attention—became increasingly prudent investments. The supply as well as the demand for campaign money was expanding; small wonder that campaign spending grew as it did.

Greater campaign costs increased the pressure to raise money and exacerbated all the problems inherent in the old system of campaign finance regulation. The potential for corruption and scandal grew proportionately, as did the problems of candidates trying to cope with a changing electoral game. Ironically, actual corruption reached its apogee in the financial dealings of the 1972 Nixon campaign, which followed (and was, in part, exposed by) the first major revision of the campaign finance laws since 1925. The Watergate investigations revealed just how corrupt the process could become if exploited vigorously, systematically, and without one iota of self-restraint.[7]

Even before such unequivocal evidence that the old system of campaign finance was no longer tolerable, action had begun to reform it. It was comparatively easy to find agreement that the current rules were hopelessly inadequate; not much defense could be given a regulatory scheme of which a congressman could truthfully say, ''there is not a member of Congress, myself included, who has not knowingly evaded its purpose in one way or another.''[8] And consensus could be found on some general purposes of reform. The real difficulty, as usual, lay in finding agreement on exactly what form a new system would take. And on this particular question, the difficulty was compounded by the peculiar circumstance that congressmen would be writing regulations applicable directly to themselves.

6. *Dollar Politics*, vol. 2 (Washington, D.C.: Congressional Quarterly, Inc., October 1974), p. 13.

7. The detailed record is found in U.S., Congress, Senate, Select Committee on Presidential Campaign Activities, *Final Report*, Pursuant to Senate Resolution 60, February 7, 1973, S. Rep. 93–981, 93rd Cong., 2d sess., 1974.

8. Representative Jim Wright, quoted in *1966 Congressional Quarterly Almanac* (Washington, D.C.: Congressional Quarterly, Inc., 1967), p. 487.

SELF-REGULATION BY INCUMBENTS

The most influential makers of federal election campaign finance policy are, of course, members of Congress. They have to live with whatever system of regulation is in force; they suffer from its defects and benefit from any advantages it confers. Their attitudes toward campaign finance issues are varied, complex, equivocal, and conflicting. One consistent thread runs through the history of congressional campaign finance reform, however. All members of Congress have succeeded at the electoral game and have little interest in altering its rules in any way that threatens further success. Just how successful they have become is clear from the figures on their reelection rates given in chapter 1. In light of all that incumbents have done to enhance their own ability to win reelection—the resources and opportunities they have provided themselves to pursue a permanent campaign—it would be remarkable indeed if the interests of incumbent members were ignored when changes in campaign finance policy are contemplated. They are not.

But other considerations certainly come into play. Most members dislike intensely the process of raising funds. Senator Humphrey called it a "disgusting, degrading, demeaning experience";[9] his sentiments are by no means unique. Senator Pastore said he felt "embarrassed and humiliated" when soliciting contributions; "it is not a pleasant thing to do. You almost feel like a beggar. . . . You are putting your self-respect on the line."[10] Senator Abourezk found the process "demeaning, corrupting, and absolutely without any redeeming value."[11] Even members who find value in compelling candidates to seek financial support from people admit

9. David W. Adamany and George E. Agree, *Political Money: A Strategy for Campaign Financing in America* (Baltimore: The Johns Hopkins University Press, 1975), p. 130.

10. U.S., Senate, Committee on Commerce, Subcommittee on Communications, *Federal Election Campaign Act of 1973*, 93rd Cong., 1st sess., hearings March 7–9, and 13, 1973, p. 130.

11. U.S., Congress, Senate, Committee on Rules and Administration, Subcommittee on Privileges and Elections, *Public Financing of Federal Elections*, 93rd Cong., 1st sess., hearings September 18–21, 1973, p. 71.

that it "can be difficult and occasionally embarrassing."[12] It is no wonder that growing campaign costs inspired renewed attention to campaign finance policy.

It is also clear, however, that incumbent members raise campaign funds much more easily than do their opponents. The data in chapters 3 and 4 leave no doubt on this point. They can raise money when they need it to combat a serious challenge. And under the pressure of necessity, most seem willing to swallow their pride. Yet the money they do raise is not always without strings, and this is another source of unease. Senator Scott's suggestion, quoted in chapter 3, that every contribution implies some obligation, however ambiguous, is instructive.

Members argue endlessly about how much of a problem this really is. At what point do campaign contributions become corrupting? Aside from direct personal bribery, the most widely recognized examples of corruption are cases where elected officials supply direct benefits to their campaign contributors in return for contributions, deliberately ignoring the interests of their constituents or of the broader public. Campaign contributions motivated by quid pro quo considerations take on the aspect of bribes—or payoffs, depending on when the funds are given—if the quid pro quo is delivered. Although it is easy to find examples—or apparent examples—of this kind of behavior, it is impossible to determine how prevalent it is. Any politician worth the name can defend almost any vote as necessary for the public good.

The minimal legislative solution to this problem has been disclosure. If voters know the sources and amounts of gifts to candidates, they can judge for themselves whether the candidate will be beholden to them or to "special interests" and "fat cats," and they can make their choice with that knowledge in mind. But disclosure may only exacerbate the difficulty for incumbent congressmen. Senator Abourezk complained during hearings on campaign finance legislation in 1973 that "there are certain controversial amendments up today that I would like to vote for, but because I

---

12. Ibid., p. 151.

received contributions from dairy farmers around the country, I am almost afraid to vote for them because it is set up now in the press that anybody who does vote for them who has taken money from the dairy farmers has been bought off."[13]

Congressional debates on campaign finance reform invariably broach the subject of corruption, but it is always dealt with gingerly.[14] Members who contend that campaign contributions from interest groups and wealthy individuals corrupt imply that at least some of their colleagues have been corrupted. Their adversaries challenge them to give specifics; they argue that certainly their own contributors want nothing more than to support the broad principles they stand for as candidates. Traditions of courtesy inhibit intramural accusations of venality, so this is a clever rhetorical ploy. In response, those supporting the corruption thesis are forced to argue that the mere appearance of corruption is sufficiently damaging to the public's confidence in its political leaders and institutions to require reforms that would prevent it. Senator Stevenson, for instance, took the position that "financing campaigns now compels us . . . to accept large contributions from individuals, also from entities which have interests in government. Those interests, either deliberately or quite innocently, are rewarded. And on the basis of circumstantial evidence, the public can draw only one conclusion—and they are drawing that conclusion."[15]

The argument over the corrupting influence of contributions is, in a sense, moot. It is not necessary to assume that members adjust

13. U.S., Congress, Senate, Committee on Rules and Adminstration, Subcommittee on Privileges and Elections, *Federal Election Reform*, 1973, 93rd Cong., 1st sess., hearings April 11 and 12, and June 6 and 7, 1973, p. 207.

14. But not without humor; witness the following exchange:
    Rep. Frenzel: "Do you feel somebody can be bought for $5,000?"
    Rep. Udall: "No, I don't think members around here can be bought by 100 times that amount."
    Rep. Thompson: "I think a couple can be rented."
From U.S., Congress, House, Committee on House Administration, *Public Financing of Congressional Elections*, 95th Cong., 1st sess., hearings May 18 and 19, June 21, 23, and 28, and July 12, 1977, p. 19.

15. U.S., Senate, *Election Reform*, 1973, p. 195.

their decisions and votes to please financial backers in order to argue that wealthy individuals and interests have an unhealthily disproportionate influence on public policy. An analogy drawn from an old controversy among evolutionary biologists is instructive. Lamarck argued that species change through heritable individual adaptions to environmental pressures. But Darwin showed that the same result could be explained through natural selection: the environment selectively enhances or diminishes the survival and reproductive chances of individuals according to their fixed characteristics, which are thus transmitted differentially to subsequent generations. By this line of reasoning, campaign contributors might influence policy just as effectively by favoring candidates who are already agreeable to their points of view; no direct venality—a member changing his position in response to a campaign contribution—is required. The financial environment affects the congressional species through differential selection of candidates. This perspective justifies Senator Stevenson's claim that "even if all of the dollars were honestly contributed and honestly spent, they would still have a corrupting influence on our politics. For the vast sums now required for political campaigns raise the unholy specter that politics in the future will be an enterprise for rich people only, for rich candidates, or at the very least candidates backed by rich contributors."[16]

OTHER CONSIDERATIONS

Members of Congress are partisans as well as incumbents and are therefore attentive to the effects of policy changes on the balance of advantages and resources between Republicans and Democrats. Partisanship is, indeed, the principal barrier to the exclusive dominance of incumbent protection concerns. Their partisan attachments are, with very few exceptions, to the two major parties, so they also have a stake in maintaining a two-party system against the possible inroads of additional parties or independent candidates.

16. Ibid., p. 185.

Broadly speaking, partisans on both sides seek, first, to protect their own sources of funds (Democrats, for example, carefully avoid imposing new limits on what labor can do for them); second, to expand those resources; and third, to cut back on the resources available to the other party.

Another complication is that members consider themselves experts on campaigning and on campaign financing. All have raised and spent money in successful political campaigns. But they are experts through experience in a wide variety of quite disparate electoral environments; each has a fund of idiosyncratic knowledge of often questionable general relevance. Senate contests are run under extremely diverse circumstances, and not only because states vary so much in population and physical size. So are House contests; compare a campaign for North Dakota's single House seat to one for New York's 20th district on the west side of Manhattan. And differences in primary election rules and customs supply another set of variables.

Members of Congress do not, of course, have total control over federal election campaign policy. Much of the legislation covers presidential as well as congressional elections, so presidential involvement—beyond that required by the Constitution for any legislation—is always possible. Typically, however, the president's role in making campaign finance policy has been comparatively limited. Congress has more than once shown itself quite willing to ignore or even act directly contrary to a president's wishes. And it has clearly been much less hesitant to enact innovative legislation applying to presidential campaigns than it has been to revise its own campaign finance practices.

Interested groups outside government have also involved themselves in campaign finance reform. Spokesmen for the television networks and individual broadcasters have testified frequently on the many reform proposals dealing with broadcasting. Minor parties and independent candidates, labor unions and business groups, ideological organizations, and "public interest" lobbies have all taken part in drafting and promoting legislation. A few groups have been particularly active and effective, and they will be acknowledged in due course.

One final participant must be mentioned: the Supreme Court. The Court's involvement is inevitable. Campaign finance policy impinges directly on political action and competition, on forms of communication and expression most explicitly protected by the First Amendment. Any restrictions on campaign giving or spending are sure to be challenged on that ground. The Court's decisions have powerfully influenced campaign finance regulation.

Still, campaign finance policy is largely the province of Congress, and the choices made have consistently supported the interests of incumbent members. The most persistent trend in the development of campaign finance regulation over the last decade has been toward restricting the financial resources available to candidates. All the evidence presented in the first part of this book favors the conclusion that this can only work to the advantage of incumbents. Ralph Winter of the Yale Law School, testifying before the Senate Subcommittee on Communications in 1971, argued that "systematic regulation of political campaigns by Congress must inevitably lead to those in power regulating in favor of themselves."[17] He has yet to be proven wrong. A review of the politics and consequences of campaign finance reform over the past decade will bear this out.

CAMPAIGN FINANCE REFORM:
FIRST STEPS IN THE 1960S

The beginning of the current cycle of campaign finance reform can be traced to the April 1962 report of a commission appointed by President Kennedy to find better ways to finance political campaigns. The commission's report established the agenda for subsequent attempts to replace the tattered Corrupt Practices Act, and a number of recommendations found their way, in modified form, into law.

In view of later legislation, the commission's suggestions are no-

17. U.S., Congress, Senate, Committee on Commerce, Subcommittee on Communications, *Federal Election Campaign Act of 1971*, 92nd Cong., 1st sess., hearings March 2–5 and 31, and April 1, 1971, p. 582.

table for what they left out as well as for what they included.[18] Election costs were straightforwardly assumed to be necessary. The commission recognized that competitive elections cost money; if they seemed expensive, the expense was the price of democracy. Of course, the era of really spectacular growth in campaign spending was still ahead. The problem as they perceived it was to ensure that candidates enjoyed sufficient campaign resources without mortgaging themselves to wealthy individuals or interests. If enough people could be persuaded to contribute to candidates they favored, campaigns would be financed adequately without the possibility of undue influence by specific contributors. Tax incentives—both credits and deductions—were recommended to stimulate small individual campaign gifts. No subsequent debate on campaign finance legislation has since passed without ritual mention of the need to broaden the base of political contributions. Measures designed to bring this about voluntarily seem destined to futility. They require economically irrational behavior, a small contribution toward the purchase of a public good (see the discussion in chapter 3). Those individuals who do make small contributions to candidates are likely to be the more extreme ideologues, not exactly the kind of "broadening" intended.

The other significant recommendation made by the commission was for full disclosure of primary and general election contributions and expenditures. This became a staple element in almost every reform package. It was a minimum step to be taken if any change in regulation were enacted. Clearly, it would be essential to any more extensive regulation of contributions and expenditures.

Conspicuously absent from the commission's recommendations were any contribution or spending limits. Experience with the Corrupt Practices Act taught that they would not work; it was preferable to have full public knowledge of where candidates got their funds and how much they were spending to win office. It would then be up to voters to judge whether a candidate would be obligated to them or to special interests. A bipartisan commission (un-

18. See the President's Commission on Campaign Costs, *Financing Presidential Campaigns* (Washington, D.C.: Government Printing Office, April 1962).

der the General Accounting Office) was proposed to administer the disclosure regulations.[19]

Other recommendations raised themes that reappeared regularly in subsequent discussions of campaign finance reform. One was suspension of the "equal-time" provision of the Communications Act of 1934 so that broadcasters could give time to major candidates for public office without having to give it to a host of minor candidates as well; from the beginning, campaign finance questions were tied in with the problem of what to do about political television. Another was the first suggestion of matching grants; the commission recommended that if tax incentives did not serve their intended purpose, thought should be given to matching all contributions of $10 or less with federal funds.[20]

Congress took no action on the commission's proposals—or any others—until 1966. President Johnson had included a call for campaign finance reform in his State of the Union speech; his proposals were much like the commission's: tax incentives for small contributions, the removal of unrealistic spending ceilings, and full disclosure of contributions and expenditures. Committees of both houses held hearings and reported bills, but no new legislation of this sort was enacted. What did pass, and quite abruptly, was a proposal to allow taxpayers to check off $1 on their returns ($2 on a joint return) to be put into a special fund to finance presidential elections. The proposal was the brainchild of Senator Long, Chairman of the Finance Committee, who got it through as a rider to the Foreign Investors Tax Act. It came as a surprise to the administration, but Johnson eventually supported and signed the bill. It never took effect. It was officially suspended the next year until Congress could provide guidelines for distribution of the money from the fund.

The handling of this legislation is revealing. The haste with which Long's proposal was pushed through contrasts sharply with the ponderously slow and elaborate consideration of legislation applying to congressional elections. Debate on the bill also raised one

19. Ibid., pp. 12–20.
20. Ibid., p. 31.

of the fundamental difficulties with any campaign subsidy scheme: what to do about third parties. Spending and contribution regulations can be applied equally to all candidates; subsidies, in contrast, either discriminate against, or encourage formation of, minor parties. Long's bill discriminated against minor parties and independent candidates; in fact, any formula that does not provide equal funding for all candidates—or at least all parties—is discriminatory. On the other hand, any subsidy system that does not discriminate against minor parties and independent candidacies threatens to bring them into existence (just because the money is available) and to keep them going long after the original purposes for which they were organized have disappeared. Think of the American Independent Party without George Wallace.

The 1966 law was suspended because it had neglected to specify how the money might be spent and because the funds were to be given to the national parties, which would then decide how to use them in the presidential campaigns. Critics felt that this gave too much power to the national chairmen. All later subsidy proposals have required that all, or nearly all funds go directly to candidates. They would thereby diminish the role of political parties even further, reinforcing the long-term trend toward ever more feeble parties.[21] This is of little concern to most members of Congress. They do not rely on the party for much in the way of financial or other help; it would scarcely occur to them to give parties control over public funds for congressional elections.

Congress never took the promised action to determine how the funds that the checkoff would have produced were to be distributed, and no further changes in campaign finance laws were made during the remainder of the 1960s. The Senate did pass a major reform package (S 1880) in 1967, but it was another year before the

21. See Herbert E. Alexander, "The Impact of Election Reform Legislation on the Political Party System" (Prepared for delivery at the 1975 Annual Meeting of the American Political Science Association, San Francisco, September 2–5, 1975); Austin Ranney, "The Impact of Campaign Finance Reform on American Presidential Parties" (Prepared for delivery at the Conference on Political Money and Election Reform: Comparative Prospectives, at the University of Southern California, Los Angeles, December 10, 1977).

House Administration Committee acted on the measure, and the bill it eventually reported was killed by the Rules Committee. The House consistently showed itself less interested in reform than the Senate. Part of the problem was simply Wayne Hays, the Chairman of the House Administration Committee; he was a persistent and unabashed opponent of almost any change in the campaign finance laws that did not flagrantly favor incumbents. And he had allies on his committee at this time: northern Democrats, who feared that new regulations would restrict labor contributions to their campaigns, and southern Democrats, who did not welcome any law that would expose primary election finances.

The main objective of opponents of this and other similar reforms was to prevent a bill from ever reaching the floor of the House. Since the old system could not be defended, and most members were committed, at least publicly, to supporting campaign finance reform,[22] any reform package reaching the floor was almost certain to pass.

THE REFORMS OF THE 1970S

The struggle to reform campaign finance practices finally succeeded in the early 1970s. Several of the reforms enacted were familiar remnants of earlier bills. But "reform" had taken on some new meanings as well; advocates of reform in and out of Congress had altered their perceptions of both the problem and its preferred solution. This probably hastened the passage of really fundamental changes, but it also shifted the purposes and consequences of those changes.

Earlier proposals—like those of President Kennedy's commission—emphasized full disclosure and a broadened base of financial support as keys to a better campaign finance system. The "public interest" organizations involved—of which, because of its

22. A poll of members taken by *Congressional Quarterly* in 1966, for example, found 208 for, 30 against more thorough disclosure requirements, including ones applying to primary campaigns. See the *1966 Congressional Quarterly Almanac*, p. 486.

expertise and its unique collection of campaign finance information, the Citizens' Research Foundation was most important—were basically interested in providing more campaign resources while allowing the light of publicity to keep candidates honest and the public confident that they were. But subsequent public interest lobbies that took up campaign finance reform—first the National Committee for an Effective Congress, later Common Cause and the Center for the Public Financing of Elections—had a more radical agenda. And they were willing to give strategic support to laws that deliberately limited campaign resources by imposing ceilings on campaign contributions and expenditures. These, it turned out, were the reforms Congress found most inviting.

The ultimate intention of these later reform groups was to limit drastically private contributions to political candidates, allowing only very small individual gifts, and making up the difference with public funds. Strategically, pursuing limits on contributions and expenditures made good sense; it appealed to members of Congress; it reduced the flow of money into campaign coffers; it required complete reporting of all contributions and expenditures; and it increased the problems of raising campaign money to the point where public funding would become a much more attractive alternative. Common Cause, working through the courts as well as the Congress,[23] was particularly effective in bringing about the changes it desired; its work to assure compliance with regulations once they were passed was especially important.

Congress enacted major campaign finance bills in 1970, 1971, and 1974. The 1970 bill was vetoed by President Nixon. Congress responded the next year with the Federal Election Campaign Act of 1971 (FECA), which was modified substantially, under the shadow of Watergate, by the FECA Amendments of 1974. The Su-

23.   See Carol S. Greenwald, ''The Use of Litigation by Common Cause: A Study of the Development of Campaign Finance Reform Legislation'' (Prepared for delivery at the 1975 Annual Meeting of the American Political Science Association, San Francisco, September 2–5, 1975); Joel B. Fleishman and Carol S. Greenwald, ''Public Interest Litigation and Political Finance Reform,'' *The Annals of the American Academy of Political and Social Science* 425 (May 1976): 114–23.

preme Court's decision in *Buckley* v. *Valeo*[24] overturned some provisions of the FECA and required further amendments, passed in 1976, to make some of its other provisions operative. A major drive to enact additional changes—the most important being public funding of congressional campaigns—has so far been fruitless.

Each piece of reform legislation was actually a package of related regulatory provisions. The progress of campaign finance reform is most clearly revealed by tracing the development of major policy components: disclosure requirements and their enforcement, spending restrictions, contribution limits, and provisions to increase campaign resources, including public funding.

Disclosure

Disclosure requirements were enacted with the least controversy. Full reports of all contributions, of the names of contributors of more than small sums, and of all campaign expenditures, were widely accepted as basic to any serious reform, and they were essential to any further regulation. Some civil libertarians and minor party officials objected to the government's compelling people to reveal their political preferences by acknowledging their campaign gifts, but this objection was overwhelmed by the far more prevalent fear that secret contributions inevitably invited corruption.

The enforcement and administration of disclosure excited much more controversy. Public interest reformers insisted that an independent commission having full regulatory authority was essential. Republican members of Congress agreed. The alternative preferred by Democrats, particularly in the House, was to make the Clerk of the House and the Secretary of the Senate (and, for presidential candidates, the General Accounting Office) responsible for gathering and disseminating the data. The Democrats, not surprisingly, preferred to regulate themselves; they were hardly likely to suffer much inconvenience from officials who were dependent on them for their positions. Nor is it surprising that Republicans and reformers outside Congress were skeptical about the vigor and impartiality

24.   424 U.S. 1 (1976).

of such regulators. The House, led by Wayne Hays, successfully resisted the creation of an independent agency in 1971; the Senate's proposal for a Federal Election Commission was dropped in conference.

Reformers did not give up on the issue. Common Cause led a continuing attack on what it took to be weaknesses in the administration of the 1971 law and helped to resist proposed changes that would weaken disclosure further. It used both litigation and information available under the new law (data that Common Cause collected, analyzed, and publicized) to support its objectives.[25] In 1974, with the Watergate scandals fresh, the FECA was amended to establish an eight-member Federal Election Commission (FEC) to enforce the law. The powers granted the commission were significant; they included authority to give advisory opinions, conduct audits and investigations, issue subpoenas, and sue for civil injunctions in court. Its structure was the result of a compromise: six voting public members, two each appointed by the Speaker of the House, the President of the Senate, and the President, with the Clerk of the House and the Secretary of the Senate serving ex-officio (not voting). The Supreme Court eventually determined that the appointment procedures violated the constitutional separation of powers, and the FEC was reorganized in 1976 to conform to the Court's requirements. The bipartisan six-member FEC is now appointed by the President and confirmed by the Senate.

Although reformers won an independent FEC with substantial enforcement authority, Congress has not given over regulation of campaign finance entirely to the commission. Under the 1974 Amendments, the House and Senate could, within thirty days of their promulgation, veto rules and regulations made by the commission, and they have done so. When the law was revised in 1976, this provision was altered to permit Congress to veto individual sections of FEC regulations, and other restrictions were imposed on the commission's authority. Members of Congress appreciate regulation no more than anyone else, and they are in a position to do something about it.

25. Fleishman and Greenwald, "Public Interest Litigation," pp. 116–17.

Reformers have succeeded in making disclosure work. Efforts to ease reporting requirements have failed; reports are now mandatory ten days before and thirty days after every election, on the tenth day after the close of each quarter (unless under $1,000 was received or spent during the quarter) and at the end of every nonelection year. Publicity for the disclosed information has so far been less effective, mainly because, as a reporter observed, "the story is unreportable with disclosure, not because it is secret but because there is such a great volume of material."[26] Beginning with the 1978 elections, however, a computerized data retrieval system set up by the FEC is supposed to make detailed contribution and spending data on each campaign available to the press and public during the campaign period.[27] It may soon be possible to observe the political effects of full disclosure—and publicity—for the first time.

Disclosure regulations, particularly the requirement in the 1974 Amendments that candidates designate a single committee to take responsibility for all financial aspects of the campaign, have clearly reinforced the trend toward more centralized, professional, candidate-oriented campaigns. The laws are complicated; the penalties for violating them can be severe; candidates increasingly depend on lawyers and accountants to keep them out of trouble. Inexperienced candidates no doubt find the regulations most bothersome, and there are indications that voluntary individual participation has been discouraged by the new rules of the game.[28]

Spending Limits

It is not hard to fathom why Congress became interested in limiting campaign contributions and expenditures. The 50 percent increase in overall campaign costs between 1964 and 1968 obviously

26. Xandra Kayden, "Report of a Conference on Campaign Finance Based on the Experience of the 1976 Presidential Campaigns" (Prepared for the Campaign Finance Study Group of the Institute of Politics, John F. Kennedy School of Government, Harvard University, 1977), p. 26.

27. Interview with Kent Cooper at the Federal Election Commission, Washington, D.C., April 3, 1978.

28. Kayden, "Finance of the 1976 Presidential Campaigns," pp. 26–38.

had something to do with it. So, too, did perceptions of where the money was coming from and how it was being spent. No fewer than twenty millionaire candidates competed for Senate seats in 1970. The most conspicuous of their campaigns made lavish use of television advertising. It is no coincidence that the first major reform passed included as its most important component limits on the amounts candidates for federal office could spend on broadcasting.

The Senate again took the lead, and with stronger reason than before. The perspective of incumbent senators is not hard to grasp. They were especially impressed by the few instances of wealthy candidates spending the family fortune on mass-media advertising to win instant prominence and statewide nominations. No matter that this extravagance rarely brought victory in general elections; it would be no pleasant thing to face such an opponent. It would seem to require an effort to match the mass-media spending and, perhaps, campaign style of the opponent, and the effectiveness of both was doubtlessly exaggerated because they were new and unfamiliar.

Senators' feelings on the matter are plain from comments made during hearings and floor debates on the 1970 bill (S 3637) to restrict broadcast spending. Senator Kennedy was moved to testify that "like a colossus of the ancient world, television stands astride our political system, demanding tribute from every candidate for public office, incumbent or challenger. Its appetite is insatiable, its impact unique."[29] Further, "the recent political landscape of America is strewn with the graves of incumbents and challengers, blitzed into defeat by an unlimited assault of television spending."[30] Senator Gore, about to be defeated in an expensive mass-media campaign, warned that "in the days of slogans, labels, image making mass communications, monopolizing the time of the television that goes into the homes of the American people is a great danger to the democratic process."[31] The examples could

29. U.S., Senate, *FECA of 1971*, p. 172.

30. Ibid., p. 173.

31. U.S., *Congressional Record*, 91st Cong., 2d sess., September 14, 1970, p. 11596.

easily be multiplied. The dubious notion that candidates could be peddled like soapflakes was widely and uncritically accepted. One congressman even introduced a bill to ban all paid political broadcasts.[32] Broadcast spending ceilings, at minimum, were deemed necessary to prevent wealth and Madison Avenue from destroying the Republic.

The 1970 bill limited the amount candidates could spend on political broadcasting to 3.5 cents per vote (in the previous general election for the office) in primary elections, 7 cents per vote in general elections. It was vetoed by President Nixon. Among his stated reasons were that it was biased in favor of incumbents and other well-known candidates, that it discriminated against the broadcast media, and that more money would simply be spent on other forms of campaigning.[33] Congress responded the following year by passing the FECA of 1971, which, among other things, extended the limits to cover newspapers, billboards, magazines, and telephone banks. Candidates could spend no more than 10 cents per eligible voter (or $50,000, whichever was greater), and no more than 60 percent of the limit could be spent on broadcasting; television was still regarded as the basic menace. The bill passed both houses with huge majorities (334–20 in the House, 88–2 in the Senate).

The FECA Amendments of 1974 finally extended restrictions to cover total spending in all federal elections, primary and general. House candidates could spend up to $70,000 in a primary or general election, plus 20 percent more to raise the money; they could also receive an additional $10,000 from their parties. Senate candidates were limited to the greater of 8 cents per eligible voter or $100,000 in primaries, 12 cents per voter or $150,000 in general elections, with similar provisions for fund-raising expenses and additional party contributions. Presidential campaign spending was also restricted under a public funding scheme enacted for those contests.

The growing emphasis on restricting expenditures (and gifts to

32. U.S., Senate, *FECA of 1973*, p. 474.
33. *Dollar Politics*, vol. 1, p. 43.

campaigns) raised the question of how such reforms would affect competition for office. Spending restrictions are likely to have the least impact on presidential elections. Ironically, these best-financed of political campaigns probably depend less on direct expenditures to get the campaign message across—at least after the primaries—than do any other federal campaigns. They are so thoroughly covered by the news media that even seriously under-financed candidates (from their perspective) will have some chance to reach the vast majority of potential voters. It should be clear by now that this is not at all the case with congressional elections. Campaign spending does have an important effect on who wins these elections, and it is the amount spent by challengers (and other disadvantaged candidates) that actually makes the difference. Spending limits, if they have any effect at all on competition, can only work to the detriment of challengers.

The question of whether or not spending limits would add to the already inordinate incumbent advantage was a central issue each time such restrictions were proposed. The argument that they would, in fact, favor incumbents, was given thorough presentation more than once in both houses. Representative Frenzel almost single-handedly carried the point to the House. During hearings on the FECA of 1971, he declared:

> What I am trying to find out from some witness is what is so bad about campaign spending. . . . I have tried to take a very unpopular position of being for a nonincumbent trying to take on the guy who has all the advantages of name recognition, popularity, access to the media, a limited franking privilege, etc. etc. This poor guy has to arise from nowhere and take on such distinguished people as you see before you. This is a very difficult task and history shows that they are very unsuccessful at it.
>
> When you establish a spending limitation you literally insure that incumbents are not going to be defeated because the only weapon the non-incumbent has . . . is to get his name known.[34]

34. U.S., Congress, House, Committee on Interstate and Foreign Commerce,

Senator Buckley made the same point most forcefully in the Senate. Elected as a Conservative, he remained very sensitive to the effects of campaign finance legislation on electoral competition (he is, of course, the Buckley of *Buckley* v. *Valeo*, of which more later). Buckley had the audacity to introduce an amendment to the 1974 bill that would have allowed challengers to spend 130 percent of the limits for incumbents. The amendment was debated, fittingly enough, on April 1; it lost, 66–17.[35]

Spending figures from 1972 congressional elections were available as evidence during consideration of the 1974 FECA Amendments; they showed clearly that challengers normally did well only if they spent a great deal of money—usually more than would be allowed under the formulas ultimately enacted.[36] Perhaps the strongest empirical testimony on the issue came from the several members of both houses who said, in effect, that had the proposed limits been in force, they never would have been elected in the first place.[37]

The reception these arguments were accorded is revealing. Those making them were accused of wanting more incumbents to lose.[38] Evidence was countered by the claim that limits equalize spending and therefore give every candidate the same chance; by the argument that incumbent advantages are more than counterbalanced by political scars inflicted by controversial legislative issues; and by utterly specious comparisons to the low spending limits for British

---

Subcommittee on Communications and Power, *Political Broadcasting—1971*, 92d Cong., 1st sess., hearings June 8–10, 15, and 16, 1971, p. 85.

35. U.S., *Congressional Record*, 93rd Cong., 2d sess., April 1, 1974, pp. 9089–91.

36. Ibid., August 7, 1974, p. 27223.

37. For examples, see the comments by Senator Tower, U.S., *Congressional Record*, 91st Cong., 2d sess., April 14, 1970, p. 11606, and Representative Seiberling, U.S. *Congressional Record*, 93rd Cong., 2d sess., August 7, 1974, p. 27247.

38. Representative Hays, responding to the argument that limits help incumbents: "The whole thrust of what I understand you to say . . . has been that there ought to be not so many incumbents reelected . . . and we have got to get rid of more incumbents." See U.S., Congress, House, Committee on House Administration, Subcommittee on Elections, *Federal Election Reform*, 93rd Cong., 1st sess., hearings October 2, 10, 16, and 25, and November 14 and 29, 1973, p. 194.

parliamentary elections. None of these arguments withstands serious analysis. Ultimately, however, demonstrations that the legislation would increase the already lopsided advantage enjoyed by incumbents were not carefully countered at all; they were simply ignored. If they were, in fact, convincing, it is of course possible that they helped gain support for restrictions rather than the contrary; few members were likely to admit such motives—except for Wayne Hays, who said, "It doesn't bother me since I am an incumbent."[39]

The actual limits were chosen somewhat arbitrarily. Bills were introduced with figures ranging from $30,000 to $190,000 as general election spending ceilings for House candidates. Lacking any better information, each member generalized from his own campaign experiences. Each argued, in effect, that campaigns could be adequately financed with whatever amount it cost to win his tightest contest.

Some members were refreshingly candid about it. Representative Frenzel thought $150,000 was a good limit if there had to be one, mainly because, he said, "that is what it cost me to get elected the first time."[40] Congressmen Hays and Dent, in contrast, claimed that $35,000 or $40,000 was plenty.[41] Hays spent $32,285 winning reelection in 1974; Dent spent $32,074 in 1972, less in 1974. Representative Young, who had just invested about $35,000 to win a primary and another $200,000 to defeat an incumbent in the general election, introduced a bill setting ceilings of $50,000 for primaries and $175,000 for incumbents and $190,000 for nonincumbents in general elections.[42] Representative Obey proposed a formula that would allow about $32,000 to be spent in a primary and $48,000 in a general election;[43] his 1972 spending was about $65,000 for both. Congressman Thompson supported a limit of $75,000, since the

39. U.S., House, *Political Broadcasting—1971*, p. 166.
40. U.S., Senate, *Public Financing*, p. 145.
41. U.S., House, *Federal Election Reform*, pp. 128–29.
42. Ibid., p. 174.
43. Ibid., p. 295.

most he had spent up to that time in ten elections was $72,000.[44]

No one, however, approached Senator Allen's capacity to draw universal lessons from personal experience. "The last time I ran for the Senate," he told his colleagues, "my campaign committee in the primary and in the general election in both races spent a total of $34,000. I feel campaigns can be run on small amounts. In the general election I did receive 95 percent of the vote. That is proof that campaigns can be run for a small amount."[45] They certainly can if, as in Allen's case, the only opponent is a Prohibitionist.

A popular alternative to the generalization from experience was the argument that since congressmen were paid only $42,500 per year (as they were at the time), they should be allowed to spend no more than this to win the job.[46] For obvious reasons, this piece of wisdom did not appeal to the Senate (nor, indeed, was any thought given applying it to presidential candidates). The Senate had to deal with the problem of the vastly differing populations of the various states; most proposed formulas provided a base amount to which more was added according to the size of the voting age population. But campaigning evidently enjoys economies of scale, so that most formulas would not limit campaign spending at all in the largest states (where the most is spent) but would do so rather drastically in the smallest ones.[47]

The House consistently favored lower limits than the Senate; those in the House Administration Committee version of the 1974 bill were actually reduced on the floor. Only the Senate conferees' insistence that they be raised (in return for dropping public funding for congressional campaigns and other concessions) prevented the 1974 bill from blatantly favoring House incumbents. The limits set

44. U.S., *Congressional Record*, 93rd Cong., 2d sess., August 7, 1974, p. 27261.

45. U.S., Congress, Senate, Committee on Rules and Administration, *Federal Election Reform Proposals of 1977*, 95th Cong., 1st sess., hearings May 4–6 and 11, 1977, p. 202.

46. U.S., *Congressional Record*, 93rd Cong., 2d sess., August 7, 1974, p. 27260.

47. See the testimony of Roy A. Schotland, Georgetown University Law School, in U.S., Senate, *Election Reform Proposals of 1977*, pp. 477ff.

by the 1974 Amendments were probably high enough to give challengers a fighting chance, provided that they spent the amount allotted for the primary campaign; those who stuck to the general election limits would be severely underfinanced.[48] These limits were overturned by the Supreme Court in the *Buckley* decision on the grounds that they interfered with rights of free expression guaranteed by the First Amendment. The Court's position did, however, appear to permit the imposition of campaign spending limits on candidates whose campaigns were publicly funded. This is plainly one of the principal attractions public funding holds for members of Congress.

Contribution Limits

The FECA and its 1974 Amendments not only put ceilings on campaign spending, but also sought to control and restrict contributions to political campaigns. Common Cause and some of its allies in Congress took the attitude that campaign contributions were inherently dangerous, that they were invariably corrupting, if only through a kind of Darwinian selection of individually upright candidates. Liberal Democrats were most likely to share this belief, more from traditional ideological premises (money is always suspect) than from any clear conception of self-interest. A brief look at the published data would have shown that among the more prominent beneficiaries of lavish campaign contributions had been liberal Democrats opposed to the Vietnam war. John Kerry ($279,746), Allard Lowenstein ($285,475), and Robert Drinan ($199,703), all "peace" candidates, were among the top spenders in 1972. Paul McCloskey, an antiwar Republican, spent $321,558. Even as recently as 1977, Representative Jacobs, a liberal Democrat, wanted to give each candidate a set amount of television time and newspaper space, then forbid any expenditures at all.[49] Nothing would do more to assure that the status quo is maintained, that those already in office stay in office.

48.   Gary C. Jacobson, "Practical Consequences of Campaign Finance Reform: An Incumbent Protection Act?" *Public Policy* 24 (1976): 14.

49.   U.S., House, *Public Financing*, p. 165.

Common Cause pushed for the prohibition of all but small individual contributions to political campaigns, banning gifts from committees and organizations (except for parties) entirely.[50] Congress as a whole showed no interest in going this far, but limits on the flow of funds into campaigns were extended with each new reform law. The 1970 bill did not limit contributions. The FECA of 1971 restricted only gifts from candidates and their families; the limits were $50,000 for presidential and vice-presidential candidates, $35,000 for Senate candidates, and $25,000 for House candidates. Congress was obviously reacting against the rash of millionaire candidates active in the 1970 elections. As Wayne Hays said, with typical understatement, "How do you balance the scales with no limit for some millionaire who moves into my district and decides he wants to go to Congress and is willing to spend a couple of million dollars of his own money to do it with? I don't want someone spending $2 million to buy a seat in the House."[51]

More extensive limits on contributions were defeated on the floor of the Senate. Republicans opposed them most vigorously, arguing that disclosure was sufficient. However, with the Watergate revelations as a spur, much more comprehensive limits were included in the 1974 FECA Amendments. And this time the limits were actually reduced on the floor of the Senate. Individuals could give no more than $1,000 to a candidate for a primary or general election campaign and no more than $25,000 total in any year to all candidates; the limit for multicandidate organizations was $5,000. Limits on contributions by candidates to their own campaigns were retained, and no individual was permitted to spend more than $1,000 on behalf of a candidate independently of the campaign.

Corporate and Union Contributions The regulation of group contributions was a particularly sensitive area. Corporate and union gifts to political campaigns had been forbidden by federal law since 1907, but this prohibition was no more effective than any other

50. U.S., Senate, *FECA of 1973*, p. 63.
51. U.S., House, *Political Broadcasting—1971*, p. 176.

campaign finance regulation. Contributions from these sources were particularly worrisome, not only out of concern for undue influence by powerful economic interests, but also because individuals could, in effect, be compelled to contribute to candidates against their wills. Union dues and corporate profits were passed along to candidates regardless of the wishes of individual members and stockholders. The issue also encouraged a sharp partisan division; as a rule, corporate contributions go disproportionately to Republicans, union gifts go overwhelmingly to Democrats. Each party was fully alert to changes in the rules that might alter the partisan balance of resources available from unions and corporations.

The FECA of 1971 permitted, and sought to regulate, corporate and union political activity. It continued the ban on direct corporate and union contributions to political candidates, but legalized the practice of establishing separate campaign funds to accept voluntary contributions from stockholders or members. Regular dues and profits could be used to administer these funds and to raise the money. The widespread violation of these regulations uncovered by the Watergate investigations led to a substantial increase in the penalties attached to these provisions under the FECA Amendments of 1974.[52]

Congress carefully adjusted the pertinent provisions of the FECA and its Amendments to treat corporations and unions evenhandedly. In 1975, however, the FEC upset this delicate balance, leading to further legislation. The FEC interpreted the law to permit corporations to solicit contributions from all employees—including union members—as well as stockholders; corporations could also use payroll checkoffs for gifts to their political action committees. Unions could only solicit their members and their families and were forbidden under the Taft-Hartley Law from gathering funds through payroll checkoffs. Labor and its Democratic supporters took the opportunity provided by the need to revise the FECA after *Buckley* to

52.   Edwin M. Epstein, "Corporations and Labor Unions in Electoral Politics," *The Annals of the American Academy of Political and Social Science* 425 (May 1976): 48–49.

undo this decision and would have shifted the balance just as strongly in the other direction had it not been for the threat of a presidential veto. A precisely balanced compromise was once again worked out: unions can now solicit only members and their families, and corporations only their stockkholders and executive and administrative personnel (carefully defined), except for twice a year, when each is allowed to solicit anonymous contributions, by mail only, from all employees otherwise proscribed. Unions may use whatever means of solicitation the company uses—including checkoffs—although they must pay their share of the cost of doing so. This law also included a provision designed to prevent a proliferation of corporate and union political action committees (PACs) as a means for circumventing the $5,000 per candidate contribution limit. All PACs from any one international union or any single company are treated as one committee for contribution purposes.[53]

It is evident from the data in chapter 3 that current regulations foster the growth of PACs and have increased their importance as a source of funds for congressional candidates. Total and proportionate PAC contributions have grown each year, with the biggest jump between 1974 and 1976, in part a consequence of the publicly funded presidential campaigns. The largest increase was in gifts from business, professional, and agricultural interests. This has worried some labor leaders; PACs have much more unexploited potential for growth than do labor committees.[54] But unions are legally permitted to engage in activities of direct benefit to the candidates they support which are not covered by campaign finance regulations. The most important of these are the "nonpartisan" voter registration and participation drives they may sponsor among their members; "in-kind" assistance of this sort favors Democratic candidates and is extremely difficult to measure or regulate.

Contribution Limits after Buckley *v.* Valeo   In *Buckley* v. *Valeo*

53. *C.Q. Weekly Report* 17 (May 15, 1976): 1223.
54. Recall from chapter 3 that 28 percent of the largest 500 companies, but only 4 percent of the next largest 500, had organized PACs by the 1976 campaigns; most labor unions have been politically active for years.

the Supreme Court declared unconstitutional restrictions on contributions by candidates to their own campaigns and on spending by individuals independent of any campaign, but upheld limits on individual and group contributions to candidates. The former are, like campaign spending itself, protected forms of political expression and therefore may not be limited. The latter are distinguished as imposing only marginal restrictions on political expression; the symbolic act of contributing can still be performed and "the quantity of speech does not increase perceptibly with the size of the contribution."[55] The Court also determined that Congress had a legitimate concern with preventing the corruption, or appearance of corruption, that unrestricted campaign gifts would foster.

The restrictions now in force have several consequences. They once again favor incumbents at the expense of the challengers. Given the way campaign spending affects the outcomes of congressional elections, any measure that limits the money available to candidates benefits incumbents. Proponents of restrictions on contributions and spending argue that, since incumbents raise twice as much money as challengers, such restrictions actually help to even things up. But they do not, because what matters is the absolute, not relative, amount the challenger spends. Incumbents also raise money in small amounts more easily. Contribution limits make it more difficult for challengers to gather "startup" money, the funds needed early in the campaign to make a show of being "viable," so that further contributions and other forms of support can be attracted. More time is spent raising money, so less is spent campaigning.

The survey taken for the FEC after the 1976 elections found agreement among candidates that the regulations made it more difficult and more time-consuming to raise money and, in general, operated to the benefit of incumbents. The study was made of a sample of 850 campaigns of the 2,150 registered with the FEC in 1976. More than half the respondents—52 percent—thought the FECA hindered fundraising; only 7 percent thought it helped.

55. Alexander, *Financing Elections*, p. 151.

Forty-eight percent found that fund raising took more time than expected; 4 percent thought it took less time. Forty-six percent thought it took too much time, 22 percent felt it did not.[56]

Most respondents agreed that the FECA favors incumbents at the expense of challengers, although, not surprisingly, challengers were more certain of this (83 percent thought it aided incumbents, 7 percent, challengers) than were incumbents (50 percent felt it helped themselves, 29 percent, their opponents).[57] Sixty-three percent felt that the Act has not put candidates on a more equal financial footing.[58]

In spite of these assessments, most candidates, including challengers, generally favored the law. Its most popular element was public disclosure of contributions and expenditures (74 percent were in favor, only 14 were opposed). Limits on contributions from PACs (59 percent in favor, 21 percent opposed) and from individuals (49 percent for, 38 percent against) were also preferred by a majority of those expressing an opinion. Contribution limits were favored more frequently by incumbents than by challengers, but the difference was small.[59]

The explanation is that challengers believe that without contribution limits, the incumbents' advantage would be even greater; 13 percent think that unlimited contributions would help them, 60 percent think they would help incumbents. Incumbents agree; 42 percent believe they would benefit if limits were removed, 26 percent think challengers would be better off.[60] The majority is right if only fund raising is considered; it is wrong if election results are at issue. The error stems from the assumption that the spending differential between candidates is what matters. But since the factor of diminishing returns applies so much more forcefully to incumbent spending, and since most challengers are underfinanced, it is clear

56. *A Study of the Impact of the Federal Election Campaign Act on the 1976 Election* (Prepared for the Federal Election Commission by Decision Making Information and Hart Research Associates, 1977), pp. 58, 60, 84.
57. Ibid., p. 118.
58. Ibid., p. 120.
59. Ibid., pp. 154–56.
60. Ibid., p. 114.

that the limits favor incumbents rather than challengers.

The survey does not consistently distinguish between House and Senate candidates, but it does contain some evidence that Senate campaigns are affected more strongly by the contribution limits. Sixty-one percent of the Senate candidates, as opposed to 52 percent of the House candidates, reported that the FECA hindered fund raising.[61] Even incumbents had problems. Senators from the two most populous states were reported to have "complained about the incredible amount of time they had to devote solely to raising money due to the limit that makes it difficult to get large chunks swiftly."[62] Senate candidates rely much more heavily on large individual contributions for funds; in 1976, 27.1 percent of Senate campaign contributions were from individuals giving $500 or more; the figure for House campaigns is 11.1 percent. Significantly, 81 percent of Senate candidates, compared to 66 percent of House candidates, thought that the FECA helped to reduce the influence of major contributors.[63] The apparent decrease (see chapter 3) in Senate campaign spending is most probably a consequence of the individual and group contribution limits.[64]

Perhaps the only candidates not bothered by existing regulations are those who are personally wealthy, a singular irony in light of the original inspiration for contribution limits. Candidates may spend all of their own money they wish (Senator Heinz put almost $2.5 million of his own fortune into his victorious 1976 race), while the size of the contributions their opponents may accept is strictly limited.

The evident difficulties raising funds under these restrictions have no doubt increased the appeal of some form of public funding for congressional campaigns (at least among Senators), just as some of their proponents intended. It is simply not possible to finance

61. Ibid., p. 61.

62. U.S., Senate, *Election Reform Proposals of 1977*, p. 180.

63. *Impact of the FECA*, p. 83.

64. Roland D. McDevitt, "Congressional Campaign Finance and the Consequences of Its Regulation" (Ph.D. diss., University of California at Santa Barbara, 1978), p. 176.

most campaigns adequately with small individual donations, and even those of the size now permitted provide insufficient funds for large, competitive campaigns. As Representative Anderson explained, "The rationale for partial public financing of campaigns is to fill the vacuum left by the elimination of large individual and special interest contributions while placing a premium on and incentive for raising small contributions."[65] So far, this rationale has proven insufficiently persuasive.

ADDITIONAL RESOURCES FOR CAMPAIGNS

Public funding is the ultimate step in a long line of proposals and enactments designed to generate broadly based funding for political campaigns. It is part of the larger effort to provide campaign resources free of obligation to well-heeled contributors. This goal has been pursued in a variety of ways. One important set of proposals has dealt with the problem of making broadcast time—particularly on television—cheaper and more accessible to candidates. Reformers have frequently suggested, for instance, that the "equal time" provison—Section 315(a)—of the Communications Act of 1934 be repealed. Section 315(a) requires that stations which give air time to any candidate must give the same amount of time to every other candidate for the same office. Its effect has been to keep most stations from giving any free time to any candidate, to avoid giving time to a host of minor party and independent candidates who would demand their legal share. It was suspended for the 1960 presidental election, permitting the debates that year, but since has been kept in force despite a number of attempts to alter or suspend it again.

The 1970 bill vetoed by President Nixon included a section repealing the equal-time requirement for presidential election only; it was widely speculated that Nixon's true reason for vetoing the bill was to avoid a debate in 1972, which would have been difficult without 315(a). The Senate's versions of the 1971 and 1974 cam-

65. U.S., House, *Public Financing*, p. 11.

paign finance reform laws also included repeal of 315(a), but for all federal candidates, not only those for president and vice president. The House once again objected; its members (led by Wayne Hays) were loathe to give broadcasters the discretion repeal would have allowed. They did not disguise their distrust of both local station owners and the national networks. Republicans were unwilling to repeal equal time only for presidential contests, since it would help whoever challenged the Republican president; Democrats chose not to push for partial repeal for fear of inviting a veto. Conference committees therefore dropped repeal in both instances.

Broadcasters have supported repeal of 315(a) most strongly; they have found other proposals to ease access to broadcast media less enchanting. The networks and local broadcasters split over the section in the FECA which requires stations to sell air time to candidates at the lowest unit rate charged to any customer for an equivalent time segment. The networks supported it; local stations, which bear the cost, did not. It is the only reform so far enacted that actually assists congressional campaigning, but it was only passed in conjunction with the 1971 limits on broadcast spending.

Other proposals designed to allow candidates cheaper and easier access to the electronic media have gathered little support. The concept of "voters' time," large segments of television time set aside during presidential campaigns for use by major party candidates, was advocated by the prestigeous Twentieth Century Fund and attracted some attention in Congress, but it never became part of any major reform package. Vaguer suggestions that free time be provided all candidates for federal office have been made from time to time, but the complexities arising from the varying structures of media markets and the distribution of congressional districts have kept these proposals from receiving any serious attention.[66] Members of Congress are not, in any case, very likely to legislate free television time for their opponents.

Neither are they interested in supplying any other campaign as-

66. See George White, "Access to Television for Lower-Level Campaigns" (Report to the Campaign Finance Study Group of the Institute of Politics, John F. Kennedy School of Government, Harvard University, 1977).

sistance. For example, one universally recognized incumbent resource of great value is the frank. Some reform-minded members have proposed extending the privilege of free mailings to all candidates in federal elections; it has not been a popular idea. During the 1973 House Administration Committee hearings, Representative Udall was asked why he had dropped a provision for free mailings from his campaign finance bill. His reply: "On practical grounds. I got my head torn off in the House dining room."[67] Congress did restrict the use of the frank during the twenty-eight days prior to a primary or general election, later extending the restriction to sixty days; but this action was only taken in response to litigation that was bringing judicial scrutiny to bear on this perquisite.[68] Congress is plainly much more willing to limit than to expand campaign resources.

Tax Incentives for Individual Contributions

The enactment of tax incentives for campaign contributions appears to be an exception to this generalization. Their actual effect, however, has been minimal. President Kennedy's commission proposed tax incentives as a means for broadening the financial base of campaigns. The question of what kind of tax incentives has drawn a strictly partisan response. Democrats prefer tax credits, which can be claimed by all taxpayers and which give each taxpayer the same benefit regardless of income. Republicans prefer tax deductions for contributions; they can only be taken by taxpayers who itemize, who fall disproportionately into upper-income brackets. A compromise was arranged and attached as a rider to the Revenue Act of 1971: credits (of one-half of political contributions up to $25, double that amount for a joint return) and deductions (of up to $50, again twice that for a joint return); these amounts were doubled in 1974.

So far, tax incentives have proven ineffective. In 1972, only 2.5 percent of taxpayers took the credit option, only 1.3 percent the de-

---

67. U.S., House, *Federal Election Reform*, p. 239.
68. *1973 Congressional Quarterly Almanac* (Washington, D.C.: Congressional Quarterly, Inc., 1974), pp. 722–25.

duction.[69] The proportion of citizens contributing to political campaigns has not increased at all. There is actually little reason to think tax incentives should make much difference. As I argued in chapter 3, the victory of a preferred candidate or party is, from the perspective of most citizens, a public good. They enjoy the fruits of victory whether or not they have borne any of the cost necessary to achieve it. Since their small contribution would have no discernible effect on the outcome of the election, it is irrational for them to incur the cost involved in making it. Tax incentives in no way alter this circumstance. Neither do they affect those for whom the act of making the contribution itself provides sufficient psychological satisfaction for it to be worth the cost. They have little effect, one way or the other.

Matching incentives for campaign contributions are subject to the same criticism, but it is less telling here because matching grants effectively stimulate candidates to more intense pursuit of small contributions. Matching grants come from public funds, however, and that raises quite another set of issues, the subject of the next chapter.

69.   Adamany and Agree, *Political Money*, p. 126.

7 ☆ THE FUTURE OF CAMPAIGN FINANCE REGULATION: PUBLIC FUNDS?

Public funding of all federal election campaigns, the ultimate goal of many reformers, is in some ways the logical conclusion of the current cycle of campaign finance reform. The 1974 FECA Amendments enacted public funding for presidential campaigns, and in 1976 the first publicly subsidized presidential contests were held. But, contrary to expectations, public funding has not been extended to congressional campaigns, and there are clear signs that the tide of reform is receding before this final step can be taken.

This chapter looks into the politics of public funding for congressional campaigns. The regression equations developed in chapter 2 are used to project the likely electoral consequences of several public funding schemes, including those of the two major bills before the House and Senate during the 95th Congress (1977–78). It concludes with speculation about the future of congressional campaign finance—of money in congressional elections—in the absence of public subsidies.

PUBLIC FUNDS FOR POLITICAL CAMPAIGNS: THE BASIC ARGUMENTS

The fundamental case for public funding is quite straightforward.[1] Competitive elections are expensive; the money is necessary, and

"Public Funds for Congressional Campaigns: Who Would Benefit?" by the author is reprinted from *Political Finance*, Sage Electoral Studies Yearbook, vol. 5, Herbert E. Alexander, editor, © 1979 by permission of the Publisher, Sage Publications, Inc. (Beverly Hills/London).

1. The most thorough case for public funding of campaigns is made by Joel Fleishman. See his "Private Money and Public Elections: Another American Dilemma," in *Changing Campaign Techniques*, ed. Louis Maisel, Sage Electoral Studies Yearbook 2 (Beverly Hills, Calif.: Sage Publications, 1976), pp. 19–54.

campaign costs should continue to grow. Privately financed campaigns will invariably give an inordinate advantage to wealthy individuals and interests, violating the democratic principle of political equality. It is simply impossible to raise enough money in small, voluntary donations to conduct serious campaigns. Candidates must therefore obligate themselves to the monied elites who control campaign funds and, once elected, will inevitably serve their interests. "By providing the capital needed for effective campaigning, the wealthy exercise political advantage. Through their influence over public policy, the wealthy are able to secure their economic advantage."[2]

Public funding, partial or complete, eliminates this problem. The prohibition of all but small individual contributions prevents the interests of the wealthy and organized from dominating; the additional funds necessary to run competitive campaigns are made up from public sources.

Indeed, Olson points out that the usual solution to the free-rider problem preventing the acquisition of public goods is coercion; it is perfectly rational for individuals to vote to coerce everyone—including themselves—to pay a share of the cost of producing a public good (assuming the benefit to them outweighs their cost); if they must pay, so must everyone else, so the good can be attained.[3] Even the most liberal governments rely on compulsory taxes, not voluntary contributions.

But this reasoning has not been applied directly to campaign finance. Theoretically, if the collective benefit is taken to be victory for the preferred party or candidate, the solution would be to compel those who support the party or candidate to finance the campaign. But the idea is too flagrantly contrary to American political values if put in those terms (not to mention the problem of implementation). The collective or public good must be conceived as something else: clean, fair, honest elections. Fleishman makes the argument: "After all, elections are at least as much of a 'public

2. Ibid., p. 25.
3. Mancur Olson, Jr., *The Logic of Collective Action* (Cambridge, Mass.: Harvard University Press, 1965), pp. 85–91.

good' as public schools, public parks, and national defense, and we all assess taxpayers for those costs whether or not they use the facilities and regardless of their opinions of the policies."[4]

The arguments against public funding are also grounded in basic political values, but they rely heavily on empirical observation as well.[5] Forcing people to supply funds for political campaigns is a direct infringement on political liberty. Even a voluntary tax checkoff scheme ultimately makes everyone pay to make up the lost revenue and so to fund indirectly the campaigns of candidates they detest. The right of free political expression includes the right to refuse to finance the expression of ideas or positions one finds repugnant.

Public funding would also inhibit voluntary participation in politics and would destroy an important link between the people and their representatives. Bernard M. Shanley, then Vice Chairman of the Republican National Committee, told a Senate committee in 1973 that "Federal financing of political campaigns is entirely contrary to America's basic concepts of participatory democracy and individual involvement in the political process of candidate selection and advocacy."[6] Representative Frenzel told the same committee that a candidate's ability to raise funds is a valuable "barometer of: (1) a candidate's popular support, (2) public approval of his record while in office, and (3) his seriousness about serving in public office."[7] Specifically, "private financing functions in a manner similar to the free market. It has been one of the traditional ways of determining the popularity and attractiveness of a candidate. Popular candidates rarely have a shortage of funds, while unpopular candidates are usually unable to raise large amounts of funds."[8]

4. Fleishman, "Private Money and Public Elections," p. 36.

5. A catalogue of arguments against public funding is found in Jewel Bellush and William J. D. Boyd, "Subsidies for Campaign Time: Some Caveats," in *Changing Campaign Techniques*, pp. 55–78.

6. U.S., Congress, Senate, Committee on Rules and Administration, Subcommittee on Privileges and Elections, *Public Financing of Federal Elections*, 93rd Cong. 1st sess., hearings September 18–21, 1973, p. 317.

7. Ibid., p. 151.

8. Ibid.

Additional common objections are that public funding is either unfair to minor party and independent candidates or unduly encourages them (depending on the rules governing the distribution of funds); that government money inevitably comes with strings, and the strings will ultimately be pulled by current officeholders to the detriment of their challengers; and that all proposed public funding schemes favor incumbents over challengers.

These and other arguments were offered repeatedly during the hearings and debates on public subsidy legislation, but it should come as no surprise that the choices made finally rested on more mundane questions of personal and partisan political advantage. So what was sauce for the presidential goose was not, it turned out, sauce for the congressional gander.

Public Funds for Presidential Campaigns

The successful drive toward public funding of presidential campaigns began with the revival of Senator Long's income tax checkoff idea. A section allowing individuals to designate on their returns that $1 of their taxes be placed in a special fund to finance presidential campaigns was attached to the Revenue Act of 1971, an important administration tax package. Division over the issue was strongly partisan, and with good reason. The Democrats were still $9 million in debt from the 1968 election with only a year to go until the next. Republicans, with plenty of money, not unreasonably saw it as a scheme to bail out the Democrats. The immediate interests of both parties dovetailed nicely with their traditional rhetorical attitudes; Democrats could support the scheme as one that would keep wealth from corrupting politics; Republicans could attack it as an assault on individual freedom and a further intrusion of government into political life. Only two Republican senators supported the measure, and only then because an amendment was adopted permitting taxpayers to designate which party would get the money—a provision that was repealed by an amendment to the Debt Ceiling Act of 1973.[9]

9. David W. Adamany and George E. Agree, *Political Money: A Strategy for*

President Nixon adamantly opposed the idea—no surprise in light of subsequent revelations—and to avoid a threatened veto, Congress delayed the law's effect until after the 1972 election and required that the money be specifically appropriated from the fund before it could be distributed to candidates. Congress did exactly that through provisions in the FECA Amendments of 1974. That law provided full public financing of major party general election campaigns for president (the amount is adjusted to the Consumer Price Index; each candidate received $21.8 million in 1976) and matching grant subsidies for primary contests. For primaries, candidates who raise at least $100,000 in amounts of at least $5,000 from twenty states in contributions of $250 or less have these contributions matched by funds from the checkoff up to a total of $5 million per candidate. The law also doubled the amount of the checkoff.

This legislation was also unpopular among Republicans and would not have become law had it not been for Watergate. President Nixon promised in March 1974 to veto any bill that included public funding; the House passed its version of such a bill just as Nixon was resigning. Gerald Ford also opposed this section of the FECA Amendments, but signed the bill anyway, saying that "the times demand this legislation."[10]

The income tax checkoff generates enough money to finance presidential campaigns at the level legislated by Congress, but it has yet to prove a great popular success, and this has probably worked against the extension of public financing to congressional campaigns. The first year it was in effect (1972), only 7 percent of those filing tax returns chose the option. When, under pressure from Congress and some reform groups, the Internal Revenue Service simplified and publicized the checkoff, participation rose to 15 percent. But since then it has remained in the range 24 to 28 percent. If public funding were extended to congressional cam-

Campaign Financing in America (Baltimore: The Johns Hopkins University Press, 1975), p. 126.

10. Herbert E. Alexander, *Financing Elections: Money, Elections, and Political Reform* (Washington, D.C.: Congressional Quarterly Press, Inc., 1976), p. 142.

paigns, the checkoff fund would probably be insufficient to cover the cost.[11]

Public Funds for Congressional Campaigns

Bills providing partial public funding for congressional campaigns were considered by both houses in 1977. Contrary to the expectations of many observers,[12] neither house enacted public funding legislation. The Senate bill (S 926) was killed by filibuster; the House bill (HR 5157) never got out of committee. Congress' failure to act was somewhat surprising because the ground seemed well prepared for this ultimate step in the transformation of campaign finance policy. In addition to the philosophical arguments mentioned above, the actual state of campaign finance regulation itself supports a solid practical case for some form of public subsidy. Campaigns are more expensive than ever. Contribution restrictions have made raising money more difficult and time-consuming. Wealthy candidates, who may spend unlimited amounts of their own money on campaigns, are at a conspicuous advantage. Since it is hard to raise money from individuals in small amounts (an especially acute problem in the more expensive Senate elections), candidates still depend heavily on contributions from interest groups. And interest groups, now largely shut out of presidential campaign funding, have redirected their resources into congressional campaigns.

Public funding offers an attractive alternative source of the necessary money. It would reduce the pressure to raise money and the time devoted to this unwelcome task. It would diminish the need for group contributions. It would also allow Congress to impose expenditure limits and to restrict candidates' gifts to their own campaigns (at least according to the usual interpretations of *Buckley* v. *Valeo*), a point of no small interest to incumbent members. The

11.   Herbert E. Alexander, "Election Reform in Its Second Stage: Momentum Passing from Reformers to Power Brokers" (Prepared for delivery at the Conference on Political Money and Election Reform: Comparative Perspectives, at the University of Southern California, Los Angeles, December 10, 1977), p. 11.

12.   *C.Q. Weekly Report* 18 (April 16, 1977), p. 707.

1976 experience with presidential campaign funding encourages confidence (perhaps unfounded) that such a policy could be effectively implemented.

Nonetheless, and despite support from the Carter administration and a large majority of the dominant party in Congress (and, it should be noted, the departure of Wayne Hays from the House), public funding legislation has foundered. During the decisive Senate filibuster, opponents of S 926 offered a variety of now-familiar arguments against the bill. It would beget a large and meddlesome bureaucracy; it would unfairly hamper minor parties; it would discourage voluntary participation and force involuntary contributions to candidates. The most telling arguments, however, dealt with the effects of the proposed bill on the competitive positions of the candidates. For it was on this basis that Republicans and southern Democrats cooperated to kill the bill.

The Republican position was that S 926 favored incumbents— hence, mainly, Democrats—because the spending limits that would accompany public funds would not permit challengers to conduct competitive campaigns. The argument that spending limits protect incumbents has been offered every time the issue has come up; the critical difference in 1977 was that Republican senators adopted it as their own, speaking, in effect, for Republican challengers rather than themselves as incumbents. Twenty of forty Republican senators had supported the decisive cloture vote that kept public funding for congressional campaigns in the Senate's version of the 1974 bill; only two of 36 voted for cloture in 1977. No fewer than 14 Republican senators switched to opposition between 1974 and 1977.

Reasons for this shift are not hard to discern. Republicans cannot ignore the diminishing strength of their party indefinitely; more attention to the fates of Republican challengers seems essential if the party is not to disappear as a political force. Republican incumbents who have survived the two post-Watergate elections may feel relatively secure. Republican candidates raise money in smaller individual contributions more easily than do Democrats. The intense pressure to support reform generated by Watergate has dissipated. And senators can no longer depend on Wayne Hays to keep the

House from supporting subsidies for congressional campaigns.[13]

Democratic proponents of S 926 argued that, on the contrary, subsidies and limits would make elections more competitive by equalizing expenditures. It would provide funds to candidates of modest means without tying them to wealthy interests and individuals—the familiar long-term reformers' goal. Incumbents now outspend challengers decisively; they also win election very consistently; any policy that makes it easier for challengers to acquire funds and cuts down on incumbent spending will increase electoral competition.

The southern Democrats who helped the Republicans sustain the filibuster did not disagree with this position, but took it as a basis for their opposition to the bill. They contended that S 926 would inspire Republican opposition in what are still basically one-party states; candidates would run simply because the money was there. Furthermore—and more critically—they argued that public funding would inevitably be extended to primary elections, something they were obviously anxious to prevent.[14]

The Senate bill, S 926, would establish a general election spending limit of $250,000 plus 10 cents times the voting-age population of the state (the bill applied only to the Senate; each house writes its own legislation). Major party candidates would immediately be eligible for 25 percent of this total as a flat grant; contributions of up to $100 per donor would then be matched up to the spending limit. A maximum of 62.5 percent of the limit might thus be publicly funded. Candidates accepting public money could spend no more than $35,000 of their own money on the campaign. Third-party and independent candidates are not eligible for the flat grant but would receive matching funds if they raised 10 percent of the spending limit or $100,000, whichever is less, in individual gifts of $100 or less. Primary elections would not be covered.

The major House bill, HR 5157, required candidates to gather a minimum of $10,000 in private contributions of $100 or less per

13. Alexander, "Election Reform in Its Second Stage," p. 6.

14. See, for example, Senator Long's comments in U.S., *Congressional Record*, 95th Cong., 1st sess., July 27, 1977, p. 13057.

donor to be eligible for matching funds; contributions (again, of $100 or less per contributor) would then be matched dollar for dollar up to a total of $50,000 in public funds. Candidates accepting grants would be required to limit their total spending to $150,000, and they could spend no more than $25,000 of their own money. This law, too, would apply only to general elections.

WHAT DIFFERENCE WOULD PUBLIC FUNDS MAKE?

The regression equations estimated earlier in this book show that the marginal return on campaign expenditures is much greater for challengers than for incumbents and is otherwise generally greater for Republicans than for Democrats. Obviously, any increase in spending by both candidates will help challengers and, *ceteris paribus*, Republicans, and any measure that effectively restricts campaign spending will have the opposite result. These are general conclusions. The effect of any particular form of public funding depends on the size of the subsidy, the rules governing its application, and the severity of the limits imposed. It is possible to project the potential impact of any public funding system by calculating how the results of the 1972, 1974, and 1976 congressional elections would have differed had it been in effect. We simply adjust the expenditure figure for each candidate according to what he would have spent under the public funding scheme and compute his expected vote using the parameters estimated for the regression equations; for several reasons, the OLS estimates are superior for this exercise, although the 2SLS estimates would support the same general conclusions.[15]

Of primary interest are naturally the matching grant systems proposed under S 926 and HR 5157, but these can be instructively compared to similar systems without spending limits, to flat grants to candidates of the full amount to which they could aspire under

15. See Gary C. Jacobson, ''The Electoral Consequences of Public Subsidies for Congressional Campaigns'' (Prepared for delivery at the 1977 Annual Meeting of the American Political Science Association, Washington, D.C., September 1–4, 1977), pp. 13–14.

the law (for example, $50,000 for House candidates), and to schemes that allow every candidate to spend to the prescribed limit.

Several assumptions necessarily underlie the analysis. First, inflation must be taken into account; $50,000 was not worth in 1976 what it was in 1972. The Consumer Price Index was used to deflate subsidies to comparable dollar amounts for 1972 and 1974. The 1972 and 1974 equivalents of $50,000 are, in round figures, $37,000 and $44,000, respectively. Similarly, $150,000 is equal to $111,000 in 1972 dollars, $132,000 in 1974 dollars. Comparable adjustments were also made in the Senate subsidy and limit figures.

Another problem is that primary and general election spending are not reported separately. Because there is no way to find out how much of a candidate's money was spent in the primary (if there was one), I simply ignored the difficulty. I assumed, for the analysis, that all reported expenditures were incurred in the general election, and the entire spending figure was used to calculate how much additional money would be due to candidates under the various subsidy schemes. The findings reported in table 5.1 suggest that whether or not a candidate faces primary competition does have some effect on how much he raises (and therefore spends), but the effect is not particularly strong and is not usually statistically significant. Candidate fund-raising strategies would certainly be affected by the offer of public money; one can readily imagine candidates using large contributions to finance primary campaigns while seeking small contributions—eligible for matching funds—to finance the general election.

The primary election problem does suggest one important reservation about the findings reported below. If primary elections are not covered by the public funding system (as would be the case under S 926 and HR 5157), candidates could avoid some of the effects of spending restrictions (to be shown presently) by spending freely in primaries. Indeed, shrewd challengers would make sure they had primary competition.

Only contributions of $100 or less would be matched by public funds under these bills. In general, only about a third of the receipts reported from 1972 through 1976 were made up of contributions this small. However, taking into account the capacity of candidates to adjust their money-raising strategies to take advantage of public funds were they to be available, I assumed for this investigation that half the reported expenditures could have been raised in small amounts, and it is on this basis that eligibility and the level of public funding were computed for each candidate.

As an example of the kind of calculation made, 1972 House candidates who raised at least $14,700 (assuming half that amount, $7,350, was raised in small gifts—this figure being the 1972 equivalent of $10,000) had half their total spending matched up to a total of $37,000 in additional funds; the maximum amount spent could not exceed $111,000 under HR 5157. The same calculation was then repeated without the ceiling. For flat grants, the designated amount was simply added to the amount actually spent. No flat grants were considered for Senate contests, but the effect of subsidizing every candidate up to the limit was analyzed for Senate as well as House candidates.

Incumbents and Challengers

The altered spending figures for each candidate were entered (along with observations on the control variables) into equations 2.1 and 2.2, which were then used to compute the expected percentage of votes for each challenger given the various subsidies and limits. The results of these calculations for House and Senate elections to incumbent-held seats are listed in tables 7.1 and 7.2. The tables show the estimated number of winning challengers, the number expected to get at least 45 percent of the vote, the challengers' expected mean vote share, and the average challenger and incumbent spending figures under the different campaign finance systems.

Notice, first of all, that the combination of subsidies and spending limits proposed in HR 5157 would have had different effects in different election years. In 1972 and 1976, the House bill would

Table 7.1.   Hypothetical Effects of HR 5157 and Other Subsidy Proposals in
House Elections between Challengers and Incumbents, 1972–76

	Challenger's Vote			Average Spending (thousands)	
	+50%	+45%	Average Percent	Chal-lengers	Incum-bents
1972 (N = 296)					
Actual results	9	26	34.5	$ 31.5	$ 50.3
Equation estimates with:					
Actual spending	5	18	34.0	31.5	50.3
HR 5157 subsidy and limit	1	27	34.7	37.8	64.7
HR 5157 subsidy, no limit	16	37	35.3	43.1	71.6
Actual spending					
plus $37,000	16	39	38.1	68.5	87.3
Exact spending of $111,000	2	80	42.8	111.0	111.0
1974 (N = 319)					
Actual results	39	82	35.5	40.2	63.8
Equation estimates with:					
Actual spending	29	58	35.3	40.2	63.8
HR 5157 subsidy and limit	40	76	36.1	49.7	80.7
HR 5157 subsidy, no limit	47	73	36.6	55.9	90.3
Actual spending					
plus $44,000	51	94	39.5	84.2	107.0
Exact spending of $132,000	90	166	44.7	132.0	132.0
1976 (N = 329)					
Actual results	11	46	34.2	51.5	83.2
Equation estimates with:					
Actual spending	8	29	34.2	51.5	83.2
HR 5157 subsidy and limit	0	47	34.8	60.2	103.9
HR 5157 subsidy, no limit	21	55	35.5	70.5	117.6
Actual spending					
plus $50,000	21	56	37.8	101.5	133.2
Exact spending of $150,000	0	101	41.3	150.0	150.0

have reduced the likelihood of a successful challenge considerably.[16] The clear implication is that the limits are too low to allow

16.   These are, to be sure, only *estimates* based on the typical pattern of effects
of campaign spending and other variables in these elections. Candidates can and do
lose even when they spend enough to be *predicted* winners, and they can also win

Table 7.2. Hypothetical Effects of S 926 and Other Subsidy Proposals in
Senate Elections between Challengers and Incumbents, 1972–76

	Challenger's Vote			Average Spending per Voting-Age Person (cents)	
	+50%	+45%	Average Percent	Chal- lengers	Incum- bents
1972 (N = 25)					
Actual results	5	11	41.4	18.0	29.0
Equation estimates with:					
Actual spending	1	8	41.4	18.0	29.0
S 929 subsidy and limit	2	13	44.9	21.5	26.3
S 929 subsidy, no limit	1	13	44.4	31.2	45.2
Exact spending at limit	2	18	46.2	27.9	27.9
1974 (N = 22)					
Actual results	2	9	42.9	24.5	44.1
Equation estimates with:					
Actual spending	3	11	42.9	24.5	44.1
S 929 subsidy and limit	6	11	45.0	23.0	26.6
S 929 subsidy, no limit	6	12	45.9	38.2	60.6
Exact spending at limit	9	11	46.1	27.0	27.0
1976 (N = 23)					
Actual results	9	10	43.8	27.0	31.6
Equation estimates with:					
Actual spending	7	15	43.8	27.0	31.6
S 929 subsidy and limit	4	18	47.4	30.1	32.7
S 929 subsidy, no limit	15	18	50.0	45.1	51.1
Exact spending at limit	4	23	49.1	33.9	33.9

challengers much chance of victory, and, indeed, inspection of individual cases shows that the spending limits are instrumental in de-
creasing the number of challengers predicted to win more than 50
percent of the vote. With the limits removed, the number of expected winning challengers increases sharply. Observe that this occurs even though the incumbent's spending advantage is even
greater in the absence of a spending ceiling (see the two right-hand

when, according to these estimates, they have not spent enough to defeat the incumbent.

columns). Further evidence that spending limits help incumbents is apparent in the results when both candidates spend to the limit; elections would be closer, to be sure—there would be fewer "safe" seats as defined by the 45 percent threshold—but fewer challengers are projected to win than would be without the subsidies and limits.

For 1974, however, the evidence is that subsidies with or without limits would have helped challengers significantly. The spending ceilings still favor incumbents—challengers are predicted to do even better without them—but if all candidates had spent the limit, challengers would have done very well indeed; the number of predicted challenger victories triples.

With the exception of 1972, a similar pattern emerges from the Senate elections. Senate Bill 926 would have aided challengers in 1974 but would have damaged their chances in 1976; in the latter year, subsidies without spending limits would have, by projection, helped them very considerably indeed. Similarly, if all candidates had spent the maximum allowable amount, even more challengers are projected to win in 1974, but notably fewer in 1976. The 1972 elections fit neither of these patterns; no system would have made much difference that year; recall that incumbent as well as challenger spending had a substantial and statistically significant impact on the outcomes of those elections.

An explanation of the difference between 1974 and the other two election years no doubt lies in the extraordinary political situation that prevailed in 1974. National short-term forces were not a prominent influence in the 1972 and 1976 congressional elections. Quite the contrary is true of 1974. Watergate, the collapse of the Nixon administration, President Ford's poorly timed pardon of the former president, and a troubled economy were the source of serious problems for the Republican party. The Democrats fielded more experienced, better-financed challengers; more than 95 percent of the projected winning challengers are Democrats under any of the public funding systems. Only Democrats were projected to defeat incumbent Senators in 1974, no matter how these campaigns were financed.

Partisan Effects

Whether or not public funding would help one party's candidates more than the other's was of course a crucial issue in the congressional debates on public funding legislation. In 1974, public funding would have helped Democrats win an even greater number of seats. The effects are much more balanced for 1972; subsidies with limits would have hurt challengers of both parties; subsidies without limits or simple flat grants would have helped them. The edge, if any, would be slightly to the Republicans. For 1976, however, seven of the eight projected winning challengers—given the actual spending figures—are Republicans. Nineteen of the twenty-one projected winners given flat grants or subsidies without limits are Republicans. Evidently, most of the vulnerable incumbents in 1976 were Democrats; indeed, no fewer than forty-nine Democrats had been elected to formerly Republican seats in 1974. Under present circumstances, the limits imposed by HR 5157 would, in fact, help keep Democratic incumbents in office.

Aside from 1974, S 926 is not projected to have any clear partisan impact on contests between challengers and incumbents. In 1976, for example, two of the four challengers predicted to win under the bill were Republicans; with the spending restrictions dropped, seven of the projected winners were Republicans.

A further idea of the partisan impact of public funding can be gleaned from an analysis of elections for open seats. Again, analysis is based on the regression estimates reported in chapter 2 (equations 2.3 and 2.4). These indicated that spending is, indeed, more important to Republican candidates and that Senate Republicans were therefore correct in assuming that spending restrictions normally work to their detriment—and not only because most current incumbents are Democrats. As candidates of a party claimed by a dwindling number of voters, Republicans rely more heavily on campaigning—and so campaign spending—to do well at the polls. On the other hand, extra funds from public sources would also do them the most good. The hypothetical effects of S 926 and HR

5157 and their variants in elections for open seats can be projected by redoing the calculations made for challenger–incumbent races for these contests. The results are displayed in tables 7.3 and 7.4.

The findings for Senate open-seat contests are most clear-cut; subsidies with limits favor Democrats, matching funds without spending limits favor Republicans. It is the typical incumbent–

Table 7.3.   Hypothetical Effects of HR 5157 and Other Subsidy Proposals in House Elections for Open Seats, 1972–76

	Republican's Vote			Average Spending (thousands)	
	+50%	+45%	Average Percent	Repub-licans	Demo-crats
1972 (N = 53)					
Actual results	37	43	51.9	$ 94.3	$ 97.6
Equation estimates with:					
Actual spending	36	44	52.4	94.3	97.6
HR 5157 subsidy and limit	40	44	53.1	96.9	85.5
HR 5157 subsidy, no limit	39	44	53.6	126.5	125.9
Actual spending					
plus $37,000	39	44	53.6	131.3	134.6
Exact spending of $111,000	41	50	53.0	111.0	111.0
1974 (N = 58)					
Actual results	13	23	42.1	79.2	102.2
Equation estimates with:					
Actual spending	9	22	42.1	79.2	102.2
HR 5157 subsidy and limit	17	29	44.2	95.8	109.1
HR 5157 subsidy, no limit	24	31	46.3	111.1	138.5
Actual spending					
plus $44,000	25	35	47.9	123.2	146.2
Exact spending of $132,000	23	42	49.0	132.0	132.0
1976 (N = 50)					
Actual results	13	26	40.7	97.7	144.1
Equation estimates with:					
Actual spending	7	15	40.7	97.7	144.1
HR 5157 subsidy and limit	5	17	41.0	98.2	125.3
HR 5157 subsidy, no limit	12	21	43.0	129.9	185.7
Actual spending					
plus $50,000	12	24	48.1	147.7	194.1
Exact spending of $150,000	5	23	45.2	150.0	150.0

Table 7.4. Hypothetical Effects of S 926 and Other Subsidy Proposals in Senate Elections for Open Seats, 1972–76

	Republican's Vote			Average Spending per Voting-Age Person (cents)	
	+50%	+45%	Average Percent	Repub- licans	Demo- crats
1972–76 (N = 25)					
Actual results	9	18	46.1	44.3	47.2
Equation estimates with:					
Actual spending	7	17	46.0	44.3	47.2
S 929 subsidy and limit	3	19	46.4	33.8	35.2
S 929 subsidy, no limit	12	22	49.7	65.1	68.9
Exact spending at limit	5	21	47.2	35.3	35.3

challenger pattern, with Republicans as challengers. The same holds for 1976 House open-seat races. For 1974, Republicans are projected to do significantly better with matching funds even if they are accompanied by limits, although without spending ceilings they would do better still. This is the only year in which HR 5157 would have increased average Republican spending significantly in these races, and Republican spending had its strongest effect on the outcome that year (see table 2.4), so the pattern is understandable. In 1972, on the other hand, the limits imposed by HR 5157 would have helped Republicans by reducing Democratic spending.

Republican senators were justified, then, in believing that S 926 was not likely to help their party rebuild. At the same time, it is not at all certain that southern Democrats were wrong in fearing that the same bill would generate more consistent Republican opposition in southern states. The availability of public funds would surely make running for federal office more inviting to candidates whose party is locally weak. Southern Democrats accustomed to no more than token challenges in general elections might well find themselves opposed more frequently and more vigorously under S 926. But Republicans were also correct in thinking that the bill would not help them actually win more frequently in the south—or elsewhere—since the limits would make it more difficult than ever to mount a successful challenge. Thus both components of the filibustering coalition reached reasonable judgments about how the bill would affect their interests, even though they offered apparently contradictory arguments to support their positions.

The Democratic majority view, that public funds plus spending limits would permit fairer competition for congressional seats by reducing the spending advantage of incumbents, is erroneous on several counts. The data in table 7.3 indicate that HR 5157 would actually increase the expenditure differential between incumbents and challengers; more incumbents would cross the threshold, and the matching grant system would magnify their initial advantage. However, S 926 would evidently reduce the average spending difference between Senate incumbents and challengers (by increasing challenger spending and reducing incumbent spending). But even this would not help challengers under normal electoral circumstances, because it is the absolute rather than the relative amount spent by challengers that matters; expenditure ceilings would diminish their chances of winning even though they tend to equalize spending.

Characteristically, no Republican support was given the alternative of public funds without limits on spending. This alternative would have the most positive effect on competition by financing vigorous challenges without inhibiting campaigning. Although the incumbent protection motivation so easily construed from previous campaign finance reform legislation[17] was not so obviously prevalent during the 1977 debates, at least among Republicans, no substantial group of incumbents, not excluding Republicans, seems ready to support public funding without expenditure restrictions. Among Democrats it is quite likely that much of the support public funding now enjoys can be traced to the desire to circumvent the constitutional ban on spending limits.

The tables reveal some additional useful information about the

17. See Gary C. Jacobson, "Reforming Congressional Campaign Finance: The Incumbency Dilemma" (Prepared for delivery at the Conference on Political Money and Election Reform: Comparative Perspectives, at the University of Southern California, Los Angeles, December 10, 1977).

workings of different public funding schemes. Notice that, in the absence of spending limits, the matching grant system proposed in HR 5157 would have about the same effect on competition—as measured by the number of projected winning challengers—as would a system of flat grants of $50,000 to each candidate. But by requiring candidates to prove some viability before receiving any money and by no more than matching private contributions, the matching grant system would be much less expensive. In every case the flat grant system is projected to cost about twice as much as matching grants without spending limits, three times as much as matching grants with spending limits. For example, a $50,000 flat grant to two candidates in 435 House contests would cost $43.5 million; a system of matching grant subsidies without spending restrictions would run to about $23.2 million; with spending limits, the cost would (given past experience) amount to about $12.8 million. If subsidies are enacted and cost is a consideration—as it surely must be—the matching grant system will stimulate competition just as effectively as would flat grants, and at a much lower cost, *provided that spending limits are not imposed.*

To recapitulate briefly: congressional elections are affected much more by what challengers spend than by what incumbents spend. The more spending by all candidates, the better challengers are likely to do. Campaign finance reforms that get more money into the hands of challengers will enhance competition for congressional seats; reforms that make it more difficult to acquire and spend money will have the opposite effect. A combined system of public funds and spending limits of the kind proposed in the two major bills before Congress in 1977 should have different effects, depending on the circumstances of the election year. When strong short-term forces favor candidates of one party, the subsidies provided should increase the number of successful challenges by its candidates; they will need less money to win in the first place, so the subsidies will be more effective, and the spending limits will be less obstructive. In the absence of compelling short-term forces, however—and this includes most election years—successful challenges will be harder to mount, and incumbents, therefore, more secure. Public funding will tend to exaggerate whatever trends exist at the time of the election.

Another tendency of such legislation will be to favor Democrats at the expense of Republicans. Apart from the fact that more incumbents are Democrats, Republicans, as candidates of a minority party, rely more heavily on campaign spending to win elections. The exception to this generalization would of course be an election in which strong short-term forces favored the Republican party, but it would be hard to argue that Republicans would therefore be wise to support such legislation on the expectation that they will benefit more often than they will suffer under its provisions.

CONGRESSIONAL CAMPAIGN FINANCE REGULATION: THE FUTURE

If public funding for congressional campaigns is now a dormant issue, still many of the practical arguments in its favor remain. The cost of campaigning will no doubt continue to grow. Candidates will continue to have trouble raising money from individuals because of the limit; the problem remains particularly acute in Senate campaigns and in the more expensive—and therefore competitive —House campaigns. The limit on individual contributions was mentioned most frequently in the FEC survey as hampering fund raising in campaigns where more than $100,000 was spent.[18]

Wealthy candidates continue to enjoy a distinct and seemingly unfair advantage; their personal spending is unrestricted, while less fortunate nonwealthy opponents must drum up many smaller contributions. And small contributions come disproportionately from the more extreme ideologues and more intense single-issue constituencies. One professional fund raiser, a liberal Democrat, advised the Senate Rules and Administration Committee in 1977 that ''if you decide that public financing is not in the public interest, then you

18. *A Study of the Impact of the Federal Election Campaign Act on the 1976 Election* (Prepared for the Federal Election Commission by Decision Making Information and Hart Research Associates, 1977), p. 81.

will have to consider seriously the repeal of the contribution limits contained in the 1974 Act. The Supreme Court . . . has left us in a position so manifestly unfair to poor candidates running against rich ones that I believe the Congress should do away with all limits and let candidates raise what they will from whomever they will in whatever amounts they can."[19]

Reform groups continue to push for lower contribution limits, no doubt intending to enhance the prospects for public funding by making private campaign money even scarcer.[20] The attack has focused on PACs. The law as it now stands encourages the proliferation of interest group committees; they provide a growing share of campaign funds, and the potential for further growth (at least of corporate PACs) is almost limitless. Since the original goal of many reformers was to reduce the influence of just such groups, it is hardly surprising that this circumstance is viewed with considerable alarm. Senator Kennedy argued that "the proliferation of such committees may be only just beginning, as more and more special interest groups and organizations join the parade. And their lobbyists are seldom far behind. . . . The interests of the average citizen, the ordinary voter, are in danger of being swamped by the rising tide of special interest groups."[21]

Organized labor has been especially concerned with the multiplication of corporate PACs. Labor's political activities have not grown under the new regulations; union and labor groups have simply continued to do what they have done for years; their potential for expanded activity is relatively small.[22] Corporate PACs have only begun to exploit the opportunity provided by current legislation, but growth has been steady. FEC data on the number of corporate PACs registered with the commission tell the story:

19. U.S., Congress, Senate, Committee on Rules and Administration, *Federal Election Reform Proposals of 1977*, 95th Cong., 1st sess., hearings May 4–6 and 11, 1977, p. 348.

20. U.S., Congress, House, Committee on House Administration, *Public Financing of Congressional Elections*, 95th Cong., 1st sess., hearings May 18 and 19, and June 21, 23, and 28, and July 12, 1977, pp. 10–11.

21. U.S., Senate, *Election Reform Proposals of 1977*, p. 187.

22. Alexander, "Election Reform in Its Second Stage," p. 1.

Date	11/75	5/76	12/76	10/77	12/77	3/78	5/78
PACs	139	294	433	508	538	595	645

The potential for further growth is enormous: "If all companies in the $10 million or more asset category (.021 percent of all corporations) are regarded as potential PAC registrants, currently registered PACs constitute a meager .027 percent of all such companies. In short, the market for potential PAC formations is virtually untapped even if we consider only the very largest firms."[23]

Labor leaders have therefore supported public funding as a way of dealing with what they perceive to be a real threat to their political clout; with public funding, they would be able to carry on their traditional registration, canvassing, and mobilization activities, while corporate involvement in campaigns would be severely restricted. Malbin argues forcefully that labor was the prime beneficiary of publicly financed presidential campaigns and would similarly benefit from an extension of public funding to congressional campaigns.[24]

Political Parties

Direct grants to congressional candidates would have left the parties with an even smaller role than they now play in congressional elections. The failure of public funding legislation has given them a reprieve of sorts. The 1976 FECA Amendments allowed national party committees to contribute up to $17,500 to a Senate candidate and $10,000 to a House candidate in a calendar year, but other party committees are treated like any other PAC and must abide by the $5,000 limit. The proportionate share of funds supplied by the parties remains relatively small. Agranoff has suggested a new role for parties under present electoral conditions: they can become centers of expertise in the technology of campaigning, giving candi-

23. Edwin M. Epstein, "The Rise of Political Action Committees"(Colloquium paper, Woodrow Wilson International Center for Scholars, June 15, 1978), p. 76.
24. Michael J. Malbin, "Labor, Business, and Money—A Post Election Analysis," *National Journal* 9 (March 19, 1977): 417.

dates the benefits of economies to scale in some of the expensive campaign operations: polling, canvassing, ad production, and so forth.[25] National Republican committees, with more money than they can legally transfer to congressional candidates, have been moving in this direction.

In March 1978 the House Administration Committee reported, on a straight party-line vote, a bill amending the FECA to lower the limits on national party contributions and direct spending for congressional candidates drastically. The move was patently partisan; at the time, Republicans had gathered $6.2 million for the 1978 campaigns, the Democrats, $1.5 million.[26] The bill did not pass, but it showed how thoroughly partisan campaign finance issues had become. The suspicion among Republicans that further campaign finance "reforms" were designed to apply the coup de grace to their party has probably solidified into a conviction, diminishing the chances for any further significant legislative change. In particular, the unified opposition to public funding is not likely to weaken.

Independent Expenditures

The Supreme Court determined in *Buckley* v. *Valeo* that restrictions could not be placed on money spent independently of a candidate's campaign. The door is therefore open to unlimited spending by any individual or group to influence an election as long as it is in no way coordinated with one of the campaigns. No one knows what the long-term consequences of this permission will be. Independent expenditures were not a prominent feature of the 1976 campaigns, but the time between the Court's decision and the election was short. Candidates and campaign managers are understandably suspicious of independent expenditures;[27] they cannot control

25. Robert Agranoff, "The Role of Political Parties in the New Campaigning," in *The New Style in Election Campaigns*, ed. Robert Agranoff, 2d ed. (Boston: Holbrook Press, Inc., 1976), pp. 123–141.

26. David S. Broder, "Democrats Tilt Reform Bill," *Hartford Courant*, March 11, 1978, p. 18.

27. Xandra Kayden, "Report of a Conference on Campaign Finance Based on the Experience of the 1976 Presidential Campaigns" (Prepared for the Campaign Fi-

what these self-designated "supporters" do, and it is easy to imagine how this kind of help could backfire: "Vote for Jones; he's not afraid to use America's nuclear might!" The independent expenditure loophole plainly adds an unpredictable joker to the campaign finance deck.

THE PUBLIC AND THE POLITICIANS

If we are to believe all sides to the campaign finance policy debate, nothing less is at stake than the public's faith in the political system and its leaders. Those who support public subsidies as a way to limit or even eliminate private campaign contributions like to argue that this is the only way people can be convinced that elected officials will not sell them out to special interests. Their opponents argue that, on the contrary, public funds and restrictions on private participation can only widen the gap between the public and its leaders. Both factions point to the steady decline in the turnout of voters since 1960 as evidence of the danger.

Actually, there is no reason to believe that anything Congress does about campaign finance will do much to raise its popularity or esteem.[28] Public opinion on campaign finance questions is ambiguous where it is not misinformed. This presents Congress with a dilemma that guarantees a goring on one horn or the other.

The public's attitude seems to be that there is too much campaigning already. The most frequently sought change in political campaigns reported by Gallup's respondents in 1974 and 1976 was to reduce spending limits; the third most popular change was to shorten the campaign period.[29] Most people think too much money is spent on campaigns. They are wrong. More often too little is spent for there to be a real contest.

---

nance Study Group of the Institute of Politics, John F. Kennedy School of Government, Harvard University, 1977), p. 41.

28. Representative Wiggins made this point during the House hearings on HR 5157: "I just want to suggest to you that we are not going to buy confidence or public esteem by the passage of this bill, or the passage of any bill. It is going to be our performance." In U..S., House, *Public Financing*, p. 158.

29. *Gallup Opinion Index*, Report No. 138 (January 1977), p. 22.

There is also evidence that the public favors public funding of congressional campaigns. In 1977 Gallup posed the following question: "It has been suggested the federal government provide a fixed amount of money for the election campaigns of candidates for Congress and that all private contributions from other sources be prohibited. Do you think this is a good idea or a poor idea?" Nationally, 57 percent found it a good idea, 32 percent a poor idea, with 11 percent having no opinion. Majorities of those expressing an opinion in all of Gallup's political and socioeconomic categories thought it a good idea.[30]

Supporters of public funding were elated. But members of Congress felt little public pressure from the folks back home to enact public subsidies. Behavioral evidence suggested that the public was not exactly smitten by the idea. Less than 30 percent of the taxpayers have opted to check off $2 for the presidential campaign fund. Oregon voters turned down a public funding proposal two to one. Only 3.5 percent of Maryland's taxpayers agreed to pay $2 extra on their state tax bill to finance campaigns in the state.[31] Given widespread public doubts about what politicians are doing with tax dollars, it is difficult to imagine overwhelming support for having them spent in political campaigns.

The dilemma comes down to this: candidates need money for campaigns. There is no way they can get enough to finance a competitive race in small individual contributions; most of the public is contented to enjoy a free ride. They must therefore rely on larger individual and special interest contributions or on public subsidies. If they opt for the former, they leave themselves open to at least suspicions of corruption. No matter how innocent, they cannot easily avoid the inference that their votes are influenced by their campaign contributors.

If, on the other hand, they accept public subsidies, they are open to the charge of going on politicians' welfare; the money they "waste" on the campaign—and the public seems to think that an awful lot is wasted—is not even their own, but the taxpayers'

30. Ibid., Report No. 144 (July 1977), p. 12.
31. U.S., House, *Public Financing*, p. 175.

hardearned dollars. It is very doubtful that the public would tolerate subsidies anywhere near the size that would permit effective competition in most congressional constituencies; it is almost certain that a public funding system that continued to permit private contributions and did not limit spending—the kind of system, in other words, that would effectively increase competition for congressional seats—would be anathema.

Since members of Congress have little to gain—or lose, for that matter—in either case, they remain free to make campaign finance policy as it suits their individual and partisan interests. They will no doubt continue to do so.

EPILOGUE: THE 1978 ELECTION
AND ITS AFTERMATH

The electoral cycle is no more sparing of scholars than it is of members of Congress. Since I completed the body of this book, another election has taken place and Congress has once more considered—and rejected—public subsidies for congressional campaigns. The Federal Election Commission has recently published preliminary data on 1978 congressional campaign finances. This epilogue incorporates the analysis of campaign spending patterns and effects in 1978 and chronicles another failed attempt to finance congressional campaigns with public money. At the risk of destroying the suspense, I will report at the outset that neither the 1978 election nor its aftermath inspired any important revision of earlier interpretations or conclusions.

CAMPAIGN FINANCES IN 1978

Congressional campaign finance practices have not remained static. Some familiar trends have continued, with increasingly pronounced effects on the politics of campaign finance regulation.

Total campaign contributions and expenditures increased more between 1976 and 1978 than over any other two-year period since reliable data became available in 1972. The average House campaign cost about $112,000; even with inflation controlled, this represents a robust 20 percent increase over 1976. The average Senate candidate spent about $950,000 in 1978; in 1972, the last time the same seats were contested, the average expenditure was about $350,000. Adjusted for inflation, Senate campaign spending has increased 70 percent since 1972.[1]

1. The campaign finance data for 1978 are from the Federal Election Commis-

These averages were driven up by some spectacularly expensive individual campaigns. Senator Helms of North Carolina spent nearly $7.5 million in his successful bid for reelection. One House challenger reported spending more than $1.1 million, nearly all of it his own money; two others, and several incumbents and candidates for open seats, spent more than half a million dollars each. But even discounting extreme cases, more money was available to campaigns than ever before.

Table E.1 lists the average campaign expenditures of House and Senate candidates in 1978 according to party and incumbency sta-

Table E.1. Average Expenditures in Campaigns for the U.S. House of Representatives and the U.S. Senate, 1978

		Democrats	Republicans
House of Representatives			
	Incumbents	$111,424 (200)[a]	$138,765 (109)
	Challengers	70,947 (109)	73,043 (200)
	Open Seats	212,671 (52)	192,514 (52)
Senate			
	Incumbents	594,230 (10)	2,065,682 (11)
	Challengers	830,291 (11)	551,990 (10)
	Open Seats	808,892 (12)	812,817 (12)

[a] Number of cases; includes candidates with major party opposition only.

Source: Federal Election Commission, FEC Reports on Financial Activity, 1977–1978. Interim Report No. 5: U.S. Senate and House Campaigns, June 1979.

sion, FEC Reports on Financial Activity, 1977–1978, Interim Report No. 5: U.S. Senate and House Campaigns (Washington, D.C., June 1979) and 1977–78 FEC Reports on Financial Activity from computer runs on March 16, 1979. These interim data are subject to amendment, but few important changes are expected and they are sufficiently complete and accurate for the requirements of this epilogue.

tus.[2] The House elections compose a familiar pattern. Campaigns for open seats raised and spent the most money, and in other contests incumbents typically outspent challengers by a wide margin.

Expenditures by every type of candidate increased between 1976 and 1978. Among Democrats, the increase was similar for all incumbency categories, ranging from 20 percent for incumbents to 35 percent for challengers (these and all other comparative figures in this section are adjusted for inflation). Republican challengers increased their spending by only 12 percent, while Republican incumbents and candidates for open seats enjoyed 31 percent and 68 percent increases, respectively. This reflects a change in Republican strategy. In 1976, Republicans went after first-term Democrats from the Watergate class of 1974. Success was very limited, so in 1978 they concentrated on taking seats vacated by retiring Democrats. This strategy was not noticeably more effective.[3]

As usual, the Senate figures are more difficult to interpret because of state population variations. Incumbents spent about 61 cents, challengers, 31 cents, and candidates for open seats, 50 cents per eligible voter. The differences in average spending between incumbent Democratic senators and their opponents was small and disappears if money spent on behalf of Republicans by the national party is included (more on this later). Republican incumbents typically outspent their rivals by a very large amount; even if Senator Helms's extravagant campaign is set aside, other Republican incumbents spent an average of $1.5 million. Political success accompanied financial prosperity. Republicans gained three Senate seats in a year when they had to defend 17 of the 38 seats they held. They understandably look forward to 1980, when only 10 Republican but 24 Democratic Senate seats are up for election.

The well-publicized examples of extraordinarily lavish campaigns and the more general growth in campaign spending predictably revived complaints about the high cost of running for

2. The focus here is on expenditures and not contributions because the interim reports contain no information on loans, debts, and candidate contributions to the campaign.

3. Republicans took eight of the 39 open House seats formerly held by Democrats but lost six of their own.

office and fears about the corrupting influence of money in politics. (It was scarcely noticed that all four House challengers who spent more than $.4 million lost—although none received less than 47 percent of the vote.) An even more potent ground for alarm was the source of the money. Contributions from nonparty political action committees—and therefore the "special interests" they are presumed to represent—led the increase in campaign contributions. Trade, membership, and health PACs were particularly active, for the first time surpassing both corporate and labor PACs in their generosity. The growth in campaign funds supplied by different sorts of PACs since the enactment of the FECA Amendments clarifying their legal status in 1974 is documented in table E.2.

The data in table E.2 explain organized labor's deep misgivings

Table E.2. The Growth of PAC Contributions to Congressional Candidates, 1974–78

	Contributions (in millions)					
	1974		1976		1978	
Type of PAC Contribution						
Labor	$6.3	(50.4)[a]	$8.2	(36.3)	$10.3	(29.3)
Corporate	2.5	(20.0)	7.1	(31.4)	9.8	(27.9)
Trade/Membership/Health	2.3	(18.4)	4.5	(19.9)	11.5	(32.8)
Other	1.4	(11.2)	2.8	(12.4)	3.4	(10.0)
Total PAC Contributions	12.5		22.6		35.1	

	Percent Change (adjusted for inflation)		
	1974–76	1976–78	1974–78
Type of PAC Contribution			
Labor	12.7	6.8	20.3
Corporate	145.9	17.3	188.5
Trade/Membership/Health	169.4	117.2	267.8
Other	73.2	6.3	83.7
Total PAC Contributions	56.7	32.0	106.4

[a] Percentage of all PAC contributions.

Source: Federal Election Commission Data.

about the system of campaign finance that grew out of the reforms of the 1970s. In 1974, labor provided more money to candidates than corporate and trade, membership, and health committees combined. By 1978, labor was matched by both groups, and together they contributed twice as much to congressional candidates. Labor organizations provided half of all PAC money in 1974; by 1978 this share was down to 29 percent.

Money from PACs more than doubled between 1974 and 1978. The striking increase in contributions from trade, membership, and health committees is the largest component of this trend. Corporate PAC contributions have also grown rapidly. By comparison, labor groups have increased their contributions very little.

The dilution of organized labor's financial impact is shown in greater detail in table E.3. Labor money has always gone overwhelmingly to Democrats. It still does. But labor money as a proportion of all contributions to Democrats has declined over the last three elections. An even steeper decline is apparent in labor contributions as a proportion of all PAC money. In 1978, incumbent Democrats actually received a larger share of their funds from corporate, trade, and professional PACs than from organized labor. These groups contribute an increasing proportion of funds to candidates of both parties.

Notice, however, that this still amounts to a relatively small proportion of total contributions to candidates. Usually ignored in the outcries against the surge of "special interest" money is that PACs as a group still provide only about 25 percent of all congressional campaign funds and that any particular PAC can only provide a very small share of the funds needed to mount an adequate campaign.[4] Individual donations have in fact kept pace with the overall increase in campaign contributions and continue to supply most of the money (about 60 percent) for campaigns. Were it not for the shift in the sources of funds within the PAC category—especially the diminishing relative importance of labor—it is doubtful that PACs would have excited so much recent attention.

4. See Michael J. Malbin, "Campaign Finance Reform and the 'Special Interests,' " *Public Interest* 56 (1979): 26–27.

Table E.3. Average Campaign Contributions by Labor PACs and Corporate, Trade, and Professional PACs to Candidates for the U.S. House of Representatives, 1972–78

	1972	1974	1976	1978
Labor PAC Contributions to Democratic Candidates	$6,429	$9,494	$11,820	$14,820
Percentage of all PAC contributions	66.3	68.8	52.7	47.8
Percentage of total contributions	12.3	14.8	14.4	13.0
Corporate, Trade, and Professional PAC Contributions to Democratic Candidates	$2,083	$2,776	$8,485	$13,999
Percentage of all PAC contributions	21.4	20.1	37.8	45.2
Percentage of total contributions	4.0	4.3	10.3	12.3
Corporate, Trade, and Professional PAC Contributions to Republican Candidates	$3,879	$6,017	$11,520	$20,701
Percentage of all PAC contributions	81.9	83.4	85.7	82.3
Percentage of total contributions	7.6	10.3	14.9	18.5

Note: Data for 1978 include all major party candidates; data for 1972–76 include only candidates with major party opposition.

Sources: 1972 and 1974, Common Cause; 1976 and 1978, Federal Election Commission.

A potentially important change in the behavior of business-oriented PACs has also raised some partisan anxiety. Although these groups are still quite willing to support incumbent Democrats (for reasons discussed at length in chapter 3), they have begun to direct more of their resources to Republicans—more likely ideological allies—who seem to be making a strong run, regardless of in-

cumbency status. Corporate PACs contributed only 53 percent of
their funds to Republican candidates through September 30, 1978;
Democratic incumbents of course greatly outnumber their Republican colleagues. But from October 1 through October 23, 71 percent of their contributions went to Republican candidates, especially to nonincumbents who appeared to have a good chance to
win. It is almost certain that this trend continued through election
day.[5]

Both the growth of corporate, trade, and professional PACs and
their increasingly partisan behavior have helped shape the current
politics of campaign finance regulation. Labor leaders feel their
influence ebbing within the Democratic party as well as within the
broader political system. Many Democrats, aware of the great
untapped potential for more corporate PAC activity and also the
ideological predilections of most corporations and trade associations, foresee serious financial disadvantages for their party in the
years ahead. Most Republicans, recognizing the same phenomena,
are understandably pleased with present trends. The effects of these
perspectives on the handling of campaign finance issues by Congress are clearly evident and will be examined below.

Another aspect of congressional campaign finance in 1978 bears
clear partisan implications. National-level Republican committees
spent $4 million on behalf of Republican candidates. Assistance to
Republican Senate candidates was particularly generous; the party
spent an average of $82,500 on behalf of each. Republican House
candidates received an average of $3,400 worth of services. The
Democrats, with only $.3 million to spend, gave their Senate candi-
dates an average of $4,800 worth of assistance, their House candi-
dates, $171. Republicans have continued to mount a much more ef-
fective national-level effort on behalf of their candidates, with a
long-term potential, well worth marking, of braking or even reversing the steady decline of party organizations. Democrats have as
yet made no serious attempt to imitate the Republicans' techniques.

The 1978 campaigns were also notable for one interesting

5. Maxwell Glen, "At the Wire, Corporate PACs Come Through for the GOP,"
National Journal 11 (February 3, 1979): 174–77.

financial innovation. Four Republicans planning to run for President in 1980—Ronald Reagan, George Bush, John Connally, and Robert Dole—established PACs which contributed a total of more than $800,000 to Republican candidates and party organizations. Present campaign finance regulations thus fostered a new variation on the old tradition of gathering political debts through local visits for campaigning and fundraising.[6] The advantage to contributors of such gifts is that it scarcely matters whether or not the candidate receiving the money wins or loses as long as he remains active in Republican politics and participates in the 1980 presidential selection process.

Finally, 1978 was notable for the prominent activity of single-issue groups (anti-abortionists in particular) and the continued growth of direct-mail fundraising, most notably by Richard Viguerie for his conservative Republican clients. Most of Helms's money was raised by Viguerie, who took a healthy share of it for his efforts. The devisive political emotions which generate this kind of campaign money have begun to worry some close observers of campaign finance practices.[7] Members of Congress who are likely targets of such campaigns have also begun to take notice, as well they might. The National Conservative Political Action Committee has already initiated public campaigns against five Democratic senators up for reelection in 1980 even though none of them yet has an official opponent.[8] The 1980 election should provide the first real test of the efficacy of independent expenditures.

THE EFFECTS OF CAMPAIGN SPENDING IN 1978

Campaign expenditures had the same effect on the outcomes of congressional elections in 1978 as they had in the previous three

6. *C.Q. Weekly Report* 20 (February 17, 1979): 307.
7. Malbin, "Campaign Finance Reform," p. 40; Xandra Kayden, "Campaign Finance: The Impact on Parties and PACs," in *An Analysis of the Impact of the Federal Election Campaign Act, 1972–1978*, a Report by the Campaign Finance Study Group to the Committee on House Administration of the U.S. House of Representatives (Institute of Politics, John F. Kennedy School of Government, Harvard University, May, 1979), pp. 10–11.
8. *C.Q. Weekly Report* 20 (July 28, 1979): 1540.

Table E.4.   The Effects of Campaign Spending in House Elections, 1978

(Estimates of Equations 2.1 and 2.3)

		Regression Coefficient	t Ratio[a]	Standardized Regression Coefficient	
Incumbents and Challengers					
	$CV = a$	14.8			
	b_1CE	.063	11.10	.51	
($N = 305$)	b_2IE	−.002	−.35	−.02	$R^2 = .61$
	b_3P	−1.76	−2.15	−.08	
	b_4CPS	.454	9.70	.42	
Open Seats					
	$DV = a$	45.3			
	b_1DE	.023	2.37	.29	
($N = 50$)	b_2RE	−.047	−3.92	−.47	$R^2 = .45$
	b_3DPS	.202	3.06	.38	

[a] See tables 2.1 and 2.4.

elections. The ordinary least squares and two-stage least squares regression equations were estimated with the 1978 data and once again showed that campaign spending by challengers and, among candidates for open seats, Republicans has the largest influence on election results. The OLS estimates (see chapter 2 for a full description of the equations and variables) for the 1978 House elections are listed in table E.4.[9] When inflation is acknowledged, the regression coefficient on CE, the challenger's expenditure, closely matches those of the previous three elections. Recall that the coefficients from 1972 through 1976 were, in 1972 dollars, .112, .143, and .100, respectively; for 1978 the figure is .101.

Incumbent expenditures again had no statistically significant im-

9.   Three extreme cases (challengers spending more than $.5 million) were dropped from the analysis. Their presence did not alter the basic pattern of challenger and incumbent spending effects but did seriously distort the estimated parameters, cutting the slope of CE in half. When they are included, a semilog model fits the data better, suggesting that these candidates spent far beyond the point where returns had diminished to zero. If they are left out, the linear model provides a better fit.

pact on the election result. Once more, the more incumbents spent, the worse they did in the election; their spending is correlated with the challenger's vote at .42. The party variable indicates that Republicans enjoyed a slight advantage in 1978, not a surprising finding. The estimates for House contests for open seats show that, as before, spending was more important to Republican than to Democratic candidates.

The OLS estimates for the Senate elections also recapitulate the findings from earlier elections. They are found in table E.5. Campaign spending makes a much greater difference for challengers than for incumbents, and contests for open seats were significantly affected only by what the Republican candidate spent.

Spending by House incumbents continued to be demonstrably reactive. Table E.6 presents the 1978 estimates of equation 4.1 (see chapter 4 for details), which measures the effects of the challenger's expenditures and other variables on what the incumbent spends. Again, incumbent spending is most strongly affected by challenger spending. The only other statistically significant variables are the candidate's party (Republican incumbents facing Dem-

Table E.5.   The Effects of Campaign Spending in Senate Elections, 1978

(Estimates of Equations 2.2 and 2.4)

			Regression Coefficient	t Ratio[a]	Standardized Regression Coefficient	
Incumbents and Challengers						
	$CV =$	a	4.8			
		$b_1 ln CEPV$	7.09	5.78	.86	
$(N = 21)$		$b_2 ln IEPV$	−3.10	−1.02	−.18	$R^2 = .73$
		$b_3 P$	−1.80	−.51	−.08	
		$b_4 ln VAP$	4.31	2.16	.35	
Open Seats						
	$DV =$	a	113.2			
		$b_1 ln DEPV$	−4.19	−.71	−.14	
$(N = 12)$		$b_2 ln REPV$	−10.05	−4.42	−.86	$R^2 = .73$
		$b_3 ln VAP$	−1.36	−.39	−.08	

[a] See table 2.2.

Table E.6   Determinants of Campaign Spending by House Incumbents, 1978

(Estimates of Equation 4.1)

		Regression Coefficient	t Ratio[a]	Standardized Regression Coefficient	
$IE =$	a	26.07			
	b_1CE	.415	7.70	.42	
	b_2P	20.67	2.40	.12	
	b_3CPS	1.80	3.77	.21	
	b_4IP	9.29	1.10	.05	$R^2 = .35$
$(N = 305)$	b_5YRS	−.92	−1.61	−.09	
	b_6PO	−5.71	−.55	−.03	
	b_7L	6.42	.48	.03	

[a] See table 4.3.

ocratic challengers spent substantially more money) and how seriously the incumbent was threatened the last time around (the best interpretation of *CPS* in this context).

Estimates of the simultaneous equation model (described in chapter 5) also produced results consistent with earlier findings. The first and second stage equations for 1978 are reported in table E.7. As in other election years, the challenger's party, district party strength, and political experience had the greatest effect on how much he managed to raise and spend. And as in every year save 1974, other things equal, Republican challengers were able to spend significantly more money. The only noticeable difference in the first stage equations for 1978 is that a primary election made a much greater difference in what the challenger spent than in previous years.

The second stage equations again conform to previous patterns. As usual, multicollinearity among the independent variables distorts the estimates of parameters of the spending variables, exaggerating them in opposite directions. A more plausible coefficient appears when IE^* is left out of the equation. None of the evidence from 1978 suggests that simultaneity bias afflicted the OLS estimates to an important degree. In short, the 1978 data nicely reinforce the central arguments of this book.

Table E.7. The Effects of Campaign Spending in House Elections, 1978
(2SLS Estimates)

			Regression Coefficient	t Ratio[a]	Standardized Regression Coefficient	
	$CE^* =$	a	-42.07			
		$b_1 P$	-34.51	-3.91	$-.20$	
		$b_2 CPS$	3.24	6.89	$.38$	
$(N = 305)$		$b_3 PO$	36.52	3.42	$.17$	$R^2 = .30$
		$b_4 YRS$	$-.88$	-1.59	$-.09$	
		$b_5 CP$	30.42	3.58	$.18$	
		$b_6 IP$	-15.30	-1.70	$-.-09$	
First-stage equations	$IE^* =$	a	8.07			
		$b_1 P$	6.75	$.74$	$.04$	
		$b_2 CPS$	3.13	6.43	$.37$	
		$b_3 PO$	9.70	$.87$	$.05$	$R^2 = .22$
		$b_4 YRS$	-1.15	-2.17	$-.11$	
		$b_5 CP$	13.62	1.55	$.08$	
		$b_6 IP$	2.51	$.27$	$.01$	
	$CV =$	a	19.7			
		$b_1 CE^*$	$.144$	4.44^b	$.62$	
		$b_2 IE^*$	$-.078$	-1.30	$-.29$	$R^2 = .46^b$
		$b_3 P$	1.08	$.68$	$.05$	
		$b_4 CPS$	$.391$	2.68	$.36$	
Second-stage equations	$CV =$	a	18.3			
		$b_1 CE^*$	$.111$	6.05	$.48$	
		$b_3 P$	$-.43$	$-.43$	$-.02$	$R^2 = .56^b$
		$b_4 CPS$	$.246$	2.80	$.23$	

[a] See table 5.1.
[b] See table 5.1.

CAMPAIGN FINANCE POLITICS IN 1979

The general rise in campaign spending, the blossoming of corporate and other "special interest" PACs, and the prominent, if atypical, examples of flamboyant extravagance, revived congressional interest in public subsidies for congressional campaigns. This time most of the action took place in the House.[10] A proposal to extend public funds to House candidates was honored with the designation HR 1. Chairman Thompson of the House Administration Committee gave HR 1 top priority, and President Carter offered a plea on its behalf in his State of the Union Address. None of this finally made any difference. The bill was killed when the House Administration Committee voted against reporting it by a surprisingly large margin, 17–8.[11]

HR 1, modified several times in futile attempts to attract more support, would have provided subsidies and imposed spending limits very similar to those of HR 5157 (analyzed in chapter 7) and hence could be expected to have the same competitive consequences.[12] Although some new considerations did arise, it failed for basically the same reasons that the last attempt to legislate public funds for congressional campaigns failed.

The most obvious and probably most critical factor was partisan polarization on the issue. Relatively few Republicans in the House supported even the concept of public funding in 1979; on all crucial committee votes, Administration Committee Republicans voted unanimously to weaken or kill the bill.[13]

Republicans appear to have reached a solid consensus that public funds accompanied by spending ceilings will harm their party. By all the evidence in this book, they are quite correct. They can hardly expect to gain a majority without defeating Democratic incumbents, and most have been brought around to the opinion that proposals such as HR 1 would aggravate challengers' problems. Republican National Chairman William Brock, in a letter sent to all

10. As of September 1, 1979, hearings had not yet been held on the Senate's public funding bill.

11. *C.Q. Weekly Report* 20 (May 26, 1979): 1000.

12. As first proposed, HR 1 would have matched individual contributions of $100 or less in $10,000 increments up to a total of $60,000. Candidates accepting matching funds would have been limited to spending $150,000, plus $30,000 for fundraising and would have been allowed $15,000 for one mailing within the district. The district mailing was later dropped. A cost-of-living escalator was included. Adjusting for inflation, the actual amount available to House candidates would be about the same as under the 1977 proposal.

13. *C.Q. Weekly Report* 20 (May 26, 1979): 1001.

Republicans in the House, expressed this view precisely: "HR 1 is a power play by the Democratic majority which seeks to control and stifle Republican challengers' access to voters. Republicans do not favor suicide. They should not vote for HR 1."[14]

In addition, it is now obvious that Republican candidates raise money more effectively under the current campaign finance system than do Democrats. They receive much more help from their party, both directly and through money spent on services for them. They have begun to benefit from the dramatic growth of corporate and other sympathetic PACs, with even greater expectations for the future. The Republican consensus is not surprising; the only surprise is that it took so long to develop.

Of course Republican unanimity would not have been effective in the face of Democratic unity. But Democrats on the House Administration Committee and in the House generally were not united on the issue. Even though a sizable majority, encouraged by traditional Democratic allies in organized labor, seemed to favor some sort of public funding, Democrats remained seriously divided over what particular form should be adopted.

Several points of disagreement arose. One major source of doubt among Democrats (and Republicans as well) involved the Federal Election Commission. Most members of Congress have little affection or respect for the agency that has been regulating their campaign finance practices. Many were reluctant to add to the size and authority of the FEC by having it certify campaigns and contributions for matching funds. FEC Commissioner Joan Aikens's testimony before the House Administration Committee—and its aftermath—scarcely quieted doubts.[15]

In an attempt to broaden support for HR 1, optional certification

---

14.　Ibid. (May 12, 1979): 907.

15.　Aikens originally testified that HR 1 would cost between $35 million and $45 million and would require the FEC to hire as many as 183 new employees. This was far above estimates made by the bill's sponsors, and under some pressure, the FEC produced revised estimates of between $22.2 million and $29.7 million for the cost of financing the 1980 House elections. The FEC explained that its original calculations were not based on the right data. See ibid. (April 7, 1979): 647, and (May 12, 1979): 908.

by state parties was added. When some members pointed out that their relations with state party leaders were less than cordial, the alternative was shifted to the secretaries of state within each state. Neither ploy attracted enough votes to matter.

Southern Democrats and some veteran northern Democrats on the Committee were doubtful supporters of any public finance measure. Representative Davis of South Carolina tried to amend the bill to cover primary elections, knowing that this would assure its defeat on the floor. Other members agreed to support the bill only if it were amended in ways that would be unacceptable to current supporters. The point was reached where any change intended to pick up votes would also lose votes, and so solid Democratic support never materialized.[16]

HR 1's problems were not exclusively internal. Although, once again, Gallup found a majority of people polled in favor of publicly funded congressional campaigns,[17] this was hardly a "consensus of decision." The proportion of taxpayers checking off two dollars for the campaign fund has yet to surpass 30 percent. There is no indication that the issue excited much public interest. The usual supporters—Common Cause, organized labor—were active once again, but this time they were opposed by better organized and more extensive lobbying campaigns against public subsidies.[18] If congressmen perceived any relevant widespread public attitude, it was that taxes were too high and that government spending and regulation were out of control. Spending more tax dollars on political campaigns did not, for the moment, seem a likely way to increase popular affection for members of Congress or for the institution itself.

16. Support for public funding was stronger among House Administration Committee Democrats than suggested by the final vote. Eight of the sixteen Democrats voted not to report HR 1, but at least three were reported willing to vote in favor if their vote was needed to win. See ibid. (May 26, 1979): 1000.

17. Nationally, 57 percent favored public funding plus spending limits, 30 percent were opposed, and 13 percent had no opinion. These figures are nearly identical to those of 1977 mentioned in chapter 7. The Gallup Poll was reported in the *Hartford Courant*, April 1, 1979, p. 5.

18. *C.Q. Weekly Report* 20 (May 12, 1979): 906–08.

Although the demise of HR 1 ended the chances of public funding for this Congress, it is unlikely, for the reasons mentioned in chapter 7, that the issue is dead. Whether it is merely dormant until after the 1980 election—with its predictable increase in spending, spectacularly expensive campaigns, increased PAC activity—or whether it remains moribund for some time to come, is uncertain.

Organized labor and reformers from Common Cause had hoped public funding would effectively eliminate PACs as important sources of campaign money, reversing the distressing changes that have occurred since 1974. The failure of HR 1 forced them to consider other alternatives. At this writing, liberal reformers had just introduced a new campaign finance bill (called the Campaign Contributions Reform Act of 1979) designed to undercut PACs directly. The maximum legal PAC contribution would be sliced in half (to a total of $5,000 instead of the present $10,000 for any candidate in a primary and general election campaign), with candidates limited to accepting no more than a total of $50,000 from PACs of all kinds.[19] The irony of this particular proposal is that, no doubt contrary to the intention of most of its supporters, it would do the most harm to labor.[20] Most PAC contributions in excess of $5,000 come from labor groups, and most House candidates receiving more than $50,000 in PAC money are Democrats who get a large part of it from labor committees. Labor organizations are inherently fewer and larger than their business and professional counterparts. If Democrats in Congress make any effort to assess the real impact of the bill, it will not pass. But it does show that the struggle to limit campaigns financially will not be abandoned easily.

An alternative set of reforms were recommended to the House Administration Committee in a study prepared for the Committee by the Campaign Finance Study Group of the Institute of Politics at Harvard. After reviewing the impact of the FECA and its amendments since 1972, the study offered a number of suggestions in-

19.   The bill also contains a section aimed specifically at Viguerie's direct mail operation; it would forbid political consultants and fundraisers to extend credit of more than $1,000 for more than thirty days. Viguerie has on occasion extended very large amounts of credit to favored clients.

20.   Malbin, "Campaign Finance Reform," p. 32.

tended to ease restrictions on fundraising and reduce the administrative burden imposed by current reporting requirements. The most important recommendations were to increase the individual contribution limit from $1,000 to $3,000 per candidate per House election, with even higher limits for presidential and senatorial contests, and to require detailed disclosure only of contributions and expenditures in excess of $500. Congress was encouraged to deal with the growing importance of PACs by providing an alternative source of the necessary wherewithall—private individuals—rather than by trying to weaken the PACs themselves.[21] One message of this book has been that Congress is rarely interested in changes that would make fundraising easier. How seriously the Committee and the Congress will entertain these proposals remains doubtful.

21. I was one of the authors of the report. The others were F. Christopher Arterton, Xandra Kayden, and Gary Orren. See *An Analysis of the Impact of the FECA, 1972–1978.*

INDEX